JOURNEYS

Journeys

Reconceptualizing Early Childhood Practices through Pedagogical Narration

Veronica Pacini-Ketchabaw
Fikile Nxumalo
Laurie Kocher
Enid Elliot
Alejandra Sanchez

UNIVERSITY OF TORONTO PRESS

19041

EC-P
P1199
2015

Library and Archives Canada Cataloguing in Publication

Pacini-Ketchabaw, Veronica, 1969–, author

    Journeys : reconceptualizing early childhood practices through pedagogical narration / Veronica Pacini-Ketchabaw, Fikile Nxumalo, Laurie Kocher, Enid Elliot, Alejandra Sanchez.

Includes bibliographical references and index.
Issued in print and electronic formats.
ISBN 978-1-4426-0943-3 (bound).—ISBN 978-1-4426-0942-6 (pbk.).—
ISBN 978-1-4426-0944-0 (pdf).—ISBN 978-1-4426-0945-7 (epub)

    1. Early childhood education—Philosophy. I. Nxumalo, Fikile, 1971–, author II. Kocher, Laurie, 1959–, author III. Elliot, Enid, 1947–, author IV. Sanchez, Alejandra, 1967–, author V. Title.

LB1139.23.P32 2014   372.21   C2014–902008–2
                                             C2014–902009–0

We welcome comments and suggestions regarding any aspect of our publications—please feel free to contact us at news@utphighereducation.com or visit our Internet site at www.utppublishing.com.

North America
5201 Dufferin Street
North York, Ontario, Canada, M3H 5T8

2250 Military Road
Tonawanda, New York, USA, 14150

ORDERS PHONE: 1–800–565–9523
ORDERS FAX: 1–800–221–9985
ORDERS E-MAIL: utpbooks@utpress.utoronto.ca

UK, Ireland, and continental Europe
NBN International
Estover Road, Plymouth, PL6 7PY, UK
ORDERS PHONE: 44 (0) 1752 202301
ORDERS FAX: 44 (0) 1752 202333
ORDERS E-MAIL: enquiries@nbninternational.com

Every effort has been made to contact copyright holders; in the event of an error or omission, please notify the publisher.

The University of Toronto Press acknowledges the financial support for its publishing activities of the Government of Canada through the Canada Book Fund.

Cover image: Sylvia Kind.

This book is dedicated to the children who co-created the pedagogical narrations we have worked with, including those we share in the book.

CONTENTS

ILLUSTRATIONS

ACKNOWLEDGEMENTS

This book is truly a collaboration—among ourselves and with many others. First and foremost, we sincerely thank our families, who have given up so much as we worked on the many drafts of this text. We also thank our editor, Leslie Prpich, who helped us to make this book a reality. The book would not have been possible without the educators we have collaborated with since 2006. Some of them are named in the book; others are not, but they were always present as we envisioned and created *Journeys*. You have been our inspiration and our companions in the process of learning to complexify our practices. We especially want to acknowledge Kim Atkinson and Christine Chan, who have generously allowed us to include their work at length in this book, as well as the helpful team at the University of Toronto Press.

We gratefully acknowledge the support from the British Columbia Ministry of Children and Family Development for the Investigating Quality Project and from the British Columbia Ministry of Education for the Early Learning Framework Implementation Project.

BEGINNING

I recall sitting around the table with a group of educators and being amazed at the wealth and diversity of perspectives that were offered. So many ideas were bounced around, each provoking new thoughts and questions. The image comes to my mind of ripples radiating out from a stone dropped into a pond, with each ripple representing so many new possibilities. (Laurie)

We—Veronica Pacini-Ketchabaw, Fikile Nxumalo, Laurie Kocher, Enid Elliot, and Alejandra Sanchez—are a group of early childhood pedagogues who live and practise in British Columbia (BC), Canada. This book describes journeys we have taken and concepts we have put to work as we collaborate with early childhood educators to complexify our teaching practices. Through our experiences working with children, families, and educators, we have become aware that pedagogy is indeed, as curriculum theorist Pinar (2012) reminds us, a complicated conversation. We have witnessed a tendency to think of early childhood practice as a simple matter that can be easily prescribed and directly applied. We write this book with the hope that readers can begin to challenge this pervasive understanding that practice is about employing specific techniques. We embrace early childhood pedagogy as an ethical political project.

Our experimentations with collaborative critically reflective communities (see chapter 1) began in 2005 with the Investigating Quality in Early Childhood and Care Project (IQ Project) and, soon after, the British Columbia Early Learning Framework (ELF) Implementation Project (detailed descriptions of these projects can be found in the appendix). Over a number of months—and in some cases several years—groups of early childhood educators in these two projects met regularly and shared moments from their practice captured through **pedagogical narrations** (see chapter 4). Together with

HOW TO USE THIS BOOK

Journeys explores complex ideas, and we have tried to present them in such a way that you can "snack" on small pieces instead of trying to digest a heavy meal at one sitting. You will notice that we come back to key ideas several times throughout the book. We want to ensure that you see that none of these concepts sits alone; they interact and are interconnected. As you explore the book, you will encounter various highlighted terms. Readers who are not familiar with these terms can refer to the section Understanding Our Language: A Glossary (pp. 195–216) for our understanding and use of these terms. Readers who are familiar with postfoundational ideas may prefer not to refer to the glossary.

Throughout the book, we include quotes from early childhood educators who have participated in our projects. Most of these quotes are from discussions in the Investigating Quality (IQ) Project learning circles (see Appendix). We also include samples of pedagogical narrations. These are not to be seen as exemplary. We discourage readers from attempting to *implement* the ideas in these narrations in their practice. Instead, we include these narrations to tell our own stories and to illustrate how we worked together to unpack difficult issues that have emerged in our journeys together.

We take a **rhizomatic** approach in our work, and *Journeys* reflects that approach. By this we mean that the ideas presented throughout the various chapters are all connected. After reading a section of the book in a specific chapter, you might find that you need to move to another section in a different chapter. In other words, you might proceed in a way that speaks to you instead of following a linear approach. We take inspiration from philosophers Gilles Deleuze and Felix Guattari (1987), who wrote about rhizomes as having multiple entries and connections (think of how blackberry plants grow). We invite you to seek out, enact, and create your own multiple connections (in the rhizome) as you encounter concepts and stories in the book.

Chapter 1, Engaging with Complexity, introduces our approach to complexifying practice with early childhood educators. We discuss our experiences in creating a collaborative critically reflective community, the inspiration we draw from diverse early childhood education contexts outside our own context in British Columbia, our shifting understandings of professional development, our use of action research as a tool to politicize early childhood education practices, and our efforts to rethink quality in the early childhood field. Engagement with these ideas provokes movement toward a **discourse of meaning-making** as we shift our focus from "understanding practice" to "making our practice more complex."

In chapter 2, Reflecting Critically, we explore how processes of critical reflection can be used to make visible the complexities of practice and to drive continual change toward ethical, creative, and equitable practices. We discuss the process of bringing a critical perspective to child development, what we mean by critical reflection, and the concept of political intentionality as the basis for critical reflection. We introduce some theoretical tools that we find useful and provide a concrete example of educators engaging in collaborative critical reflection on a pedagogical narration.

Chapter 3, Challenging Assumptions, critically examines some images of the child, the educator, and the family that are prevalent in the early childhood field. Taking inspiration from Reggio Emilia and postfoundational perspectives that situate childhoods within sociocultural, historical, and economic contexts, we explore how dominant images and taken-for-granted assumptions may limit our practices, and consider ways to use postfoundational approaches to complexify them. We discuss children's participation in curriculum-making and explore some dominant and alternative images of the child, the educator, and the family. We consider what might be involved in rethinking a "diversity" perspective, using a **sociomaterial** perspective to move beyond discourse.

Chapter 4, Thinking Together, explores the theories and processes of pedagogical narration. We briefly investigate innovative approaches to pedagogical documentation from three different contexts: Italy, New Zealand, and Australia. We critique the "McDonaldization" of pedagogical documentation and discuss our concerns with how this revolutionary tool is being used as part of an evolutionary project in most North American contexts. Using examples from our collaborative work with early childhood educators, we consider pedagogical narration as a discourse of meaning-making, as a political tool, as a vehicle for public dialogue, and as a **materializing apparatus**.

Chapter 5, Opening to Possibilities, highlights the theoretical lenses that we find useful to complexify practices, interpret pedagogical narrations, and expand our view of early childhood pedagogies. We explain the processes we use to analyze, **deconstruct**, and make meaning of pedagogical narration. Here we put to work the postfoundational theories we presented in chapters 1 and 2 and the ideas about pedagogical narration we explored in chapter 4.

In chapter 6, Opening to Ethics, we explore some of the ethical challenges that confront us in our daily work with young children and families. We elaborate on how we foreground an ethical approach, particularly in the spaces of uncertainty, discomfort, and complexity in which we often find ourselves in early childhood pedagogy. We clarify our understanding of an ethical approach; we investigate ethics as relational, as attitude, and as political action; and we discuss some ethical difficulties of working with pedagogical narrations, the idea of pedagogical narration as a **nomadic** ethical act, and ways to centre ethical potentials in our practice.

At the centre of the book, between chapters 3 and 4, we include a selection of pedagogical narrations created by some of the educators we have worked with. We engage with these narrations (and others) throughout the book to illustrate the many ways that critically engaging with different theoretical lenses to interpret children's meaning-making and identity negotiations opens possibilities for complexifying practice.

We hope that as you read the book you will engage with its multiple perspectives and the complexities we bring to our collaborative reflection processes. We encourage you to keep in mind your own questions as well as the comforts and discomforts you experience daily in your practice. We particularly hope that our work will inspire you to think about complexifying practice in your own contexts.

CHAPTER I

ENGAGING WITH COMPLEXITY

This chapter introduces our approach to complexifying practice with early childhood educators. We discuss:

- Our experiences in creating a collaborative critically reflective community.
- The inspiration we draw from diverse early childhood education contexts outside our own context in British Columbia, particularly the questions that emerge from our engagement with pedagogical approaches from New Zealand, Sweden, and Italy.
- Our shifting understandings of professional development.
- Our use of action research as a tool to politicize early childhood education practices.
- Rethinking quality in the early childhood field.
- Moving toward a discourse of meaning-making.
- Shifting our focus from understanding practice to complexifying practices.

Creating a Collaborative Critically Reflective Community

Collaborating with educators has been an eye-opener for me in terms of pushing boundaries and creating spaces of possibility—spaces that theory alone cannot open. (Veronica)

Two of us—Veronica and Enid—began the work with educators that this book describes in September 2006 through the Investigating Quality in Early Childhood Education and Care Project (hereafter called the IQ Project).

About 20 early childhood educators participated in the first two groups, one in Vancouver and one on southern Vancouver Island, both on the west coast of Canada. The educators came from a variety of settings, including Aboriginal, multicultural, rural, urban, college- and university-based, preschool, full-time childcare, infant and toddler care, and family childcare. When they joined the IQ Project, educators committed to being involved for about 10 months through a series of learning circles, sharing circles, online discussions, and site visits. (We describe these project components below.)

In 2008, Laurie and Alejandra joined our community as group facilitators. By then we were working with five different groups of educators in several locations across BC. Fikile came to our meetings as a project participant in 2009 and now facilitates a group.

Many other colleagues have facilitated group discussions, including Sylvia Kind, Ahna Berikoff, and Iris Berger. While not co-authors of this book, they are very much part of our collaborative community. This diverse group shares two things in common: a concern for the challenges we face in our current childcare context, and an interest in postfoundational approaches. Together we work to create opportunities for early childhood educators to network and to critically reflect on their practices.

Learning Circles

In the IQ Project, small groups of educators come together in monthly learning circles to share and talk about established and emerging practices and to become familiar with, reflect on, discuss, struggle with, and challenge postfoundational critical approaches to practice. Educators collect moments of practice in their centres using the tool of pedagogical narration (see chapter 4). A pedagogical narration, whether it is shared through photos, video, or written text, is a documented fragment of children's learning that spurs thought, curiosity, and understanding. Through journal writing, photography, and audio and video recording, educators capture children's ordinary moments and then share these moments with the group. Together we critically reflect on each educator's documentation and explore how we might work with postfoundational theories to extend our practices and build curriculum.

Sharing Circles

Annual or semi-annual sharing circles bring together all of the educators from the different groups to interact and share the work they have produced as a result of their involvement in the learning circles. Scholars and pedagogues from Australia, New Zealand, Sweden, and Canada have been invited to join us and respond to the work we present. The sharing circles give each group the opportunity to learn about other groups' work and allow us to see different points of view. Sometimes groups agree; sometimes they disagree with each other's work, and these discussions enrich our critically reflective communities.

Online Discussions

An online space allows educators and researchers to communicate between our face-to-face meetings and to circulate materials of interest. We also use this space to extend our critical reflection on the ideas we address in the learning and sharing circles. These online postings allow us to keep our critically reflective community alive and to share our struggles and successes.

Site Visits

In addition to facilitating the workshops, members of the research team provide individual support to each educator through visits to early childhood education centres. The visits provide opportunities for one-on-one conversations between the educators and the researchers. This component of the program also allows us to find out more about the work educators do in their centres.

To date, more than 100 early childhood educators have participated in the IQ Project, and some have been involved for several years. Even those who are not involved right now stay connected. From time to time, we receive emails from them updating us on their current situation, their challenges, and their successes. Some of the educators have moved into leadership or public positions; our connections continue and our discussions become more important as their potential to effect change grows.

Connections and Disruptions: Encounters with Diverse Perspectives

Our journeys as a critically reflective community involve connecting with pedagogical approaches outside our own context in British Columbia and then disrupting these lines of connection through continual questioning. In particular, we draw inspiration from Sweden's Stockholm Project, the Reggio Emilia preschools of northern Italy, and groundbreaking programs in New Zealand (Aotearoa in the Maori language). These approaches to early childhood education, among others that we haven't singled out here, embrace diversity, multiplicity, and experimentation.[1] For many participants in our projects, engaging with these approaches opens up multiple ways of understanding practice.

1 For more on pedagogical approaches in Italy, New Zealand, and Sweden, see Carr, 2001; Carr & May, 1992; Dahlberg, Moss, & Pence, 2007; Project Zero, 2004; Government of New Zealand, 1996, 2002.

Back in the beginning, I had my Reggio knowledge—or what I thought was knowledge and experience. I thought I was at the head of the pack! But I struggled with the idea of critically reflecting on my ideas and philosophies as an early childhood educator—trying to understand what things needed to change in my supposedly cutting-edge stellar practice. Now the ideas we're discussing have moved me beyond any understanding I thought I had about Reggio. I know now that I never truly understood it before. I was teaching through some surface ideals, but not much more. (Kate)

In the early days of the IQ Project, our discussions raised some key questions that sparked and sustained our ongoing processes of inquiry. We include them below. Exploring these questions with educators helped us build a sense of community and generate new trajectories for knowledge and action in early childhood education.

We engage with these questions not to seek definitive answers, but to unsettle our ways of viewing children and the roles of early childhood educators. We invite you to consider how these questions might stimulate your thoughts about your own practices.

What counts as knowledge of how children learn, and of what they can learn? What possibilities exist for disrupting taken-for-granted understandings?

Based on our reading of the reconceptualist literature (e.g., Cannella, 1997; MacNaughton, 2003) and our own practices, we began our journey with an awareness that our own assumptions, knowledge, and ideas about childhood and early learning needed to be considered from a critical perspective. We tried to recognize that the authority we have automatically granted to developmental theories is problematic at best because it privileges certain voices and silences others.

How might we work to foreground other social, cultural, and political constructions of the child?

In our work, we challenge the idea that a single, universal story about childhood can be told. We believe we need to think about childhood more as a phenomenon than a "natural" developmental path. This means working to understand how our society **constructs** childhood. In our work, we attempt to analyze how particular constructions of childhood, such as the "independent child," are grounded in Western capitalist values, and how such constructions silence perspectives that come from other cultural knowledges.

How can we pay attention to children's theories, hypotheses, dreams, and fantasies in early childhood pedagogies?

Listening to children is an important component of complexifying practices. We have learned, from the writings of our colleagues (e.g., Dahlberg &

Moss, 2005; Rinaldi, 2006), how challenging—and rewarding—it is to listen to children. Our engagement with pedagogical narrations throughout this book illustrates the complexities of listening to children as part of a process of complexifying our theories and ideas.

How can we disrupt the theory/practice divide that has been the norm in traditional early childhood education discourses?

We have heard it many times: academics do theory; early childhood educators engage in practice. Our Swedish colleagues challenged this idea in their work with educators (see Lenz Taguchi, 2009). We wanted to challenge it, too, to make visible how our practices are, in fact, already theoretical.

What possibilities exist for challenging the project of modernity?

Modernity, according to Dahlberg, Moss, and Pence (2007), "[holds] out the prospect of a continuous and linear progress, certainty and universality, predictability and control" (p. 133). Following their suggestion, our work seeks to recognize uncertainty, diversity, non-linearity, multiple perspectives, and specificities of time and space—all notions that challenge the concept of modernity. For example, one of our learning circles explored what Deborah Britzman (2003) calls *a pedagogy of uncertainty*. We wondered how this idea might fit into our practices in early childhood. As we thought about a pedagogy of uncertainty, we opened our discussions to a place of not-knowing.

How can we put theories to work in ethical ways that move us closer to social justice?

We felt it was integral to our practice to embed issues of social justice. To do that, we needed to question our own understanding of ethical practice. Ethics became about asking difficult questions about our practices, such as: who benefits from our choices and who is silenced?

We want to avoid the idea that practice can be approached with predetermined answers. We recognize the need to understand how we situate children and families, how we position ourselves as educators in relation to children and families, and what effects our actions have on children and families.

Rethinking Professional Development

Our intent in engaging with perspectives from Sweden, Italy, New Zealand, and other locations is not to reproduce this work but to engage with ideas that have the potential to disrupt normalized practices and inspire action in our own contexts. We are particularly interested in exploring possibilities for reconceptualizing professional development in early childhood education beyond its **normative construction** in North America. One prevailing approach to professional development that we wish to unsettle is the assumption that professional development is about transferring knowledge to early childhood educators that can then be applied to create high-quality early childhood education.

The idea that a textbook or a workshop can prescribe what is appropriate or inappropriate in an early childhood setting, and that these prescribed ideas can then be easily applied by an educator in a classroom, ignores the complexities educators encounter in their daily practices. Often, professional development approaches assume that the educator is an empty vessel to be filled with knowledge. In the professional development work we do with educators, we assume that educators are complex human beings who already have a lot to say about their practices and that they will respond to issues that affect them deeply.

Taking inspiration from Carlina Rinaldi's (2006) conception of *relational* professional development, we believe that professional development can take place only if we engage with educators in asking questions about their own practices, as this is the context in which they make sense of what teaching and learning could become. This kind of professional development involves educators in thinking deeply about issues they encounter. Rinaldi, who is president of Reggio Children and a professor of pedagogy at the University of Modena and Reggio Emilia (Italy), says:

> Personal and professional development, like education, should not be seen as static or unchangeable qualities, achieved once and for all, but rather as a process, an ongoing path that we follow from birth throughout our lives, now more than ever. Personal and professional development and education are something we construct ourselves in relation with others, based on values that are chosen, shared and constructed together. It means living and living ourselves in a permanent state of research. (Rinaldi, 2006, p. 137)

Envisioning professional development as ongoing research provides us with possibilities to stay in motion. Our critically reflective processes can be seen as intensely relational journeys taken with others to continually seek new ways to transform taken-for-granted pedagogical approaches into spaces in which new practices can grow. We cannot maintain an open, dynamic practice without further theoretical insights; neither can we create theories without extending them through moments of practice.

This relational approach to professional development disrupts two common assumptions among early childhood educators: first, that they need to have all the answers, and second, that practice is simple, consisting of easy textbook solutions to predefined problems that arise in the classroom—as opposed to theory, which is often thought of as more complex.

In reality, practice is even more complex. It is filled with many unknowns. Countless moments arise that are not in the textbook, moments where we don't know what to do. A child brings paint to the nap room, for example. The easy solution is to simply say, "Moving paint away from the easel is not allowed." The book tells us not to allow children to engage in inappropriate practices. But as educators, we need to think about what is meant by "inappropriate." When we stop a child in the name of appropriateness, we may be interrupting rich processes of discovery, of making meaning, or of art making.

Clean/Mess

Educator Vanessa Clark describes a situation she found herself in as an art teacher visiting an early childhood classroom to engage in art explorations with the children.

Varied patterns of yellow paint are smeared on the paper-covered table. The patterns may be read as intentional and mounted on the wall, but to me they are by-products of an event that just took place. Brushes lie strewn around the table, chairs, and floor. I sit stiffly in my chair as I watch the last child with the brushes. I notice my body become more and more uncomfortable as the tension mounts in the room. The paintbrush is cradled in Sarah's right hand and is moving slowly on her left arm. Her arms are suspended in the air, and she is silent. I look to the other teacher in the room and notice her face becoming red. She moves to another spot in the room where she does not have to see Sarah. The tension in my body melts away as I become engrossed in what Sarah is doing. I think to myself, "I have never seen anything like this before." I begin to break down and lose myself in the moment. Sarah's arms and hands are suspended in the thickness of space. Breath is slow and heavy in my chest. The smell of tempera paint lingers in the air. Supporting the paintbrush in her hand, Sarah's right arm is raised, and the bristles from the paintbrush move back and forth slowly across her left arm. The paintbrush is then guided toward her mouth and is embraced by her teeth and lips. Paint creeps from the paintbrush held in her mouth onto her right arm ...

All of a sudden, our focus is broken by a loud, angry voice. The teacher wants Sarah to stop. I look at Sarah and notice a faint smile on her face as she takes the brush from her mouth. My stomach is in knots, and I feel my face become hot and red.... I am reminded that the children are not supposed to put things in their mouths and that it is best if their clothes are not covered in paint ... I go over to Sarah and say to her, "I am so sorry, but we need to stop now." I feel my eyes well with tears, and I start to understand how disruptions can become violent. I hear a voice scream in my head, "How can we get educators to open their practice?" I feel my acts of disruption being met with the structuring power of policy and a fear of difference. As I clean the table, I wonder how I can disrupt this powerful structure and view it from another angle. (Clark, 2012, p. 23)

A classroom's ordinary moments are filled with complexity. It is our belief that the normative construction of professional development that is typical in North America fails to recognize this complexity.

Listening to Bubbles

In another example, Louise, an early childhood educator participating in the IQ Project, recounts her story of changing her practices after reading, critically reflecting on, and discussing an article on listening to children.

[Carla Rinaldi's] idea of a "pedagogy of listening" is a great way to get staff not to jump in without listening first. This week I had an experience that changed the way I understand what it means to listen to children. I set up a large table for bubbles, with large trays of soapy water, and I watched. Right away, I heard the children saying: "Don't!" "Stop!" I was about to jump in but I stopped myself. My first thought was, "This isn't going to work. They are too young." Then I remembered what we discussed in the last workshop about listening with all the senses and seeing the whole context before making assumptions.

It turned out the four-year-olds wanted to build a mountain of bubbles, while the two-year-olds wanted to pop the bubbles. The two-year-olds weren't even answering the four-year-olds' pleas of "Don't!" "Stop!" They just kept popping the bubbles! I held myself back and watched to see what would happen. While all of this was happening I was consciously aware of my staff watching. I could sense they wanted to jump in and were wondering why I wasn't intervening at the first cry of "Stop!" from the children.

I reminded myself that the children were only playing with soap and water, that they couldn't hurt themselves. I looked at the whole situation and asked myself what was going on besides the warnings of "Don't!" and "Stop!" I waited to see what they would do about the situation. I held back on my underlying judgment about the children's ability to deal with this and was happily surprised to see that the kids sorted it out amongst themselves, quickly and without further conflict. The two-year-olds moved to the other end of the table and the four-year-olds got to build their mountain of bubbles.

It's hard to admit it, but I keep hearing and seeing how our own underlying judgments, preconceived ideas, and hidden motives might be hindering change, both in the staff and in our centres. Listening to the children as they played with the bubbles opened up a whole new world of meaning for me, and it's leading all of us to a place of change, sometimes uncomfortable, but change nevertheless. It's really amazing. We are holding ourselves back from jumping in too soon, we are allowing the children to lead us to new and exciting projects with them, and we are getting excited by this new perspective. We are all learning together, the children and the staff. (Louise)

We further explore how we complexify professional development in our discussions of the image of the early childhood educator in chapter 3.

Collaborative Action Research and Politicizing Practice

Why Action Research?

We designed our projects as action research because we wanted to actively engage educators in discussions and actions that relate to their current circumstances in early childhood education (MacNaughton, 2005). An important goal of action research is to effect change through action by generating knowledge that people can then use in their everyday lived situations (Carr & Kemmis, 1986; Brydon-Miller, Greenwood, & Maguire, 2003; Kemmis, 2009).

One way we pursue this goal is by always starting our conversations in the learning circles with issues that emerge in the educators' classrooms. We ask educators to bring to the group a moment from their practice that is challenging, meaningful, or provocative to them. For example, when two children in Trina's centre began calling each other Chocolate and Vanilla, Trina was unsure of what these names signified for the children. She brought the issue to her learning circle for input from and collaborative critical reflection with her colleagues. We discuss Chocolate and Vanilla on pp. 19–20 and pp. 31–32.

Once an educator brings an issue or a pedagogical narration to the learning circle, we invite the whole group to engage in this moment of practice from an inquiry perspective, trying to unpack assumptions (by using questions like the ones we posed in Connections and Disruptions on pp. 3–5) and brainstorming ways to address these issues in the classroom.

Educators extend their critical reflection on these practice moments through journalling. For example, here is an excerpt from Fikile's journalled reflections on Becoming Rapunzel (see pp. 86–95):

> Perhaps it is my own entangled subjectivities and assumptions that tend to charge this drawing as a gendered, racialized representation framed by normalizing ideals of desirable beauty. (Fikile)

Readings from a wide range of theoretical perspectives provoke us to generate responses in the form of actions that challenge practice as usual.

Our online space and monthly meetings allow us to follow up on issues over time.

Through these varied processes, opportunities emerge to change our practices.

Why Politicize Practice?

The political orientation of collaborative action research is also important to our work. We are interested in practical change (e.g., using more natural materials in the classroom), but we also want to provoke ideas about participants' theories and everyday actions in relation to equity and **social justice**. We encourage educators in our projects to engage with issues such as **power/knowledge** and social inequities. We focus on ways to enact an activist approach in our practices, and we attempt to shift power relations by foregrounding voices that have been marginalized by particular power/knowledge structures. These processes are never straightforward, as the following journal reflection underscores:

> Another educator asked me if I thought my conceptions of identity might be influencing my interpretation of a child's self-view. She wondered whether my interpretations were based on what I had directly gathered from the child or if they reflected my own beliefs regarding positive/strong black female identity. Her question brought to mind Glenda MacNaughton's words about "asking children to be part of political discourses that I struggle with myself" (MacNaughton, 2005, p. 142). I agree that I cannot separate my own individual perceptions, cultural influences, and personal experiences of female blackness from how I interpret the children's meaning-making. I also hold certain ideals regarding the importance of self-acceptance in children, yet I wonder about ascribing my notions of "positive identity" to children who are negotiating their identities

in different times and places and with different people from those I have experienced. (Fikile)

We work with the assumption that all the work we do is political and that therefore our actions and thoughts need to be embedded in activist frameworks.

What Does Political Engagement Look Like?

In an early childhood setting, what does political engagement look like? To return to the example above of including more natural materials in the classroom, we might politically engage by unpacking our own seduction by "natural" materials. In other words, we don't just get rid of all the plastics in the classroom; we ask, "Why?" Why are many early childhood educators interested in bringing natural materials to their settings? What are the implications of this shift for children, educators, families, and the earth? What assumptions do we make about incorporating natural materials in the classroom? How have we come to think about plastic materials or toys as normal in our classrooms? How are we implicated in the production of plastic toys in the world?

An important goal of our work is to practice from a position of ethical responsibility. This means not transcending problems, but engaging and situating ourselves and our own practices in them. A key tool we use to engage at a political level is pedagogical narration—documenting ordinary moments of practice to build curriculum. The examples of pedagogical narration we present in this book deal with social issues such as racialization, gender, special rights, gun play, and sexuality.

For examples that engage with racialization, see:

Chocolate and Vanilla, pp. 19–20

No Chinese-Face Homeless, pp. 131–133

Stand Up, p. 152

Becoming Rapunzel, pp. 86–95

For examples that engage with sexuality and gender, see:

Princesses and Pirates, pp. 76–83

The Tiara, pp. 83–86

For examples that engage with gun play, see:

Hunters, Good Guys, and Bad Guys, pp. 37–38

Building a Fort, pp. 105–112

For examples that engage with special needs/rights, see:

Entangled Bodies, pp. 96–105

Rethinking Quality in the Early Childhood Education Field

I was introduced to thinking critically about quality as a graduate student in 1999, reading Beyond Quality in Early Childhood: Postmodern Perspectives. *From that time on, I thought about how the ideas in that text would change practice. When the* IQ *Project emerged as a possibility, I realized the possibilities. (Veronica)*

The work we describe in this book began with a question: What does quality mean in early childhood education? That question provided the impetus for the Investigating Quality (IQ) Project.

The quality of early learning programs in North America has been a concern for some years. Two important reports rank Canada and the US among the lowest of the world's richest countries in terms of providing quality early education and care (Doherty, Friendly, & Beach, 2003; UNICEF, 2008). The primary strategy for improving quality is through regulations that set minimum standards (for group size, adult–child ratios, educator training levels, health and safety) and promote "best practices" that outline prescribed activities for young children, ostensibly to foster their optimal development (Doherty, Lero, Goelman, LaGrange, & Tougas, 2000). The Early Childhood Environment Rating Scale (ECERS) and Infant Toddler Environment Rating Scale (ITERS) are well-known and widely used examples of these tools.

In recent years, measuring quality in terms of children's developmental outcomes has gained currency in the early childhood education field. An example is the assessment of children's school readiness using the Early Development Instrument (EDI), which measures children's physical, language, social, and cognitive development in kindergarten. The EDI, which is widely used in British Columbia, has enabled classification of the "risks" and "vulnerabilities" of particular classrooms, schools, and neighbourhoods (Guhn, Janus, & Hertzman, 2007).

But who selected these standards as the defining indicators of quality? What assumptions underlie these conceptions of quality? What views of children and educators are privileged in these definitions, and what views are marginalized?

In these narrow framings of quality, the educator implements already-specified developmental and learning goals which were articulated outside the complex sociopolitical contexts within which children live and within which practice is shaped and enacted. As Moss and Dahlberg (2008) argue,

quality has become reified, treated as if it was an essential attribute of services or products that gives them value, assumed to be natural and neutral. The problem with quality, from this perspective, is its management. How can quality be discovered, measured, assured and improved? What goals, to be achieved by technical means, will enhance performance and increase value? (p. 3)

In our discussions with early childhood educators, we examine and problematize our assumptions around the meanings of powerful concepts such as quality. We use our discussions as an opportunity "to create a disturbance, to avoid stagnation, and to continue to challenge ourselves and others" (Lyon et al., 2006, p. 16).

"The language of quality is the language of the early childhood institution as producer of prespecified outcomes and the child as empty vessel, to be prepared to learn and for school, and to be helped on his or her journey of development." (Dahlberg, Moss, & Pence, 2007, p. 86)

Questioning Quality

We see early childhood settings as spaces where children, families, educators, and communities can engage and interact, opening up possibilities for program quality that are much more dynamic than those that can be achieved through a "minimum standards" approach. Situating meanings of quality outside of the dominant social and political landscape requires looking beyond uniform definitions of quality and asking critical questions about complex issues as they arise in practice. Some questions we might ask include:

- How do children negotiate subjectivity?
- How do they engage with their **material** and **discursive** environments?
- How do they understand and enact democracy?
- How do children learn and become, with others, in the context of the classroom?
- What kinds of learning do we make visible? What kinds do we silence?

Asking questions like these enables us to look beyond the emphasis on measuring and improving developmental outcomes that dominates conceptions of quality in early childhood education. Asking questions like these complexifies practice.

Moving Toward a Discourse of Meaning-Making

Quality, rather than being discussed in terms of abstract measures, can be viewed as a situated pedagogical experience. By this we mean that quality isn't located somewhere "out there"—it is found in the here and now of each educator's everyday practice. In this way, quality emerges as a response to local circumstances and interactions, including particular social and cultural contexts. Engaging with quality as subjective, contingent, complex, and multi-faceted has moved us toward a discourse of meaning-making, which is

> first and foremost about constructing and deepening understanding of the early childhood institution and its projects, in particular the pedagogical work to make meaning of what is going on.... The discourse of meaning making calls for explicitly ethical and philosophical choices, judgments of value, made in relation to the wider questions of what we want for our children here and now and in the future. (Dahlberg, Moss, & Pence, 2007, pp. 106–107)

A discourse of meaning-making lets alternative pedagogies emerge—pedagogies that encourage children and educators to co-construct knowledge and resist dominant understandings that have become normalized. These new forms of pedagogies are reflected in some of the recently created early childhood education frameworks in Canada (e.g., BC's Early Learning Framework, New Brunswick's Early Learning and Child Care Curriculum Framework–English, Saskatchewan's Play and Exploration: Early Learning Program Guide). These documents embrace the tool of pedagogical narrations as a means of engaging educators and children in processes of meaning-making.

A DISCOURSE OF MEANING-MAKING

In our view, a discourse of meaning-making (Dahlberg, Moss, & Pence, 2007):

- requires an active, engaged early childhood educator.
- accommodates diversity, complexity, and multiple perspectives.
- encourages individual judgements and uncertainty.
- views consensus and unanimity as neither necessary nor desirable.
- requires individuals to make ethical philosophical choices and judgements.
- draws on concrete experience.
- involves critical, reflexive thinking about pedagogies.
- contextualizes everyday practices within a particular social location and time.
- produces meaning in dialogue with others.

We expand on each of these points below.

Meaning-Making Requires an Active, Engaged Early Childhood Educator

In this conceptualization, educators are not external, passive observers of children and objective producers of knowledge about children (e.g., in relation to children's developmental paths). Instead, they are immersed in experiences with children. They have an ethical responsibility, not to "know" the child, but to participate with the child in making meaning, to live alongside children.

During a learning circle, Veronica reflected on the complexities of an educator's active engagement with a child:

> *Levinas talks of respect and responsibility—It's my responsibility to be there but not to define the Other.... We stay in that space and struggle with it.... Christine in her pedagogical narration is trying to be very careful not to assume that she knows the child, but she's also trying to make a connection, establish a relationship, so she doesn't detach herself from the child. There's still a responsibility to connect with the child, but with humility. (Veronica)*

Meaning-Making Accommodates Diversity, Complexity, and Multiple Perspectives

Dahlberg and Moss encourage us to be "multiplicity thinkers" instead of "simplicity thinkers" by extending our thinking to that which has been marginalized and excluded (2005, p. 112). Pedagogical narration gives us a tool through which we can open up to multiple views of the child, multiple voices, multiple interpretations. We can open to diversity.

Jennifer, a participant in the IQ Project, reflects on a pedagogical narration about a boy who requested a tiara to be drawn on his forehead (see the pedagogical narration The Tiara, pp. 83–86):

> *I'm thinking about developmental theory and the whole idea that children need to learn gender constancy—that understanding of gender as a fixed or stable category. You would read that situation and say he doesn't have a sense of gender stability or constancy, so therefore he hasn't moved to that stage of gender understanding. It's a very different way of looking at it to say that he's contesting or questioning our [dominant] understanding of gender—that once you know you're a boy or a girl, you "know."*
>
> *This is why it's important to unpack our own views. If we're not aware of our own views on gender and how they are influenced by dominant discourses, we won't notice it because it just seems "natural." (Jennifer)*

Meaning-Making Encourages Individual Judgments and Uncertainty

In seeking to participate with children in meaning-making, we find opportunities to resist modernist assumptions of universal truths that can be applied to all children. Instead we can embrace the uncertainty that comes with recognizing that truth and knowledge are socially constructed within discourses that may privilege particular ways of knowing and working with children (MacNaughton, 2005).

Dianne, an IQ Project participant, reflects on the powerful influence of **dominant discourses** and how the possibilities brought by multiple readings of children's play have complexified her practice:

> *I think even understanding that there are discourses.... In the past I didn't think about the way I felt and how it's shaped by discourses. I thought I was smart when a parent challenged me and I could tell them all the mathematical concepts their child was learning through block play, but to actually look at it differently now, to pick it apart.... It's taking it way beyond "Are they fed?" "Is it naptime?" I thought I was doing a good job, but it's way more than that. (Dianne)*

Meaning-Making Views Consensus and Unanimity as Neither Necessary nor Desirable

As this excerpt from a learning circle discussion highlights, our work with pedagogical narration disrupts the view that it's possible to uncover an objective consensus of the meaning of children's encounters.

DEBBIE: *This pedagogical narration is resisting the modernist way of saying, "This happened, then this happened, then this happened."*

VERONICA: *It stays in the contradictions and ambiguities that we in early childhood education sometimes think cannot be part of our practices.*

BRIANNA: *There isn't one way in each particular moment or project. We need to be more open to that.*

Meaning-Making Requires Individuals to Make Ethical Philosophical Choices and Judgements

In the universalist approach to ethics that dominates the early childhood field, ethics is viewed as a "categorical distinction between right and wrong, applicable to and by everyone irrespective of social or historical context or circumstances" (Dahlberg & Moss, 2005, p. 66). In contrast, a discourse of meaning-making requires us to make ethical choices rather than apply predefined rules.

Kim, an IQ Project participant, reflects on her political and ethical choices to resist the dominant lenses used in her centre to view and regulate children. Kim has become aware of the difficulties of practising from an ethical and political stance.

I am interested in your concept of "silencing moments." As often happens when a topic is brought up, examples miraculously occur. A 4-year-old boy in our centre was playing outside, jumping, climbing, running, all the while holding his shirt up to reveal his stomach. I asked what he was doing and he replied that he was Blue Woman. Being completely out of touch with pop culture, I assumed it was a character from a movie. I mentioned it later to his mom, who groaned and related this story: Her son found the Victoria's Secret catalogue and asked if he could look at it—in his room with the door closed. She said ok, and then checked on him a few minutes later. He was gazing adoringly at the pages, and said they were "so beautiful." Then he said "I want to act it out!" (We act out lots of stories at preschool.) He told his mom she was to be Brown Woman, he was going to be Blue Woman, and Ruby the dog was to be Yellow Woman, naming the characters according to the colour of the underwear. He set up pillows and lounged like the models in the photos. The next day at preschool, he was holding up his shirt to be Blue Woman.

Sexuality in children is definitely a silencing moment for most of us. (Kim)

Meaning-Making Draws on Concrete Experience

A discourse of meaning-making uses the children's and educators' experiences as a starting point from which to reflect critically. Lauren, an IQ Project participant, draws from a child's experience with paint to make visible how we make meaning of the idea of special needs/rights. She intentionally resists the dominant discourses surrounding this child, who has been normalized as a child with special needs. In her words, the child

has a lot of intervention, so I really set out for time, to not have so much of his life being guided, interrupted. I really want him to explore. I sense that he is figuring out the world in his way. There is all that learning happening, but it isn't seen through a checklist.

He paints long lines down the length of the paper. His actions are slow and deliberate; he changes brushes, choosing different colours. He watches the brush intently. He seems to be watching the movement of the bristles. Some of the brush strokes accidentally go over his open hand. He stops and looks at the blue paint now on his hand, then he slowly begins to paint his fingers. Only when his hand is covered does he look at me, holding out his hand as if to say, "Look, I covered the whole hand." (Lauren)

Meaning-Making Involves Critical, Reflexive Thinking about Pedagogies

In complexifying practices, we strive to embrace a pedagogy of listening in which, as Rinaldi (2006) describes, the educator creates "a context in which children's curiosity, theories and research are legitimated and listened to, a context in which children feel comfortable and confident, motivated and respected" (p. 126).

Penny, an IQ Project participant, responds to a pedagogical narration in which a child, while painting on paper, became interested in painting his body. She reflects critically on how dominant pedagogical practices, where educators take on an authoritative, interventionist role, may marginalize children's capabilities and limit their meaning-making.

> Often we step in and say, "It's too messy, there's paint everywhere." We're so quick to jump in, but I think just giving that space—it's amazing what the child is capable of doing.... That makes the teacher vulnerable as well, allowing something to happen that is outside the comfort zone. It's not that easy to let go. (Penny)

In another example, Diana reflects on the process of deepening her questions about the children's learning in ways that resist developmental discourse.

> I felt like I was taking a risk by saying that, at the end of the day, they don't know the difference between these spiders, but they've learnt so many other things so much deeper about working together, respecting someone's opinion, if someone is saying something you disagree with, finding those answers to challenge that.... That's what was happening with these children. I felt strong enough to take a risk and say "I'm not going to go with this developmental route." That's the shift that's happening—it's reflecting on what's happening in the classroom, things that are so much deeper. (Diana)

Meaning-Making Contextualizes Everyday Practices within a Particular Social Location and Time

Contextualizing is a critical aspect of practising for social justice and equity because it creates a shift away from viewing all children through the same universalizing lens. It makes visible the discourses that may act to shape children's experiences, such as their encounters with difference.

An educator recounted in a learning circle how a child in her centre told another educator to go away, he didn't like her because she was brown. In responding, Veronica situated issues of racialization within the Canadian context of multiculturalism.

> If you think about developmental theory in that situation, you would say he's being racist—we would put it on the individual. Instead we need to see racism as

a discourse in our society, and then we can look at how the dominant discourses around racialization are actually reproduced in the classroom. Children also do racialization. If we look at that, we can read it very differently. It's uncomfortable to talk about those things, especially in Canada where we are a multicultural society. We've learned that we're multicultural and that being multicultural makes us non-racist, but in fact, racism exists everywhere. (Veronica)

Meaning-Making Produces Meaning in Dialogue with Others

As we discussed in the opening to this chapter, collaboratively reflecting with others is a key part of our learning. The dialogue below illustrates how we enrich each other's perspectives—not through seeking answers, but by opening up many possibilities for ethical response and interpretation. In this dialogue, a group of educators in the IQ Project discusses a pedagogical narration that Trina brought to the learning circle about two children—one White and one African Canadian—who called each other Chocolate and Vanilla.

TRINA: *I'm not just sure if I should make a big deal of this or if it's nothing. I don't know if I should bring it to the children and start talking about race. I don't know if I want to go that deep into it, because I don't know if that's where they are going, but ...*

JOANNE: *There is a very interesting chapter about race in a book called* Nurture-Shock: New Thinking about Children *by Po Bronson and Ashley Merryman (2009) about the need for discussion. They say that example is not enough. Children actually do want to talk about these things; these discussions are important to them. And when we don't talk about it, then it becomes the thing we don't talk about in the classroom.*

LISA: *It becomes invisible.*

TRINA: *Back in the fall we had the incident when the other little girl didn't want the brown baby ... so it's interesting that this is happening within the same year because we never experienced this before. I mean, it wasn't an issue last year. So, I'm sort of on the fence. I don't want to make a big deal out of this because it's very innocent at this point in time.*

VERONICA: *What do you mean by innocent?*

TRINA: *They're both laughing about it. They're calling each other Chocolate and Vanilla. It's very much a give and take that is happening. There is no exclusion. It seems to be just between the two of them at this point. Nobody else is engaging.*

VERONICA: *Maybe this is a good learning space for us to engage with as educators because it seems as if the children want to engage with the issue of skin colour.*

JENNIFER: *You know, it makes me think of the event that Glenda MacNaughton writes and talks about in her presentations, how, as white educators, we always have our Caucasian eyes to think about these events. Now every time that a conversation about race comes up, I think to myself, "Do not go to that place"—the place I normally go to through my Caucasian eyes where I end up saying that everything is okay. Maybe there is more to it than we know, or we can ever know … because we don't have those experiences.*

JOANNE: *I keep thinking, too, about our conversation around meeting children in their own minds. This idea comes often when I've got a dilemma going on, and then I ask myself, "How can I go about this?" So, meeting children in their own minds brings me back to "What makes me curious about this? And why?" When we show our curiosity to children about what's going on and we don't have a specific agenda of what needs to come out of it, they'll let us know how far they want to go with it.*

TRINA: *Yes, thank you. Sometimes you stray away from that piece of it. And that's what I mean, because I don't think this is big.*

JOANNE: *And they might surprise you.*

TRINA: *Yes, you're right, they might surprise me. I think I need to go back to the children and figure out what might be happening for them.*

For an illustration of how we use pedagogical narration toward a discourse of meaning-making, please see chapter 4.

Shifting Our Focus from Understanding Practice to Complexifying Practices

When we complicate our ways of knowing and doing with children, we move beyond one "best" way of responding and open up to many possibilities, thus we refer to a shift from understanding practice (singular) to complexifying practices (plural).

Using pedagogical narration to make visible what might be happening for children is a key component of our journeys in complexifying early childhood education practices. We explore this tool in depth in chapter 4. In addition, at the centre of the book, between chapters 3 and 4, we have included a selection of pedagogical narrations created by some of the educators we have worked with. We visit and revisit these narrations throughout the book to illustrate the many ways that critically engaging with different theoretical lenses to interpret children's meaning-making and identity negotiations opens possibilities for complexifying practice. In no way are these pedagogical narrations intended to signify "best practice." Rather, they suggest multiple directions that our practices might take.

If you like, please take some time now to read the pedagogical narrations in the centre section. They illustrate some of the complexities of practice that we have introduced in this chapter. The educators who documented these ordinary moments engage with and make visible multiple layers of children's meaning-making and curriculum-making. In these examples you will see the richness of children's imaginations, the complexities of their gendered identity negotiations, the shifting power dynamics in their narratives, and the particular contexts of their meaning-making—for example, in relation to popular culture.

The questions the educators ask the children and each other in these narrations are not intended to seek "truth," nor are they attempts to categorize what children know as right or wrong. Instead, they are grounded in what the children are saying and doing *at that moment*; they show a respect for children's fantasies and a curiosity about how children construct theories. They use these moments to create curriculum.

Through these dynamic processes of complexifying practice, the pedagogical narrations illustrate how "knowledge is irreducible to a static body of facts but constitutes a dynamic process of inquiry as an experimental and practical art embedded in experience" (Semetsky, 2009, p. 443).

Next, in chapter 2, we explore how processes of critical reflection and **diffraction** can be used to make visible the complexities of practice and to drive continual change toward ethical, creative, and equitable practices.

REFLECTING CRITICALLY

This chapter explores how processes of critical reflection and diffraction can be used to make visible the complexities of practices and to drive continual change toward ethical, creative, and equitable practices.

We discuss:

- The importance of bringing a critical perspective to child development.
- What we mean by critical reflection.
- Political intentionality as the basis for critical reflection.
- Some theoretical tools for critical reflection.
- A concrete example of educators engaging in collaborative critical reflection on a pedagogical narration.

Bringing a Critical Perspective to Child Development

> A preschool teacher once told me that being involved in processes of questioning taken-for-granted thinking and habits of doing pedagogical practices at first felt frightening and difficult. Soon, however, it turned into the most exciting feeling she had had during her career. However, it felt somewhat like walking through a quagmire, not knowing when she would fall into traps of taken-for-granted habits or encounter unknown situations and not immediately knowing what to rely on and do next.
> (Lenz Taguchi, 2009, p. 20)

Developmental theory forms the backbone of early childhood education practices. Theorists like Vygotsky, Bowlby, Piaget, and Erickson have provided support for the concept of developmentally appropriate practice (DAP), upon which many early childhood settings base their programs. These theories—and DAP—describe a universal path of human development that is rarely questioned or problematized.

Several authors argue that a focus on developmental theories, and on DAP, silences other ways of thinking about young children and how they learn (see, for example, Cannella, 1997; Dahlberg, Moss, & Pence, 2007; MacNaughton, 2005).

This argument is foundational to our collaborative work with educators.

Reconceptualizing Developmental Theory

Reconceptualists seek to bring perspectives to the early years field that situate theory and practice within their economic, social, cultural, historical, and political contexts. Reconceptualists draw on the multiple perspectives offered by postfoundational theories—including postmodern, poststructural, feminist, anti-racist, queer, and postcolonial theories—to politicize the "truths" of early childhood pedagogies and create spaces for "complexity, values, diversity, subjectivity, indeterminacy" (Dahlberg, Moss, & Pence, 2007, p. 108).

An important goal of the reconceptualist movement is to disrupt the centrality of child development theory—that is, to critically reflect on the assumptions and values embedded in developmental theories.

Valerie Walkerdine (1984) was one of the first feminists to challenge our field's reliance on child development theory. Arguing that ideas cannot be taken for granted without understanding how they emerge in particular social and political contexts, Walkerdine invited us to engage critically with "truths" that are created in our field. She noted, for example, that Piaget's child development theories were grounded in evolutionary biology and a quest for rational knowledge—ideas that were emblematic of his times. She also troubled the term *child centred*, arguing that, rather than liberating children, child-centredness is

> a mode of observation and surveillance and production of children. Given this, it is difficult to conceive of these practices as being the basis of any kind of pedagogy which could potentially liberate children and respect the diversity of the world. (1984, p. 195)

Erica Burman (1994), building on the work of Nikolas Rose (1985, 1990) John Morss (1996), and others, also questioned well-known child development theories (such as Bowlby's attachment and Piaget's cognitive theories) and their role in creating oppressive environments for children and women.

Feminist thinker Elly Singer (1992) showed from a historical perspective how the psychological and educational theories that formed the basis for childcare policies failed to integrate the realities of contemporary societies.

While Walkerdine, Burman, and Singer were working in Australian and European contexts, an interesting group emerged in early childhood education in the United States. A key text, *Reconceptualizing the Early Childhood Curriculum: Beginning the Dialogue* (edited by Kessler and Swadener, 1992), brought together a group of scholars in the US in a reconceptualist early childhood movement. The contributors to this text reflected on assumptions embedded in the work on DAP (Bredekamp & Copple, 1997) of the key North American professional organization, the National Association for the Education of Young Children (NAEYC). The reconceptualists argued for critical thinking about concepts such as play-based pedagogies, school readiness, discourses of care, and quantitatively focused research. They also offered alternative views of cultural and linguistic diversity.

In our projects with educators, we work with ideas brought forward by these and other scholars to broaden the lenses through which we view children. We strive to move beyond the dominant child development lens and make visible the political aspects of teaching. As we explore examples of educators' pedagogical narrations throughout this book, our readings of postcolonial, anti-racist, queer, feminist, and **poststructural** early childhood education literature have led us to new spaces of critical inquiry that have complexified our practices in ways that would not be possible if we relied solely on developmental understandings of children.

In our projects we seek to create possibilities for alternative early childhood pedagogies that allow children and educators to co-construct knowledge and to resist dominant developmental understandings that have become normalized as the singular and natural way to shape practices. Our goal is to *contextualize* and *politicize* ideas about child development that tend to be taken for granted.

This is not to say that we dismiss child developmental theories; we do not. We do, however, seek to shift their dominant position as the lens through which children are viewed. By exploring multiple lenses and contexts, we endeavour to question the acceptance of child development ideas as neutral facts.

Central to this disruption is continual critical reflection on what is marginalized or left out when children are *normalized*—that is, when they are subjected to universal developmental norms. Critical reflection allows us to think beyond developmental theories. In our collaborations, we use the tool of critical reflection to think about DAP's assumptions and effects.

Critically Reflecting on Development Theory

Critically reflecting on practices using postfoundational ideas enables us to engage with issues such as power relations, the role of dominant discourses in children's understandings, and, more broadly, questions of social justice and equity in the classroom. In other words, thinking critically about child development allows us to make visible issues that remain hidden or marginalized in developmental understandings.

Some issues we explore in our work include:

- the ways that dominant discourses privilege certain gender identities as more desirable than others
- the ways in which multicultural discourses (so prevalent in Canada) silence the multiple ways in which racisms are reproduced
- the complexity of issues related to popular culture and young children
- the need to move beyond explanations of cause and effect when we encounter them in our classrooms

These ideas are explored throughout the book.

What Do We Mean by Critical Reflection?

Prior to the first months of the IQ project, I believed I was a reflective practitioner. I would have argued strongly that I reflected regularly on my practice. That at the end of each day I looked back on what happened and gave that day some type of measurement.... I started to realize that even though I looked at how the day went for me, I neglected to go a step further and look at how the day went for the children. Then to take that reflection even further and to work with it to improve my practice [and] to make it more than a measurement of "was this a good or bad day" but to actually look at what happened ... and how to extend the learning. (Jenny)

Reflection Is Not Necessarily Critical

One risk of engaging in self-reflection is that of reflecting only at a personal level, as Jenny describes above, without recognizing that practices are embedded in social and political circumstances. Poststructural and feminist scholars warn of the dangers of using reflection in research to search for inner feelings (Burman, 2009; Davies & Gannon, 2006) without deconstructing historically, socially, and politically implicated discourses. Fendler (2003) notes that "some reflective practices may simply be exercises in reconfirming, justifying, or rationalizing preconceived ideas" (p. 16).

Without a critical orientation, reflecting on one's practices may not be productive, and it may not hold the potential for transformation. As Jenny describes, an important aspect of critically reflective practice is to move away from a focus on "how the day went for me" to engage with the broader implications of our practices.

What Purpose Does This Practice Serve?

In our learning circles, for example, we ask questions about how the day is structured in participants' childcare centres. When we ask this question, we notice that we all follow a similar schedule. Circle time, for instance, is a key feature in many centres. But why do we engage in circle time? When we ask why circle time has such a dominant presence in our practice, the answer is often "because we have to."

Next, we unpack the links between circle time and broader social and political issues. We might ask:

- What purpose does circle time serve?
- Who benefits from circle time practices?
- Can we trace circle time to developmental theories?
- How does circle time relate to surveillance practices designed to regulate children's behaviours?

Here is when our discussions turn into critical reflection because these questions have a political intent.

Critically reflecting on our practices moves us to question the beliefs, assumptions, and understandings that frame how we view and respond to children and that shape the learning experiences we make available for them. It involves reconsidering practices—seeing practices not as truths that can be categorized as good or bad, but as complex and contradictory. Critical reflection allows us to see that practices *always serve a purpose in how societies are structured.*

Group Time in Kim's Classroom

Kim engaged in critically reflecting about circle time in her classroom.

> *As I became more aware of issues around power and democracy, I was uncomfortable with the idea of the traditional circle time, so I arranged our group area with sofas and stools so children had a choice of where to sit. More*

FIGURE 2.1: Group time in Kim's classroom

importantly, as illustrated in the photo, group time was used for discussing our projects, acting out and telling stories by children, and/or engaging in conversations that the children wanted to explore. Everyone was welcomed in our group times. This photo shows that siblings and other family members often participated in group time. (Kim)

Critical reflection does not imply that answers will emerge easily. Making social inequities like processes of racialization visible in early childhood classrooms can create spaces of discomfort (see Becoming Rapunzel, pp. 86–95). Critical reflection is an active process of engaging with difficult concepts, tensions, and uncertainties.

It's a place where we sometimes become uncomfortable, because we don't have all the answers. Nobody has all the answers ... but critical reflection provides opportunities for more exploration. (Kelley)

Critical reflection requires us to approach our practice with curiosity and political intent. It requires us to look closely at the dynamics in the early childhood classroom. By challenging the image of the "expert" educator and the idea that children's development follows a "natural" developmental path, critical reflection highlights the inherent complexities, contradictions, and multiplicities in early childhood practice. As we reflect on our practices, we can consider ways to resist the familiarity of taken-for-granted knowledge. By doing so, we can extend children's learning and our curriculum in multiple ways.

We return to the concept of using multiple lenses or perspectives in chapter 5.

DECONSTRUCTING CLAIMS TO TRUTH

Garrick and Rhodes assert that "all claims to truth must be deconstructed to disrupt privileged ideas and critically re-examine taken for granted ways of seeing the world" (1998, p. 179).

Deconstructing (i.e., critically reflecting on) taken-for-granted ideas in early childhood education is central to our work. Here are some of the questions we ask:

- What ideas do we privilege in our early childhood education practices?
- What assumptions, values, and beliefs are we using to inform our views of practices?
- What other perspectives might we use to critically rethink the "truths" we hold about teaching and learning?
- What rules, routines, expectations, and norms limit or shape our views of desirable early childhood practices?

Critical Reflection and Political Intentionality

Critical reflection is about making discourses visible and interrupting dominant ones. We need to acknowledge how powerful discourses are, to be able to look at what is so deeply ensconced that we can't step back. (Veronica)

In our view, the basis for critical reflection is political intent. As Dahlberg, Moss, and Pence (2007) assert, "too much discussion of early childhood occurs in a social, political, economic and philosophical vacuum, as if young children exist apart from the world" (p. 10). In fact, children are very much part of the social, cultural, political, and economic worlds in which they live.

Critical reflection requires us to consider how knowledge and practice in early childhood are underpinned by historically, politically, and socially constructed forces that shape what is seen, said, and done—as well as what is hidden or marginalized (MacNaughton, 2003). Once we identify these discourses, we can challenge those that maintain inequities in our everyday practices, particularly those taken-for-granted ways of knowing and acting that remain unquestioned precisely because they seem natural to us. Critical reflection, then, should be seen as part of an ongoing effort to disrupt and resist "oppressive and inequitable power relations in the classroom" (MacNaughton, 2005, p. 10).

In our work with educators, we strive to bring the political into our early childhood practices by engaging with critically reflective questions like the ones below. We invite you to consider some of these questions.

- Where have our ideas about early childhood education practices come from?
- Who generated these ideas?
- Whom do they benefit?
- How does power operate in maintaining these ideas?
- What are some of the reasons I hold these ideas?

Deborah Thompson, an ELF Project participant, engages with the possibilities and limits that come from holding fixed ideas:

> Often the various roles that I take up to position me as "the expert" who "knows": my knowledge is placed above that of children, families, students, and other caregivers. Responsibility and commitment demand knowledge, but "knowing" can limit my ability to learn new ways and new ideas. On the other hand, resisting the impulse to know sometimes challenges my ability to respond in the midst of practice and to commit. And, while I strive to be open to new ideas and to others' beliefs and values, I also have passionate ideals (my own beliefs and values) that sometimes work to close off particular practices. (Thompson, 2010, p. 80)

- **How can we consider the broader social, cultural, and political contexts of our locations as we strive to understand the world from the perspective of groups who are consistently marginalized and silenced in our practices?**

An important goal of contextualizing our perspectives is to resist the linearity and certainties of the modernist discourse that views all children from developmental psychology's Euro-Western image of childhood (Pence & Hix-Small, 2009). By engaging in critical reflection, we can consider the social, political,

and economic contexts in which we practise, as well as the diverse realities
of children and families.

- **How can we make visible how issues of gender, class,
  and "race" emerge in the classroom and change our
  practices to act in socially just ways?**

Critically reflective practice doesn't mean fixating on what is wrong or right
about a particular representation of gender, "race," or class that emerges in
the classroom. Instead it moves us to seek new potentials and ethical relations,
asking, for example, Where else could this go? What kinds of new encounters
are possible? How might the material and discursive environments be rearranged to increase children's capacities for ethical action?

In chapter 1 we included a discussion about two boys in an early childhood program who called each other Chocolate and Vanilla. Here Trina, the
educator who brought this encounter to the learning circle in the form of a
pedagogical narration, reflects on it.

> Over the past month and a half, two boys in our class have been calling each other
> Chocolate and Vanilla. One child has white skin tone and the other has brown.
> These children have been together since they were in our infant/toddler classroom.
>
> Chocolate and Vanilla all started when Vanilla said to Chocolate, "You
> look like chocolate ice cream, yummy."
>
> I thought about this encounter over our two-week spring break. Am
> I allowing racism to happen without stopping it? Should I stop it? How
> innocent is this? What are the boys exploring right now? Is this a good time
> to talk about race? Should I speak to the boys quietly and ask them to stop?
> How do I explain my feelings to the children about such a large topic? Is this
> bigger than I realize? Are families going to worry? I do my best every day to
> teach these children how to be caring ...
>
> These questions followed me. I thought I would leave it alone and keep
> my eyes and ears open after spring break to see if the situation progressed any
> further. Maybe it was just a silly little game the boys played.
>
> After spring break a parent came to speak with me. She said her daughter
> had mentioned that two boys in the class were calling each other Chocolate and
> Vanilla. The mother expressed her discomfort with this. She was worried that
> the boys might create an unhealthy environment. Race is a complicated subject,
> she noted; she teaches her daughter that people are all the same on the inside.
>
> She wasn't the only parent to express discomfort. It happened with a couple of
> other families. There happened to be student-led conferences that week, so it was a

perfect time to speak with a few of the parents, especially Chocolate's and Vanilla's
families, about how they feel about this event. I knew that Chocolate's mom was
aware of what was going on. She had heard them talk about it in the hall just
before spring break. She seemed ruminative about it at the time, but she smiled and
laughed. I didn't hear anything from her, so I just thought it was okay.

I felt I needed to bring this reflective documentation—and, more
importantly, my many questions—to the group so we could talk about what
might be possible. (Trina)

As this example shows, the process that we engage in during learning circles
of critically reflecting on educators' pedagogical narrations provides us with
opportunities to make issues of "race," class, and gender visible when they
emerge in the classroom.

> ▪ **How can we honour the understandings of diverse groups**
> **by deconstructing and reconstructing what we do and**
> **think in our practices?**

Critical reflection enables educators to become aware of power relations and
privilege in interactions with children and families. Through critical reflection, we can question and shift our practices. For instance, we can consider
ethical approaches to cultural and linguistic diversity, and challenge hierarchies
based on colonial histories and immigrant status. Through critical reflection,
we can move beyond merely acknowledging diversity to enact social justice.

Throughout the book we use examples of pedagogical narration to illustrate how critical reflection can be used as a political tool.

For pedagogical narrations that engage with racialization and colonization, see:

No Chinese-Face Homeless, pp. 131–133

Stand Up, p. 152

Becoming Rapunzel, pp. 86–95

For pedagogical narrations that engage with sexuality and gender, see:

The Tiara, pp. 83–86

Princesses and Pirates, pp. 76–83

For pedagogical narrations that engage with gun play, see:

Hunters, Good Guys, and Bad Guys, pp. 37–38

Building a Fort, pp. 105–112

For examples that engage with special needs/rights, see:

Entangled Bodies, pp. 96–105

Theoretical Tools for Critical Reflection

The goal of reflective practice is not to find solutions to use in our every-day practices, but to use theoretical tools to reimagine new worlds and create openings for ethical possibilities in practice.

In the early years field, reconceptualist perspectives enable critical engagement with the power effects of privileging particular types of knowledge about children and families. This engagement opens up possibilities for the ongoing transformation of early childhood education and care in the direction of ethical practices (Lenz Taguchi, 2009; MacNaughton, 2005). While we explain our understanding and use of key reconceptualist concepts in chapter 5 and in the section Understanding Our Language: A Glossary (pp. 195–216), below we outline how some of these perspectives support collaborative critical reflection processes and discuss how we employ these theoretical tools to complexify our practices. For each perspective, we've suggested an example of a pedagogical narration that illustrates it, but we certainly don't mean to imply that the example is the only one in the book that relates to a particular perspective.

Social Constructionism Perspectives

Social constructionist perspectives enable educators to critique the assumption of universal truths about children, families, and what constitutes "good practice." Using a social constructionist lens for critical reflection, educators can, for example, question how children's knowledge and meanings are co-created and negotiated in social relationships and mediated by **discourses** in their particular contexts.

See Princesses and Pirates on pp. 76–83 for an example of an educator using a social constructionist perspective.

Poststructuralist Perspectives

Poststructuralist perspectives provide conceptual and pedagogical tools for contesting taken-for-granted knowledge through critically reflective practice. Poststructuralism views knowledge (including the discourses that inform views of children and early childhood practices) as socially constructed; that is, as shaped by particular economic, social, cultural, and political contexts. In bringing poststructural understandings to critical reflection, educators can question inequities and their impacts on every-day practices. They can also critically examine the marginalizing effects of some dominant discourses and begin to generate alternative discourses (Ryan & Grieshaber, 2005).

See Building a Fort on pp. 105–112 for an example of an educator using a poststructuralist perspective.

Feminist Poststructural Perspectives

Feminist poststructural perspectives provide useful lenses for considering issues of gender in early childhood classrooms. These perspectives consider the ways in which children continually negotiate their gendered subjectivities and make meaning within complex and contradictory discourses according to what is desirable or powerful in their particular contexts (Davies, 1989, 2000; Walkerdine, 1990). Critically reflective practice using feminist poststructural lenses opens possibilities for educators to consider the inequitable effects of dominant gender discourses, including how power shapes the construction of knowledge (MacNaughton, 2003, 2005), and to create pedagogies that open spaces for disrupting hierarchical gender constructions (MacNaughton, 2005).

See The Tiara on pp. 83–86 for an example of an educator using a feminist poststructuralist perspective. Also see chapter 5 for a related perspective, queer theory.

Postcolonial Perspectives

Postcolonial perspectives offer possibilities to acknowledge and resist the unjust effects of coloniality. Postcolonial theories enrich critical reflection by making visible and confronting practices whose oppressive potentials may be hidden or subtle in taken-for-granted understandings (Viruru, 2005). For example, educators can contest and question the power relations embedded in the universal categorization of all children under the normative gaze of Western neoliberal models of early childhood development and care. Postcolonial theories encourage practices that embrace "divergent thinking, characterized by movement away from set patterns and goals and toward a more whole perspective, one that includes rather than excludes" (Viruru, 2005, p. 23).

See Becoming Rapunzel on pp. 86–95 for an example of an educator using a postcolonial perspective.

Social Justice Perspectives

Engaging with social justice and equity is an intrinsic aspect of politicized critical reflection. Critical reflection requires continual attention to practices that marginalize others and create or maintain inequities and injustices. Critically reflective attention to the ways in which young children's and educators' identities are constantly negotiated within different and oppositional discourses is an important part of creating socially just pedagogical possibilities. By considering the discourses at work in the classroom, educators and researchers can act toward social justice. For example, when encounters with social injustices emerge in the classroom, educators can deconstruct dominant understandings, such as dominant constructions of gender and "race" (MacNaughton, 2005).

See Entangled Bodies on pp. 96–105 for an example of an educator using a **social justice perspective**.

Sociomaterial Perspectives

Considering the social and material worlds as mutually transformative can generate many possibilities for critically reflective practice. Educators can consider how particular materials take an active part in shaping learning; they can critically reflect on how to read, interpret, respond to, enrich, and problematize encounters with materials. Sylvia Kind, an IQ Project facilitator, provides an example of how we might critically reflect on children's encounters with materials:

> What if we thought ... of encounters and negotiations? We might see a young child sitting on a large slab of clay on a mat and begin to imagine how the clay becomes a medium for negotiating power and strength. The child presses into the clay, working her hands and feet and body into the dense clay. As she presses in, the clay resists, it doesn't bend easily. In its resistance the clay speaks back—in its strength, density, weight, heaviness it is a force to be struggled with. In this sense clay also has a voice and a presence. It is ... a medium for negotiating and interacting with. The clay becomes a partner in the creative process, an object of encounter rather than a medium for re-presenting thought. (Kind, 2010, p. 125)

Sociomaterial perspectives also bring attention to the role of the physical or material in creating identities. These perspectives suggest that subjectivities, including gendered and racialized subjectivities, not only are created through language or discourse, but also emerge in the very moments of encounter between bodies, things, and discourse. Critical reflection would bring attention to the material aspects and effects of the classroom to ask what particular discursive and material **assemblages** gather to charge a particular encounter. For example, in Becoming Rapunzel, what elements have been arranged in that particular moment (e.g., hair, pencils, books, educator, children) to assemble **racialization**? Considering these assemblages opens space for new arrangements to emerge that may create movement toward social justice and equity. In relation to racialization, for example, critically reflective questions might consider what systemic and discursive forces are at work, as well as how "race" acts, how it comes to matter, and how it functions in that particular moment. Sociomaterial understandings allow for critical engagement with racialization in its many different variations—and offers the potential to encounter difference from an ethical standpoint.

See Jacob's Encounter on pp. 140–141 for an example of an educator using a sociomaterial perspective.

See Becoming Rapunzel on pp. 86–95 for an example of using a sociomaterial perspective in relation to racialization.

In chapter 5, we use specific examples to illustrate how educators in our projects have put reconceptualist ideas to work to capture and interpret moments of practice with pedagogical narrations.

Pedagogical Narration: A Tool for Critical Reflection

In our individual and collective work, we use pedagogical narration as a tool for critical reflection, planning, and action within the discourse of meaning-making. Working with pedagogical narration allows educators in our projects to collaborate while provoking, stretching, and challenging each other's thinking in relation to theories and practices. The contingencies, uncertainties, and complexities of practice—including how they are situated within particular political discourses—emerge through intensive discussions of the pedagogical narrations in our learning circles.

Our use of pedagogical narration embraces values that are foundational to the work conducted in the Reggio Emilia early childhood education centres in Italy, in preschool programs in Sweden, and in early childhood programs in New Zealand. These innovative programs:

- regard the child as an active learner
- value the roles of community and relationships in learning
- view curriculum as an experiential, dynamic, relational process
- view learning and life as ongoing experimentation (Dahlberg, Moss, & Pence, 2007).

Pedagogical narration is a useful tool for critically reflecting on, and creating curriculum that builds on, the multiple and emergent influences of children's relationships with social and material worlds. Our dialogue and critical reflections make visible the complexities of the meaning-making that occurs in children's encounters and interactions with early childhood spaces, materials, other children, and educators, and the influence of dominant discourses on these encounters and interactions. From a postfoundational perspective, pedagogical narration does not claim that what is documented is "a true account of what has happened" (Hultqvist & Dahlberg, 2001, p. 23). Instead, what we document is a social construction in which we as educators participate with children to co-construct meanings (Hultqvist & Dahlberg, 2001).

We explore pedagogical narration in depth in chapter 4. Here, to highlight some of the critically reflective processes we have discussed in this chapter, we present a pedagogical narration and some excerpts from discussions that emerged from it. As you read the pedagogical narration and the reflections that follow, think about the ways they illustrate critical reflection.

HUNTERS, GOOD GUYS, AND BAD GUYS[1]

A group of children was offered large DUPLO blocks to play with outside. The teachers were challenged when different variations of guns and gun play appeared. While the teachers wanted to respect and support the children's interest in trying on different roles of power, it was difficult to control the impulse to intervene and "shut it down."

> *The four boys were clear about being on a bear hunt. They were serious hunters, propping their rifles upright on their shoulder because "that's how it's done." They paused in different areas, watching closely for their prey. They rushed in to retrieve the meat when the animal had been brought down.*
> *"Follow me!"*
> *"We are the bad guys!"*
> *"We're going to shoot all of the bikes, anything with wheels!"*
> *"Ready, set, shoot!"*
> *The boys continued stalking and posturing for 25 minutes.*
> *I stepped in when a gun was pointed into the playhouse and William shouted: "I'm going to shoot your eyeball out!"*
> *At a loss for how to deal with the situation, I thought the extreme. I asked, "How would you feel if this was your mother?"*
> *William quickly put down the gun and went to play soccer instead.*

....
1 We also discuss gun play in relation to the pedagogical narration Building a Fort (see pp. 105–112).

The next time we were outside, William asked for the big LEGOs. He immediately clarified: "I know, they are not for shooting at people, only for pretend shooting."

William's tone of voice really got me. He reminded me of an impatient teenager, ready to borrow the car. "Of course I will be careful!" (Just short of rolling his eyes.) After some serious reflection, it was no wonder to me that he was making a statement like that. I had witnessed his instructions to "shoot at all of the bikes." My discomfort had led me to be on the watch for any "crossing of the line" which, for me in this case, came with the statement "I'm going to shoot your eyeball out." My discomfort led me to shut down the children's play. Now I wonder where their play would have gone if I hadn't intervened. Would William have discovered a too-gruesome reality on his own? Would his friends have eventually demanded their turn in a leadership role?

William's mother showed up at the fence one afternoon. I described the scenario to her, including my trepidation and uncertainty. She said that William probably gets to see more adult-content viewing than he should, but she added that she is there when he is watching it and she is careful to interpret what he sees. She felt quite certain that William knows what is real and what is imaginary. It was a helpful, respectful conversation. (Tracey)

Educators' Reflections on Tracey's Narration

We and some of the educators in our projects critically reflected together on Tracey's pedagogical narration. Some excerpts from our discussions follow.

ANGELIE: *I've been reflecting about gun play in our centre over the last 20-plus years. When I went through the early childhood education program back in the 80s, it was drilled into us that gun play had a very negative effect on children. So I spent the 80s and 90s redirecting the children away from gun play/sword play.... Last week two boys were creating guns out of Tinkertoys. One of the educators calmly suggested that they could make a really cool plane out of the materials. The boys had no interest in changing their shooting game. I noticed that one of the guns had a pointed end; that concerned me for safety reasons. The boys were running back and forth in the room trying to shoot the invisible bad guy. I suggested that the child put a round tire piece on the end of his gun so that no one got accidentally poked. I went on to explain that now it looked like a machine gun that could shoot several bullets at once. The child listened intently as I explained about machine guns, then gave me a big smile as he ran off with his revised gun.*

KIM: *Interesting thoughts, Angelie. I have gone through much the same evolution as you. I disallowed my own boys gun play and redirected that kind of play at work. And now I'm letting it go. Like you, I'm happy to not be nagging about it. Even when I redirected it, the play was more or less the same, just using something similar to a gun and calling it something else. I wonder what I was afraid of? Did I think these boys would turn into gun-toting maniacs? Not really. I see it now as drama, trying out roles of leader and follower, power, courage, bravery, fear, the thrill of the chase, and working collectively for a common goal.*

ENID: *I would like to think more about what we mean by aggressive and assertive. Do children need to experience different ways of being and relating in order to understand more about power and relationships? If we are pretending to be aggressive are we really being aggressive? Or are we just pretending? When is a line crossed—if there is such a thing as a line? Where do our feelings of discomfort fit in and why? Do we allow our feelings of discomfort? Do children know that guns kill or hurt? What is pretend for children? What does it mean to us?*

RITA: *Maybe we want children to be children and not have to worry about things we consider to be in the adult realm. Children do seem to grow up so quickly these days. I wonder if we're hoping to slow it all down just a little.*

DANIELLE: *I myself as a child played cops and robbers a lot and I turned out fine. So what are we really afraid of? I wonder, do we as adults feel a sense of failure that we didn't instill "morals" or "ethics" about peace and getting along? I have never completely bought into the "no weapons" rule. Yet I still use those words more than I care to and it's almost automatic. Who am I using those words for? The children? The parents? Or the onlookers?*

KIM: *Rita's thoughts on our view of children as innocent and how that influences how we handle gun play brings up lots of questions. When children play out behaviour we consider "adult only" it makes us uncomfortable— sexualized play (girls posing and flaunting), swearing, violence without guns (bashing the dolls), racist language, using power manipulatively. I feel we have an obligation to intervene in many of these areas, [or maybe] all of them.*

ENID: *What does gun play mean for the children? How is it gendered? (I remember playing guns with my brother and wrestling with him.) What is safe? Tracey was listening deeply to the child in question and she responded from that place—honestly and directly. We all wonder many times about what we said and if it was the right thing. My thinking is that the places of discomfort are the places we need to learn from … they are signals to us to pay attention!*

In the above interpretations of gun play, we see disruptions of dominant ideas like the innocent child, the expert educator, and the marginalization of family perspectives. These are just some of many potential disruptions. The educators' comments underscore Glenda MacNaughton's contention that "critical reflection means there are always far more questions than there are answers" (2005, p. 7). Here are some questions that we find helpful; we invite you to reflect on them.

- How does Tracey, the educator who presented this narration, invite others (e.g., family, other educators) to make meaning of children's experiences?
- How does she embrace uncertainty, complexity, values, and subjectivity (Dahlberg, Moss, & Pence, 2007) in her interactions with and responses to the children? In her engagements with William's mother? With the reflective questions she poses in the narration?
- In what ways do the educators' discussions disrupt a "single, fixed truth" (MacNaughton, 2005, p. 130) of the children's play through the questions they pose?
- How do these discussions challenge the image of the "expert" educator?
- What are some contradictions in the educators' and researchers' reflections? For example, how do the educators conform to and resist the image of the innocent child?
- In both the pedagogical narration and the educators' discussions, how are children's encounters interpreted from the multiple perspectives we introduced in this chapter, such as developmental, feminist poststructural, and social constructionist perspectives?
- What possibilities emerge for extending the children's understandings and disrupting hegemonic masculinities? What possibilities remain hidden?
- How is the children's play situated, through the educators' and researchers' reflections, within historical, social, and political contexts? For example, how are the workings of neoliberalism, capitalism, and heteronormativity made visible and deconstructed? What further possibilities come into view for making these effects visible?
- How might we consider the active role of the materials provided to the children? What might happen if we consider everything that acts in this narration (e.g., the educator, the children's bodies and their movements in the room, the materials children use to make the weapons, what is said at that moment, and memories of various popular media) as an assemblage whose elements intra-act to create this event as a complex sociomaterial encounter?

From Reflection to Diffraction

As we noted earlier in the chapter, reflection—particularly reflection that is enacted as self-expression—may result in fixity of thought and perspective that tends to "hold the world at a distance" and maintain boundaries between the educator and the object of reflection (Barad, 2007, p. 87). Hultman and Lenz Taguchi (2010) explain this phenomenon where

> reflection is thought to be an inner mental activity apart from the image: the researcher takes a step back and reflects about how and what s/he sees or thinks. The [educator] is understood to make her/his reflections at a distance from or from the outside of the [practice or pedagogical encounter].... Subjects (knowers) and objects (known), as well as discourse and reality, words and things, are still seen as separated entities. (p. 536)

The concept of diffraction can help to move us away from this fixity. Diffraction disrupts the construction of emotion and intention as fixed concepts to be excavated from one's interior by reflection. This disruption occurs through an emphasis on the mutual transformation and material entanglements that are a part of critical reflection. As Højgaard and Søndergaard (2011) explain, the term *diffraction* is drawn from the field of physics; it refers to the way in which water, sound, or light waves combine and move (p. 7). The movements, they explain, suggest differences that are generated from within. They apply this concept to the act of reflection:

> Where reflection operates with a distance to the object and with assumed fixed, absolute boundaries between subject and object [and] between objects, representations, and knowledge producers, the concept of diffraction implies such possible differences and boundaries as results of movement from within the interconnected/mutually saturated phenomenon you are dealing with. (p. 7)

In this way, "diffraction does not produce 'the same' [thing] displaced, as reflection and refraction do" (quoted in Barad, 2003, p. 803). A diffractive educator can thus be seen as resisting the notion that reflection can be performed separately from practice. One does not relate a story of one's inner thoughts and then stand outside the pedagogical encounters that one is reflecting on. As Hultman and Lenz Taguchi (2010) assert, "we can never reflect upon something on our own; to reflect means to inter-connect with something ... reflection is always done in the midst of a complex network" (p. 536).

Diffraction disrupts the separation of the discursive, material, and linguistic elements that form pedagogical encounters. These elements exist in interconnected and interrelated emergent relationship with each other—and with the educator and the educator's thoughts or reflections.

The concept of diffraction helps us to complexify our practices by challenging us to consider critical reflection *as an encounter whose meaning cannot be isolated within the individual educator*. Diffraction moves us away from representational reflection and helps us to visualize assemblages of different matter (such as people, early childhood spaces, materials) and discursive meaning in an encounter. In other words, "a diffractive strategy takes into account that knowing is never done in isolation but is always effected by different forces coming together" (Hultman & Lenz Taguchi, 2010, p. 536).

Below we illustrate the concept of diffraction with an example of children's explorations with sand and water that were documented by an educator participating in the IQ Project. We then offer a reading of these encounters. We invite you to engage with the images using the concept of diffraction and consider what might be occurring between the materials and the children.

The Pool

(Kate)

FIGURE 2.2: Children playing in pool of water

FIGURE 2.3: Child taking care of pool of water

If we think about the concept of diffraction as we view these images, we can see that the children are not simply playing with water and sand, nor are they mirroring or representing the world (Hultman & Lenz Taguchi, 2010). The intent of **diffractive visualization** is not to reveal the reality of events or to describe, as an outside observer of either the images or the event, the children's encounters with the water and sand. Instead, diffractive visualization is itself an event that involves actively immersing yourself in the images. In so doing, it produces reflections that are shaped by the material and discursive events of encountering the images.

As Hultman and Lenz Taguchi (2010) explain, diffraction does not mean imagining ourselves sitting in a puddle or playing with water or holding wet sand.

In a diffractive reading of the children's encounters with sand and water, we can bring together and consider both our perspectives and the "agentic force and intensity" (Lenz Taguchi, 2009, p. 81) of the materials—not as static, separate, or independent, but as interrelated and active elements of an assemblage that includes the educator's reflexive encounter with the images. For example, in Fikile's encounter with the images of children playing with sand and water, she says:

> *I see the ripples, waves, splashes, and other movements in the water that emerge as the children place their hands in the water to be some of the ways that the*

water is "acting back" in provocation, resistance, and mutual transformative processes. How might we see the water acting as it slows down the children's movements as they walk through it, so that they have to exert a force to make splashes, and adjust their leg movements to make different-sized splashes and push back against the water's resistance? The cold air, the educators' watching, the proximity of children's bodies to each other as they splash, the shifting shadows and patterns in the water all come together to create a diffractive and creative assemblage, an event that cannot be simplistically represented as children playing with water. (Fikile)

In practice, then, diffractive thinking moves us away from assigning fixed meanings and representations; it seeks the "*events* of activities and encounters, evoking transformation and change in the performative agents involved" (Hultman & Lenz Taguchi, 2010, p. 535). The water, the sand, and the children's bodies

> all become different in themselves as a result of the intra-action, while what they were before the intra-action still remains in what emerges and becomes: each body becoming anew. (Hultman & Lenz Taguchi, 2010, pp. 535–36)

As this chapter has discussed, critical reflection involves rethinking taken-for-granted images of children, families, and educators. In our collaborative work with educators, we complexify critical reflection by using the concept of diffraction to move us away from fixed meanings or representations that might arise from our reflections.

Next, in chapter 3, we discuss in more depth our engagement with post-foundational ideas as a means to disrupt and reconceptualize dominant images of the child, the family, and the educator.

CHALLENGING ASSUMPTIONS

In this chapter we critically examine some images of the child, the educator, and the family that are prevalent in the early childhood field. Taking inspiration from Reggio Emilia and postfoundational perspectives that situate childhoods within sociocultural, historical, and economic contexts, we explore how dominant images and taken-for-granted assumptions may limit our practices, and consider ways to complexify them.

We discuss:

- Some ways to rethink dominant images of the child.
- Using postfoundational approaches to complexify our image of the child.
- Children's participation in curriculum-making.
- Alternative images of the child.
- Moving beyond a "diversity" perspective.
- Using a sociomaterial perspective to move beyond discourse.
- Dominant and alternative images of the educator and of families.
- Complexifying the learning journey by challenging assumptions.

Images of the Child

What if we create a different image of a child? What if we look at what a child can do, at what they can express? What if we have been vastly underestimating and "cute-ifying" what children are capable of? What if we see children as continually forming theories and then testing them? (Kim)

In our context in North America we tend to see children as having needs and vulnerabilities, mostly defined through developmental lenses. Children are seen to have emotional needs, social needs, language needs, cognitive needs, and physical needs that vary according to their stage of development. Some dominant images of children include:

- the child as incomplete adult
- the child as future citizen
- the child as nature—an essential being with universal characteristics and inherent capabilities whose development is viewed as an innate process
- the child as innocent, living in a golden stage of life
- the child as weak and in need of guidance, security, and direction from adults
- the child at risk
- the child as vulnerable and in need of protection/surveillance
- the child as an empty vessel to be filled with knowledge
- the child as deficient and in need of adult intervention

While these images of children are not "wrong," we can look at them as **dominant discourses**. We use this term to describe the way things are named, spoken of, and written that become experienced as objective and true—what Foucault (1980) called "regimes of truth." As regimes of truth, discourses hold power over individual and societal ways of understanding the world; they organize our everyday experience of the world, govern our ideas, thoughts, and actions, and determine "what can be said and not said, what we consider normal or not normal, appropriate or inappropriate" (Moss, 2001, p. 10).

Rethinking Dominant Images of the Child

Alternatives to these dominant images are emerging. In their work in Australia, for example, MacNaughton, Hughes, and Smith (2007) promote a model of the child that reflects "a new concern with young children's rights as citizens and new knowledge about the significance of young children's early experiences" (2007, p. 458). This image of the child is influencing policy documents, training materials, and practices in some parts of Canada. As one example, the British Columbia Early Learning Framework (BC ELF) views young children as social actors who shape their identities, generate and communicate legitimate views about the world around them, and have a right to participate in that world. The framework states:

All children are born with a curiosity about themselves, other people, and the world around them, and in this sense are born learners.... This framework ... views young children as capable and full of potential, as persons with complex identities, grounded in their individual strengths and capacities and their unique social, linguistic, and cultural heritage. In this image, children are rooted in and take nourishment from a rich, supportive ground comprised of relationships with their families and communities, their language and culture, and the surrounding environment. As children grow and learn, they ask questions, explore, and make discoveries, supported by these roots and branching out to new experiences, people, places, and things in their environment.... Every child belongs and contributes. (Government of British Columbia, 2008a, pp. 2–4)

We refer to the BC ELF in our projects, in part because it highlights the importance of pedagogies that build on every child's potential. We also acknowledge the dynamism, diversity, and contradictions inherent in the images of childhood we all hold—and the challenge of resisting the powerful influence of dominant social constructions of children in early childhood pedagogies. In our discussions, we consider how we always work from specific images of the child yet rarely make these images explicit in our practices. Together we discuss ways to deconstruct dominant images (e.g., the child in need) and reconstruct alternative ones (e.g., the gendered child, the racialized child). In such perspectives, children may be seen as:

- curious, competent, rich, and full of potential (Rinaldi, 1993, p. 114)
- having voices to be listened to as citizens and members of social groups (MacNaughton, Hughes, & Smith, 2008)
- agents of their own lives (Moss & Petrie, 2002)
- co-constructors of knowledge, identity, and culture who constantly make meaning of their lives and the world (James & Prout, 1997)

These alternative images allow us to interrupt, if only momentarily, our dominant images and create more complex subjectivities for and with children. We don't argue that these alternative images are better, but rather that they are necessary in our journey of complexifying practice. We are ethically obliged, from this perspective, to always question our images, even our alternatives to dominant narratives.

We view this process of continual reflection about the images of the child as key to understanding why we do what we do in our practices with young children. Some of the questions we critically reflect on include the following (drawn from MacNaughton, 2003, and Moss & Petrie, 2002):

- What is my perspective on the child?
- How is that perspective reflected in my practice?
- Who do I think children are?
- What assumptions are embedded in the way I look at children, talk about children, work with children?
- Which sciences do I bring in to my image of the child? (e.g., child development, anthropology, history, genetics, biology)
- What views are missing from my understanding of who children are?
- What meanings of words or concepts are key to my understanding of children?
- What meanings are marginalized, silenced, or "othered"?
- How do these meanings lead to taken-for-granted assumptions about children?
- Are there other ways of understanding what these concepts mean?

These discussions are an important component of our work with pedagogical narration, which we find to be a valuable tool for making visible the images we hold of the child and challenging some of the images presented by developmental theories. One example of a pedagogical narration that creates and makes visible alternative views of the child—including the child as meaning maker, as gendered, as not necessarily innocent—is Princesses and Pirates (see pp. 76–83). Below, Kim, the educator who created this pedagogical narration, reflects on the richness she sees in children's meaning-making and expressions of imagination.

> *Having the chance to listen to children's stories and imaginative play is a gift. The trick is to actually listen. The conversations I hear are rich with imagination and they tell me something about the children participating. Listening to children—really listening—opens up their world to us, allows us a glimpse into how they may think, how they are interpreting what they see around them. We can get clues as to how they make sense of media and of what their families and their friends do. And we can be filled with wonder to see just how much children know. (Kim)*

We return to Princesses and Pirates later in this chapter to explore how children's play is embedded in societal discourses of gender.

Complexifying the Image of the Child:
Postfoundational Approaches

Reconceptualist scholars resist viewing children through a primarily developmental lens that imagines a universalized, innocent child and views childhood as a progression of stages toward adulthood. This lens is resisted, in part, because "a developmental knowledge base is inadequate to the task of teaching children in current times" (Ryan & Grieshaber, 2004, p. 44).

Reconceptualist perspectives on children represent a significant shift in early childhood educator training in British Columbia. As ELF Project participant Kathleen Kummen reflects below regarding her experiences as a teacher of early childhood educators, the discourse of a universal child is a dominant one that is challenging to shift:

> Do the students I work with see the child as a universal concept that can be "known objectively" and "governed rationally" (Rose, 1996)? From my perspective, a large number of the students describe all children as "x" with no provision made in their image for the absence of "x".... Children are complex, contradictory, and unknown. When we tell and retell one story of a child, we construct a singular universal child. Chimamanda Adichie (2009) warns us of the danger of this single story. A universal image of the child silences, marginalizes, and oppresses the everyday lived experiences of "real" children. (Kummen, 2011, p. 3)

In our projects we draw from feminist poststructural scholars in early childhood (e.g., Lenz Taguchi, 2009; MacNaughton, 2005), among other theorists, to make visible how children are aware of race and gender and the power they hold in particular contexts. We consider pedagogical responses that move beyond developmental appropriateness, and we strive to be aware of the discourses that are at work in framing children's interactions.

Differing Perspectives on Identity Formation

In early childhood development texts that are based on psychological understandings of identity, children are depicted as coherent beings who develop their identity in a progressive path toward a final adult sense of self. A postfoundational perspective understands children's identities differently. Poststructural feminists, for instance, foreground the concept of **subject formation** (subjectivity) and describe processes of subjectivity as those in which the individual becomes a subject in the world through discursive negotiations. Feminist poststructural theorists bring attention to the way that children's identities, or subjectivities, are always embedded within discourses, such as those that shape gender, "race," ethnicity, class, language, and immigration status (Davies, 2000; Robinson & Jones-Diaz, 2005). We become subjects, Lenz Taguchi suggests,

> in a simultaneous process of being subjected to dominant discourses and subjecting ourselves to them by picking up normalized meanings. Alternatively we might go against the grain of these meanings and formulate resistant meanings and discourses.... The subject can be understood as an individual patchwork or weave of materialized negotiated meanings. (2010, pp. 42–43)

As adults we act differently within different contexts. Children do the same. You have undoubtedly noticed that children act one way with you, the educator, and in other ways with their families. An educator may report, for example, that a child is very well behaved. The parent may appear shocked, saying this is not what they experience at home. Understanding that we all have many subjectivities opens up the possibility of understanding children's complex identities.

From a poststructural feminist standpoint, an individual "emerges through the processes of social interaction, *not as a relatively fixed end product,* but as one who is constituted and reconstituted through the various discursive practices in which he or she participates" (Davies, 2000, p. 89).

In this perspective, human beings have multiple, complex, and contradictory ways of being and acting in the world, and the person is seen to emerge from discursive practices. The subject is understood not as consistent and rational, but as emerging in response to the positions that are made possible by a given situation. Thus young children (and educators) may have multiple and even contradictory positions by which they know and understand themselves.

In the following example (from Pacini-Ketchabaw, Kummen, & Thompson, 2010), a practitioner named Robert is contradictorily positioned in relation to developmental knowledge. Robert feels at ease when developmental knowledge is at his fingertips. He

> thinks about the instruction he is about to give the children. He is planning to ask them to write down their names and the things they are good at doing. He starts to hand out the pieces of construction paper—it feels thick and smooth between his fingers. He positions a

box of markers in the middle of the table, next to the plate holding the remnants of cheese and crackers. He thinks about his developmental theory class—drawing upon the information about stages of cognitive development as he prepares to deliver his instruction. As he recalls the learned information, he feels a calming of his stomach and a loosening of his muscles. He is about to try out some of his learning.

When he delivers his instruction, the children look to him as they pay attention to his voice. The children continue to look at him—time appears to freeze. The lights get brighter and more piercing. One child says quietly, "I don't understand." Another child says the same. Then another. His hands start to feel wet and clammy. The chair feels hard underneath him as his muscles tighten. He feels a flush of warmth down his face and neck. His stomach tightens and doesn't release. He feels the eyes of the other facilitator looking at him. He imagines a hole underneath his chair opening up gradually encompassing his body. He thinks he doesn't belong here. He realizes it is him who doesn't understand. He got it wrong. (pp. 348–49)

For Robert, the desire to have developmental knowledge in his professional repertoire is produced through developmental discourses themselves. A developmental worker who can use and create technologies of developmental theory to know and understand the child is also one who can be in control and feel at ease. Not having expert knowledge or not being recognized by others is risky, something to be hidden. When he fails to get developmental knowledge right, Robert jeopardizes his viability as a subject. His story shows that processes of subject formation are complex.

Children, too, construct their identities in relation to dominant discourses—discourses that create social institutions like the family, the early childhood centre, the community, popular media, and so on. In Princesses and Pirates (pp. 76–83) we can see how young children position themselves in relation to—and how they constantly negotiate—dominant gendered discourses. Please take a few minutes to read it now.

It is important to keep in mind that not only are children *influenced* by discourses, but they also *constitute* and *contribute to* these discourses.

Subjectivities, then, are interdependent and mutually constituted in relation to discourses of the media, the family, the childcare centre, and so on. And again, sometimes these discourses are contradictory, and children do not always choose to position themselves within the same discourse. It depends on their specific context. For example, a child might feel comfortable experimenting with makeup at home, but not in their childcare centre.

As children encounter various meanings, such as discourses of gender, "race," class, and culture, they actively:

- read, interpret, and understand those meanings
- desire or reject them
- live, embody, and express the meanings they desire by taking them up as their own (Hughes & MacNaughton, 2001, p. 128).

By doing so, children negotiate these meanings. This is not to say that they

> are free to construct any meanings or any identities they wish. The meanings and identities that children can construct may be many and variable, but they are restricted to the alternatives to which children have access. Children do not enter a free market of ideas but a market in which some meanings [dominant discourses] are more available, more desirable, more recognizable, more pleasurable, and therefore more powerful than others. (Hughes & MacNaughton, 2001, p. 128)

Hughes and MacNaughton (2001, p. 122) remind us that:

- Identities are multiple: They have many facets, including gender, "race," ethnicity, class, sexuality, ability, geographical location, and so on.
- Identities are (at least potentially) contradictory: Their many facets are not necessarily coherent and can often conflict with each other.
- Identities are dynamic: Subject formation is never complete and fixed, but is always changing and in the process of being formed [even in adulthood].

We can illustrate these ideas by once again returning to Princesses and Pirates. Whereas the image of the child that we see in the developmental discourse is devoid of gender, by looking at the children's dialogues through a feminist poststructural lens, we can see that the children's play is embedded in discourses of gender.

Now we might consider questions like these:

- How are these children reproducing dominant social constructions of masculinity and femininity?

- How are they disrupting dominant gender discourses?
- What material, linguistic, and discursive elements come together to shape which masculinities and femininities are seen as desirable and are taken up by the children in this particular context?
- How do the children use their bodies to express their "understandings and enactments" of gender (Keddie, 2006, p. 108)?
- How are the children taking up popular culture in ways that maintain or disrupt taken-for-granted gendered assumptions (Keddie, 2006)?

Reconceptualizing children's subjectivities as being formed within the dominant discourses of their particular contexts brings attention to the ways in which issues of power and equity may be marginalized in early childhood classrooms. For example, we can consider how viewing children's play as what is "normal" for boys or girls at a particular age can lead to missed opportunities to question values and meanings. A narrow view of what constitutes normal behaviour may lead educators to avoid dealing with issues that have far-reaching effects on those with less power and privilege.

By looking beyond what is considered normal at particular ages and stages, and by situating children's knowledge and experiences within their social and discursive contexts, we can begin to see how even very young children, like the four-year-olds who participate in the Princesses and Pirates dialogue, constantly negotiate their understandings of complex issues like gender and class. We can also see that, in working out their identities, children are likely to reflect and negotiate the mores and belief systems of the society in which they live (Ryan & Grieshaber, 2004).

Educators Are Not Separate from the Images They Hold of the Child

One question that has emerged in our conversations with educators is how we can change our image of the child from a child who is in need of intervention to a child who is competent, rich, and full of potential. In our view, the idea that educators can simply shift from seeing children as deficient to seeing them as competent involves two assumptions: one, that an educator can sit outside her own practice, and two, that the image of the child is an objective entity. We see the image of the child as continually emerging through educators' practices. In this view, the image that educators hold is not a fixed essence, but is always shifting, always in the process of becoming—and it does so through the material and discursive effects that educators materialize in the moments of pedagogical encounters.

It is not realistic to think that educators can directly transport a new image of the child from the reconceptualist readings we do in our learning circles to their practice. What we find is that educators are actively entangled in configuring and reconfiguring the material and discursive elements of the image of the child. Educators are not mere observers who bring their image of the child to life in the moment. They are *part of* the image—and of an ongoing articulation of the image of children in the moments of practice. As Lenz Taguchi (2011) explains, "pedagogical practices create and enact particular children and particular learning subjectivities" (p. 37); therefore we need to carefully consider what is created by particular practices.

Ethic of Resistance

If early childhood education is a site for politics, as we discussed in chapter 2, it can become a site for resistance (Dahlberg & Moss, 2005). Lenz Taguchi (2006) invites us to engage in **an ethics of resistance** to contest early childhood education's often unchallenged spaces of governance, which include the dominant images of the child that we have been discussing in this chapter. As Lenz Taguchi explains,

> An ethic of resistance refers to conscious acts of thinking deeply about the assumptions and taken-for-granted notions we bring with us (often without awareness) as we engage in our daily work with children. As we practice an ethic of resistance, we deconstruct, or take apart, what we "know to be true," to reflect on it, analyze it, criticize it, and resist its seductive powers arising from its familiarity. (2006, p. 259)

Through critical reflection and ethical resistance, we can create new ways of seeing, understanding, and working with children. As we do so, we also engage in resisting and reworking dominant discourses that emerge in our lives and our practices. As we mentioned above, we need practices that respond to (and resist) discourses that are important in the lives of the children and families we work with. For example, we need to critically understand how newcomer families with young children experience immigration, how their experiences are socially and historically situated, how these families constantly negotiate their way through immigration discourses, and how those discourses position them. With this kind of understanding, we can experiment with practices that are respectful and ethical based on both current experiences and historically and socially situated discourses. This is what we mean by complexifying our practices. It's about much more than simply understanding the child as a developing child.

Children's Participation in Curriculum-Making

Rethinking the image of the child leads us to consider ways to reconceptualize children's participation in curriculum-making (Chan, 2010). While most child-centred approaches in early childhood emphasize children's right to be listened to, actually involving young children in curriculum development presents many challenges. Truly involving children is about more than providing spaces that allow them to feel confident to express their opinions. It is about situating the child in a social and political context that is both contemporary and historical simultaneously. It requires ongoing ethical resistance. And it involves seeing both children and ourselves as complex subjects.

Before we continue with our discussion of the complexity of involving children in curriculum-making, we briefly outline some of the prevalent approaches to children's participation (adapted from Chan, 2010). Drawing on the reconceptualist ideas we introduced above, we then discuss ways to disrupt developmental approaches and move toward complexifying how we think about participation.

Developmental Approaches

In approaches that focus on universal developmental stages, educators act as arbitrators, overseeing the children and evaluating them against predefined categories of normal development. Educators then develop curriculum for the children based on these judgements, with the objective of helping them develop "normally."

In such approaches, rather than the child being an active participant throughout the whole learning process, including making decisions about what they will learn, the adult is expected to observe and interpret children's interests and develop curriculum based on them, according to "developmentally appropriate" guidelines.

A Rights-Based Approach

A rights-based approach views participation as the base on which a democracy is built and the standard against which democracies are measured. While this approach does not assume that children are too immature to participate in decisions about their lives, it typically implies that adults should decide for children the knowledge, skills, behaviours, and experiences they need to become socially competent.

A Strengths-Based Framework

Early childhood educators who work within a strengths-based framework see children as co-constructors of meaning and adults as facilitators who provide opportunities for learning. In this approach, educators look for practical ways to develop curriculum that responds to the "the child" and recognizes young children's competencies (Clark & Moss, 2001). A strengths-based framework begins with what children have to offer, as opposed to highlighting children's vulnerabilities.

A Child-Centred Participatory Rights-Based Approach

A child-centred participatory rights-based approach prioritizes engaging young children as active citizens who are competent, capable, and socially responsible. MacNaughton and Smith (2008) outline the implications of such an approach. They argue that it is not enough to observe and document what young children say. To engage them as active citizens requires taking seriously the *politics* of what children say and acting on these thoughts accordingly. Doing so, they argue, enables children to see their thoughts, feelings, and ideas as valid, and creates spaces to support young children to learn about the complexities of including diverse perspectives in a democratic society.

An Alternative View of Children's Participation

While some of the approaches outlined above offer great potential for providing children with opportunities to participate in the societies to which they belong (including that of the early childhood centre), children's participation in these approaches still tends to follow a linear, progressive path that centres adults as the experts (Chan, 2010).

To incorporate children's participation in ways that allow for transformation of early childhood practice, Olsson proposes we

> imagine the child in more open and complex ways, trying to avoid falling into the trap of thinking, talking and acting in a simplified way through the notion of the "competent child." The ambition has been to open up this image of the child to many other expressions; to find more and unknown ways of being a child than being defined through one's competencies. (2009, p. 14)

From this viewpoint, participation is a dynamic process that involves continual transformation through learning. The focus is on what is going on in the learning process, not on attaining knowledge or achieving goals. In other words, educators and young children may seek to expand curriculum-making in new and creative ways—ways that treat learning as "impossible to predict, plan, supervise or evaluate according to predefined standards" (Olsson, 2009, p. 117).

That children's learning is impossible to predict or plan is illustrated in these pedagogical narrations:	Building a Fort, pp. 105–112 Becoming Rapunzel, pp. 86–95 The Tiara, pp. 83–86

Alternative Images of the Child

The complexified approach to thinking about children that we have outlined here challenges us to move past notions of "truth" and to think critically about children and the world. For many educators, this shift in thinking causes a "crisis in thought" as we struggle over how to give meaning to the world around us (Dahlberg, Moss, & Pence, 2007). Dahlberg, Moss, and Pence maintain that this struggle over meaning produces opportunities to see children, early childhood institutions, and early childhood pedagogy with new eyes (2007, p. 123). These new ways of thinking have the potential to enliven the concept of children's participation in curriculum development and to transform early childhood policy-making, training, research, and practice.

Framing children's growth as occurring concurrently across a series of domains in irregular, diverse, and constantly changing processes (Deleuze & Guattari, 1987) complexifies early learning. It "replaces certain 'hard facts' with shifting and multiple truths" (MacNaughton, 2004, p. 92), thereby opposing notions of standards-based programming that base young children's education on the achievement of particular knowledge and skills.

This work embraces the importance of educators and children working together in an ongoing process of constructing and reconstructing a given problem, always paying attention to the shifting contexts in which children live. Children, educators, families, and community members are all situated within contexts that are unpredictable. As educators, we need to engage in practices that allow for this unpredictability. One way of doing this is to create opportunities for everyone involved in the children's learning to express their views through a meaningful dialogue. Pedagogical narration provides such opportunities.

Moving beyond a "Diversity" Perspective

As we have seen from the examples we have been discussing, engaging in deeper listening and consultation with children requires additional conceptual tools. Using **postcolonial** and anti-racist perspectives helps us to pay attention to the experiences of Indigenous and other minoritized children as we complexify and politicize our practices. It is important to us to make visible how North America's colonial history is permeated by racisms and injustices. Colonialism is not a thing of the past; it continues today in the form of social, economic, and political structures and other discursive and material formations that sustain and spread inequities. We call this ongoing structural arrangement "coloniality."

Examples of postcolonial and anti-racist perspectives can be seen in these pedagogical narrations:	Becoming Rapunzel, pp. 85–95 Stand Up, p. 152

To remain vigilant against early childhood education practices that marginalize Indigenous and other minoritized children, we can

- interrogate the colonizing effects of assessing Indigenous children against Eurocentric developmental norms.
- incorporate culturally appropriate assessments and images of the child.
- consider ways to work against the forces of cultural appropriation and colonial governance that emerge in children's everyday lived experiences.

As an example of the latter, IQ Project participant Carol Rowan collaborated with children, educators, and elders in an Inuit community in northern Québec to create children's books in the Inuttitut language.

Caribou by Annie Puttayuk (2008) is an example of the books that were created. The book includes eight pictures with Inuttitut-language text. The English translations are as follows.

People go hunting for caribou.
They cut caribou into pieces.
Inuit eat caribou boiled, frozen, dried, and fried.
Inuit make clothing from caribou skin; we make caribou skin parkas, kamiks, mittens, and snow pants.

FIGURE 3.1: From the cover of *Caribou* (Puttayuk, 2008)

ᑐᒃᑐᖅ

ᐊᓂ ᐳᑕᔪᒃ

> When the caribou are hungry, they eat grass.
> Caribou go swimming when they don't like mosquitoes.
> Caribou crouch to hide when they are tired.
> Inuit kill caribou for food and clothing. (Puttayuk, 2008)

Books like this one are not available in the commercial market. The text and images in *Caribou* resonate with Inuit children. The story is important because almost every Inuit family has hunted caribou. Butchering caribou is an essential skill. The hunter who provides food and the person who makes clothing from the skins are respected and valuable community members. Inuit people live in relationship with caribou, so the story is rich with community-specific meanings (Rowan, 2010).

Here Carol reflects on how children's books that draw on local knowledges disrupt neocolonialisms that have privileged the English language and Euro-Western norms for children from diverse contexts. Carol wondered,

Would the books present an opportunity to investigate Inuit ways of being and becoming? Could the bookmaking project help to uncover and reaffirm Inuit knowledge by telling stories about Inuit ways of knowing and being?... In many childcare centres serving Indigenous communities the educators are trained in developmental approaches, the majority of the books are in English, and most of the toys and materials reflect Euro-Western norms. Few books are available in Indigenous languages for children to pick up and read. Many of the story books originating from publishing houses in North America, Great Britain, and Europe show pictures and tell stories depicting the dominant discourse of the colonizer such as the cute little bunny, the domesticated doggie, trees, princes and palaces, tall city buildings, farms, highways, white-skinned nuclear families—stories that employ visual references far removed from, and written in languages foreign to, the contexts of many Indigenous children. I have wondered how these stories and images interfere with and disrupt the grounding of [Indigenous] knowledge. (Rowan, 2010, p. 161)

When we view children as actively constructing meanings within discourses, such as those that shape gender and "race," we can move beyond simply recognizing or tolerating diversity to actively engage in issues of social justice in early childhood settings. Drawing from anti-racist and postcolonial theories presents possibilities for approaching social responsibility and diversity issues in early childhood settings (see, for example, Pacini-Ketchabaw, 2007). Because we see practising for social justice as a critical aspect of complexifying early childhood pedagogies, we return to these ideas throughout this book.

The early childhood education field takes several approaches to addressing social justice. In Canada, multiculturalism has been a preferred approach. However, recent developments question or problematize the effectiveness of multiculturalism to eliminate racisms and other forms of social injustice. Early childhood scholars such as MacNaughton (2005), Robinson and Jones-Diaz (2005), and Vandenbroeck (2004) argue that multicultural approaches present fixed views of culture based on the assimilationist idea that children acquire success by becoming more like the mainstream population. Multiculturalism is also, for some authors, a legacy or a reimagining of colonial structure and practice. As a conceptual framework and approach, multiculturalism is limited in its ability to understand and address the complexities of racisms and social injustices; therefore, it is necessary to consider other frameworks and approaches.

Theories such as anti-racism and postcolonialism can provoke new thinking about the role of social justice in early childhood education. These approaches use a critical literacy of "race" and racialization to explore how power operates and shapes social relations.

In a similar fashion, bringing queer theories to our project discussions has allowed us to engage in deeper listening and participation and engage differently in social justice pedagogies (see The Tiara, pp. 83–86). Queer theories allow us to unpack heteronormativity and see how certain practices can be unjust. We expand on queer theories in chapter 5.

Moving Beyond Discourse: Sociomaterial Perspectives

In our work with educators, we also bring a **sociomaterial (or material-discursive)** lens to our thinking about **subject formation**. As we discussed above, subject (or identity) formation can be understood as the processes by which we (including children) position ourselves (in both normalizing and subversive ways) and are positioned within dominant discourses. Subject formation can also be understood in terms of the material processes that come into being in a particular encounter. Deleuze and Guattari (1987) emphasize that bodies (both human and non-human) operate in conjunction with other bodies to form assemblages. They highlight the relationships that exist between these bodies that are constantly engaged in a network of relations that shift over time. Their interest lies not on materials' meaning, but on what the materials can do and how they relate to the human and non-human bodies they encounter.

In the early childhood classroom, for example, subjectivity emerges as bodies and their actions, perceptions, and emotions interact with objects, spaces, and discursive elements (including dominant discourses of "race," gender, and class) in an embodied assemblage of multiple belongings; one's identity is made, remade, and potentially transformed in relational connections (Braidotti, 1998; Deleuze & Guattari, 1987; Gallacher & Gallagher, 2008).

To illustrate this complex concept, let's return to Princesses and Pirates. As we think about this pedagogical narration, we can consider not only the discourses that are at work in the children's play, but also how the clothing the children are wearing, the materials they are provided with, the words that are said, the distribution of boys and girls around the room, the children's and the educators' memories of Disney movies and other media, and many other human and non-human materializations all come together to shape

Other examples of engagement with sociomaterial perspectives can be found in:

The Pool, pp. 42-44

Becoming Rapunzel, pp. 86-95

Stephanie and the Sticker Moment, pp. 97-100

the children's play as gendered in particular ways—and to create children's gendered subjectivities in those particular moments of encounter.

Images of the Educator

Just as particular images of the child dominate the early childhood field, certain images of the early childhood educator are also prevalent. Four common ones, among many,[1] are the educator as substitute maternal care, as expert, custodian, and technician. In this section, we engage with the question "Who do we understand the early childhood educator to be?" We consider how dominant images of the educator might shape and limit the work educators do. Then we juxtapose these dominant images of the educator with alternative images that have inspired us in our journey to complexify practices.

Dominant Images of the Educator

The Educator as Substitute Maternal Care
The idea that early childhood educators should substitute for maternal care flows from the societal discourse that a mother's love is required for a child's development and that any alternative to maternal care should be similar to a mother's. This ideology is deeply embedded in North America, due in large part to its entanglement with social, political, and economic histories that came together to create a particular image of childhood (Pence, 1989). Peter Moss critiques this image:

> The early childhood worker as substitute mother produces an image that is both gendered and assumes that little or no education is necessary to undertake the work, which is understood as requiring qualities and competencies that are either innate to women ("maternal instinct") or else are acquired through women's practice of domestic labour ("housework skills"). (2006a, p. 34)

The educator as maternal substitute reinforces gendered discourses and devalues the role of families in their relationships with their children; therefore, it requires critical engagement.

------

1 For more images of the educator see Britzman, 2003; Ellsworth, 1999; Fendler, 2003; Moss and Petrie, 2002.

The Educator as Expert

Child development discourse positions the early childhood educator as an expert with specialized skills and knowledge of young children over and above those possessed by parents and families (Elliot, 2010, p. 7). The idea of expert knowledge implies that the educator knows what children need; it also suggests knowledge or power to which others—including families—must defer.

Educators do, of course, have specialized knowledge that allows them to engage with young children in meaningful ways. However, the concept of the expert educator tends to obscure the complexities that may be revealed when we engage with young children from a stance of not-knowing.

> *Often the various roles that I take up position me as "the expert" who "knows": my knowledge is placed above that of children, families, students, and other caregivers. Responsibility and commitment demand knowledge, but "knowing" can limit my ability to learn new ways and new ideas. (Deborah)*

The Educator as Custodian

As custodian, the educator is expected to keep children healthy and safe. Requirements for hygiene, nutrition, and safety are carefully prescribed, and educators are expected to adhere to them. Custodial images of educators can be found in places as varied as licensing regulations and the media (Elliot, 2010, p. 7). We also see the custodial image in how we regulate children by stopping play we believe is inappropriate. IQ Project participant Kim thinks critically about her involvement in regulating children's play:

> *In my experience, when a child does something that we call inappropriate, their goal is actually quite appropriate, and it doesn't take much probing to figure it out. For example, years ago a group of boys were playing soccer. One boy went around systematically knocking down the other players. When asked, the boy said quite sincerely that he never got a chance with the ball so he HAD to knock them down to get a turn. Very logical. (Kim)*

The Educator as Technician

The image of the early childhood educator as technician is intimately connected to strong neoliberal forces that construct the child "as a redemptive agent who can be programmed to be the future solution to our current problems" (Dahlberg & Moss, 2005, vii). The focus of early childhood education in this perspective is to create children of the future—children who are ready for school, ready to be prepared for the future demands of the work force. This notion of children reaching their "economic potential"—and the accompanying assumption that childhood is a progression toward adult-defined outcomes that are easily quantified—works in tandem with the image of the child as an empty vessel. It fails to value childhood in the here and now and to recognize childhood as an important life stage in its own right. This discourse holds little space for a critically reflective educator. As Enid writes,

> Children's growth and development is often represented as sequential and predictable, with a primary focus on children's acquisition of skills. Children's growth, as measured through articulated norms of skills and behaviours, appears simple, even straightforward. Within this vision of normatively ranked children, the educator appears as a technician whose job is to ensure the achievement of children's demonstrable skills and abilities; her role is to facilitate children's movement from one stage to the next. Within a developmental viewpoint (Copple & Bredekamp, 2009) is an implicit belief that each progressive stage is "better" as children move to the end product of adult. The child's contribution to society as an adult is valued as part of the future. When judging children in terms of a prescribed set of norms, lost within this view are the children's individual patterns of growth, diverse histories and perspectives, and possible contributions in the present moment. (Elliot, 2010, p. 7)

The technician embodies "the possibility of an ordered world"—a world that is certain, controllable, and predictable (Moss, 2006a, p. 38). In our view, the image of the educator as technician erases childhood's diversity; thus it needs to be challenged.

Complexifying Practices: Toward Alternative Images of the Educator

The images described above are not inherently "bad," but we contend that they are limiting perspectives that lead to viewing early childhood practice as simple and straightforward. As we have been expressing throughout this book, we believe that early childhood practice is a complex journey. As such, it requires that we complexify our image of the educator.

Below we present two images of the educator that have allowed us to extend our discussions and the work in our projects: the educator *in relationship* and the educator as researcher. Many other images are possible. We encourage readers to generate additional images of the educator that might help to complexify taken-for-granted understandings of what it means to work with young children. For example, we might also think of the educator as an artist, the educator *in question* (Vintimilla, 2012), or the educator *in process*.

The Educator in Relationship

Relationships are essential in the work we do as early childhood educators. In our projects we encourage educators to critically engage with the idea of relationship. We dig deep into understanding how we are engaged in relationship with children, families, and other educators. We challenge ourselves to unpack the assumptions we make in these relationships. How does power come to matter in our relationships? How can we challenge our assumptions about how relationships ought to be developed? What happens when relationships do not materialize in the way we anticipated? How do we value relationships that are difficult, challenging, or unwanted?

Pedagogical narrations such as Hunters, Good Guys, and Bad Guys (see pp. 37–38) reveal some of the complexities and ethical tensions we encounter in our relationships with children when we try to provide space for the questions and issues with which children struggle. These are the moments when we test what it means to be in relationship with children. Edmiston (2008) notes: "To be addressed by a child means we must be listening. To be able to answer, and to create spaces for children to address one another, we must be in radical dialogue with children" (p. 174). This statement resonates for us when we think of the image of the educator in relationship. The educator in relationship involves struggle, tension, and embracing the unknown of being with others.

> All of the pedagogical narrations in this book reveal the complexities and ethical tensions we encounter in working with young children. See, for example:
>
> Stand Up, p. 152
> Building a Fort, pp. 105–112
> Entangled Bodies, pp. 96–105
> The Tiara, pp. 83–86

The Educator as Researcher

As we mentioned above, our work with educators in British Columbia has taken inspiration from the complex roles educators play in the early childhood centres of Reggio Emilia, Italy. In Reggio Emilia, educators do not simply guide and observe children, nor do they follow a prescribed curriculum. They seek ways to extend children's learning and engagement, and they make children's theories and ideas visible through **pedagogical documentation** (see chapter 4).

The early childhood educator as researcher "is open to the other, striving to listen without grasping the other and making the other into the same" (Peter Moss, 2006a, p. 37).

Importantly, the Reggio Emilia educators are committed to what Carlina Rinaldi (2001) terms a **pedagogy of listening** in creating an environment that is open to multiple perspectives and is deeply respectful of children and their families (p. 65). As co-constructors of knowledge, educators partner with the children, families, and their colleagues to collaboratively research, document, critically reflect on, deepen, and share their contextualized understandings. The educator as researcher and co-constructor considers new provocations and resources to build on the children's questions, learning, and interests (Rinaldi, 2001).

This commitment to research and the co-construction of knowledge complexifies our idea of early childhood learning processes beyond the prescriptive transmission of knowledge that we see in images of the educator as expert or technician. As Moss explains, this approach reconceptualizes knowledge as

> perspectival, partial and provisional, where the image is a rhizome ... something which shoots in all directions with no beginning and no end, but always in between, with openings towards other directions and places. This is very different to learning understood as the transmission of a body of knowledge, proceeding in a linear way to a predetermined outcome, passing through progressive and predictable stages. (2006a, p. 36)

Rather than seeking conformity to predetermined outcomes, the early childhood educator as researcher is open to the unexpected, open to learning that is, as we described above, "impossible to predict, plan, supervise or evaluate according to predefined standards" (Olsson, 2009, p. 117).

When we move away from images of the early childhood educator as technician, custodian, expert, or maternal substitute and embrace images of the educator in relationship and the educator as researcher, among many possibilities, the idea of professional development changes. If the educator's role is a complex one that negotiates subjectivities, seeks social justice, and embraces "curiosity, the unknown, doubt, error, crisis, [and] theory" (Rinaldi, 2003, p. 2), then professional development cannot be simply a linear, finite process of acquiring and then applying prescribed knowledge.

Reconceptualizing Professional Development

Alternative images like these ones we discuss above allow us to reconceptualize professional development for early childhood educators. By exploring the notion that change is both constant and intra-active, we hope to turn the idea of professional development on its head.

As we noted in chapter 2, professional development programs for early childhood educators in North America tend to aim at changing educators' knowledge, beliefs, skills, and practices to effect improvements in children's learning outcomes. The emphasis is on changing the educators and their practices by implementing a specific source of change, such as a program (Smith & Gillespie, 2007).

We problematize three interrelated assumptions embedded in this idea of professional development; these assumptions are:

- That professional development is a neutral, objective, passive event in educational processes.
- That professional development is linear and sequential (e.g., that you start at point X and as you do more professional development you travel in a straight line, always getting better).
- That the educator who participates in professional development is a stable, unchanging subject.
- That change is something exceptional, while stability and order are the norm.

In our work, we do not presuppose a static, knowable educator. Instead, we view the educator "as an incomplete project" (Britzman, 2007, p. 3). This alternative view shifts the focus of professional development from *being* to *becoming*. A focus on being—which is typical of professional development in the North American context—concerns itself with the organized state of things—their unity, identity, essence, structure, and discreteness. In contrast, a focus on becoming allows for dissonance, plurality, change, transience, and disparity (Chia, 1995). We explore this shift in focus below.

Moving Beyond Representational Thinking

In modern thought, **representational thinking** works through language to deem objects, concepts, and events as real and as having a concrete entity unto themselves. Underlying this view is "an unshakeable assumption that reality is essentially discrete, substantial and enduring" (Chia, 1999, p. 215).

The term *professional development* is understood to accurately represent "an external world of discrete and identifiable objects, forces and generative mechanisms" (Chia, 1999, p. 215). Guskey (2002) acknowledges that professional development involves different processes at different levels, but he views them as purposeful endeavours that need to be carefully evaluated to determine whether they are achieving their purposes.

This normative depiction of the effects of professional development assumes that the learning that takes place in professional development involves responding "to pre-formulated questions and eventually arriving at pre-existing answers" (Bogue, 2004, p. 333)—a passage from non-knowledge to knowledge, from ignorance to enlightenment. Reflected in this model is an individual who can be known, defined, and represented.

By giving priority to being—and consequently to representation—the transformation that is professional development's primary goal is seen as something exceptional that takes place under specific circumstances with the help of certain people who are referred to as agents of change (Chia, 1999). This view privileges outcomes and end-states. Through this lens, individuals are viewed as primarily unchanging entities. As one example of professional development that takes this view, Michael Fullan (2001), a leading scholar on educational change, writes that real change "represents a serious personal and collective experience characterized by ambivalence and uncertainty; and if the change works out it can result in a sense of mastery, accomplishment, and professional growth" (p. 32). Fullan contends that people need pressure to change; he identifies dos and don'ts that support the view that change is an exceptional process through which individuals need to be led, and which must be carefully orchestrated (2001, pp. 108–109).

In contrast to this view, Tsoukas and Chia (2002) borrow from process-oriented philosophers Bergson and James to argue that change is not an exceptional capacity of individuals, but a pervasive state of life:

> Individuals ... are themselves tentative, and precariously balanced but relatively stabilized assemblages of actions and interactions. (Tsoukas & Chia, 2002, p. 592)

Below we discuss some pedagogical narrations that capture how change took place during the IQ Project. Here, rather than thinking about the early childhood educator (in this example, Christine), as the main change agent, we think of change as **intra-action**.

Change as Intra-Action

Christine was interested in challenging dominant ways of thinking about the child. She was troubled by the material-discursive meanings that were commonplace in her centre regarding Stephanie, a girl with special rights. After being introduced to the idea of a competent and rich image of the child in the IQ Project learning circles, Christine wanted to challenge and unpack the ways in which she viewed and worked with the children in her classroom.

In Stephanie and the Sticker Moment (pp. 96–101), Stephanie has an encounter with another child and a much-prized sticker. Stephanie approaches Sally, taking her hand, and walks across the room with her. Sally is surprised by the gesture, and she is even more taken aback when Stephanie removes Sally's sticker from her shirt and places it on her own. Christine watches the girls from a distance as they resolve the situation.

In two other examples, Stephanie and the Art Supply Cart (pp. 101–103) and Stephanie and the Paints (pp. 104–105), Christine observes the gentle acts of kindness offered by several of Stephanie's classmates as they make silent gestures of friendship to her. Kindness, generosity, and connection are the focus of Christine's analysis.

In these examples, Christine's practices are agentive in that they play a role in producing the very phenomenon (the image of the child) they set out to grasp (Barad, 2007). The observations Christine makes of Stephanie's engagement with her classmates, the sticker, and the art materials are part of the configuration of the image of the child in its intra-active becoming.

The image of the child is always shifting, always in the process of becoming. It is made to matter through material-discursive practices—through the intra-actions materialized in the moment as well as the intra-actions that materialize themselves in the process of writing about and discussing the pedagogical narration.

To read that Christine moved from applying an image of a deficient child to conceptualizing competence is to assume both an educator who can sit outside her own practice, and that the image of the child is an objective entity. Neither of these assumptions is accurate. Regarding the first, an educator is always entangled in her own practices. Regarding the second, the image of the child is constituted and constitutive; it is always configuring and reconfiguring itself—and the educator, the children, the environment, the intelligibility of practice, and so on.

The image of the child that we see in Christine's pedagogical narrations is not a fixed essence that she transported directly from her readings during our meetings to her practice. Rather, Christine is actively entangled in configuring and reconfiguring the materiality and discursivity of the image of the child. "Reality," Barad says, "is an ongoing dynamic of intra-activity" (2007, p. 206).

In her pedagogical narrations, Christine not only brings to us the intra-actions that are enacted between the children and the materials. She also makes visible the intra-actions in which she herself is entangled. Christine is not a mere observer who brings her image of the child to life in the moment.

Rather, she is part of the image—part of the ongoing articulation of the image—of the children.

More analysis of Christine's pedagogical narrations can be found on pp. 96–105.

Images of the Family

Thinking about relationships with children is complex, but what about relationships with family members? Aren't most of us still finding our way through those? How do we view a child as competent in relation to a parent who is struggling? (Kim)

The importance of family–educator partnerships has long been emphasized in the early childhood education field. Partnership, though, as Laurie and her parent co-authors point out, "is an amorphous term that does not always make explicit either the nature or the unresolved terrain of family–educator relationships" (2010, p. 177).

Evidence suggests that many relationships between early childhood educators and the families of the children in their care are strained, with communication between them perceived as "highly complex and problematic" (MacNaughton, 2003, p. 259). Many factors may contribute to strained relationships. Both educators and parents may be stressed and tired, for example. Cultural differences may exist, and these—among other differences—may lead to conflicts about the focus and content of the early childhood programs.

MacNaughton (2003) identifies another potential point of tension between educators and families: educators often hold views of families that conform to dominant normalizing discourses. For example, she points to evidence that educators tend to judge their knowledge of children as more important than families' understanding of their own child because educators tend to see their knowledge as research based while parents' knowledge is based only on their own child. As a result of this perception, when educators think about working with families, they often focus on parent education. Kim, for example, wondered early on in her involvement with the IQ Project:

How do we view a child as competent in relation to a parent who is struggling?... I keep coming back to parent education! But I see that there are a lot of problems with this concept. (Kim)

We touched on some of the problems Kim alludes to in the section above on the image of the expert educator. **Power dynamics** is one of them. Educators are often seen as experts, and they may use their knowledge and position to maintain existing social relations of power. MacNaughton (2003) suggests the following ways that educators can transform their relationships with families.

- Always be aware of potential power dynamics between educators and families.
- Avoid judgements and seek instead to understand families through respectful dialogue, negotiation, and compromise.
- Be conscious of one's stereotypical and discriminatory reactions to families.
- Engage families in discussing their children's learning.
- Allow for time to negotiate shared meanings and understandings about the child.
- Be culturally sensitive to parents' comfort level with sharing information about the family.

To illustrate the challenges of embracing these ideas, below we share a situation that emerged in Sabrina's preschool. Our intent is not to present Sabrina's story as an exemplary piece, but to demonstrate the complexity of educator–family relationships and the critical engagement required to transform them.

Staying Alive to Complexities: Sabrina's Story

Sabrina's preschool group meets twice a week in the afternoons. Sabrina is experiencing multiple pulls and anxieties in relation to the preschool community. Her concerns are interconnected, but to explain them, it is easier to separate the components (the children, the structure, and the families) and discuss each individually. Keep in mind, however, that Sabrina's concerns are not like layers of sediment lying calmly one on top of the other; they intermingle. Sabrina's biggest concern is that, until recently, she was not seeing signs of a cohesive learning community coming together.

The Children

The children are a diverse, lively group. There are four or five very young and nearly 3-year-olds who are coming to a group setting for the first time, and Sabrina has her hands full preventing pokes and punches and keeping an eye on the youngest ones as they make their way through the day. A pair of twins have their own shared language (mostly non-verbal), another child has significant language delays, and an autistic child has an aide. The classroom routine has been simplified to create a minimum of transitions, and snack is served as early as possible. The children arrive excited, and they happily wave goodbye to their families as they leave.

The Program

Sabrina is the only educator in the group. Because the preschool is a co-op, the teacher and families make up the ratio for licensing. To qualify to be assistants, family members must have training, which takes place at the beginning of the year and in parent meetings throughout the year. Sabrina has a class coordinator who helps schedule the parents for their duty hours and keeps everyone informed about classroom issues and activities. There has been a lot of confusion about the schedule, and many days have begun with a scramble for qualified duty parents to assist that day. A number of the children have food sensitivities, and three are strict vegetarians. Because the class shares a snack provided by the duty parents, the children's dietary needs pose an extra challenge every day. The class went through two coordinators before a third settled in and was able to organize the duty schedules to accommodate everyone. The time for the afternoon class was moved back half an hour because parents were having difficulty eating their lunch and getting to the preschool on time. Sabrina has spent more time than usual on administrative tasks like making duty lists and guidelines for assisting in the classroom. Time and energy spent on classroom organization means less time for pedagogical narration and other planning.

The Families

The diversity of families in the preschool group has been an added challenge for creating a community. There are young families, lone parents, a military family, a family from Libya and one from Germany—families in very different circumstances.

Sabrina is concerned about her relationship with the family from Libya, whose members are Muslim and speak Arabic. With the barrier of language and culture, Sabrina feels it is taking longer than usual to get to know the family. When she speaks with them, she is not always sure that she and they understand each other. They are the parents of the twins, so they have double the number of duty days, and only the mother takes on the task. So far she has been scheduled for eight duty days but she has done only one because, with all the confusion regarding the schedule, she was not aware of her days. One time when she was ill, the father came to substitute, but since he hasn't had the training required or undergone a criminal record check, Sabrina worried that they would not be in compliance with the licensing regulations. Because of the language difficulties, Sabrina finds it hard to explain her concerns to the twins' parents. She also wonders how she can share with them the many things that happen at preschool. She doesn't know how much they understand when she shares anecdotes about their children.

Transforming the Educator–Family Relationship

No simple solution exists for the complexities of working with children and their families. In our efforts to collaboratively transform educator–family relationships, however, we engage with Glenda MacNaughton's (2003) work to help us examine how inequities based on taken-for-granted assumptions may shape these relationships. We are also guided by questions like the following, which are drawn from BC's Early Learning Framework (Government of British Columbia, 2008a).

- How do the children's families contribute to creating the learning community?
- How do we nurture and encourage contributions from home, including from families of children with additional support needs?
- Have we spoken to the families of children with additional support needs to discover their expectations and goals for their children?
- How can we engage families whose first language isn't English?
- How do we help the children's parents, families, elders, and other important community members feel welcome in our programs?
- How do we ensure that our assessments of children reflect the diversity of cultures in our learning community?
- How do we foster acceptance of diversity within our learning community?

In our projects, just as we seek to think of children as competent and full of potential, we seek to engage with families with the same respect. Laurie, writing with a group of parents in her learning community, suggests that

> rather than approaching families with the agenda of teaching them how to be better parents or to simply support the school's agenda, [a] relational approach engages families around their own interests and values and respects their contributions. In this process, both educators and families can grow and change, and a new kind of relationship can emerge—one that centers on shared understandings of children's learning. (2010, p. 198)

In our work, pedagogical narration has proven to be an invaluable tool for fostering shared understandings of children's learning among educators, children, families, and the wider community. For example, in her reflections on Building a Fort (see pp. 105–112) Kim describes presenting the pedagogical narration to the children's parents at their monthly meeting. An open discussion followed in which the parents shared stories of feeling vulnerable and judged when their children engaged in gun play in public. While an undercurrent of tension could be felt through the discussion, Kim noted that the mood was warm and forgiving. Similarly, in her reflections on Princesses and Pirates (see pp. 76–83), Kim describes discussing the play with family members. One of the themes that emerged from their discussion was the difference in children's dramatic play at home and at school. Both of these examples highlight how sharing pedagogical narrations with families provides a means for children's families to be active participants in a pedagogical community and to contribute vital knowledge about their children.

Challenging Assumptions Complexifies the Learning Journey

This chapter has explored our journeys in rethinking images of the child, the educator, and families. Among the many lessons we have learned in our projects is the need to reconsider our assumptions—both about children and childhood and about the purposes and goals of early education. Complexified images of the child, the educator, and families allow us to design early childhood programs that centre children's learning and build on the potential that all children possess.

As in Reggio Emilia, our approach recognizes educators as researchers who not only have knowledge about pedagogical theories but who also, and more importantly, construct educational theory. We encourage educators to enjoy learning as much as they enjoy teaching, to appreciate questions as well as answers, and to view alternative points of view as opportunities for discussion. Together we rethink how we position families in our classrooms, and how we privilege certain images of families and silence others.

Having explored how engaging with complexity, reflecting critically, and challenging our assumptions about children, families, and early childhood educators can help us to complexify our practices, we now present several examples of pedagogical narrations created by participants in our projects. Please explore the narrations at your leisure. In addition to the reflections and analysis presented with them, we refer to these examples in various places throughout the book.

Following the pedagogical narrations, in chapter 4 we explore theories and processes of this valuable tool and discuss how it can be used to make visible both children's learning and the dominant discourses that shape their learning, and to keep curriculum alive.

PEDAGOGICAL NARRATIONS IN THE MAKING: FROM OUR WORK WITH EDUCATORS

In this section we include five examples of pedagogical narrations that were created by educators who participated in the IQ Project learning circles. We hope they hint at the wealth of possibilities that exist for making children's learning visible through pedagogical narration. For example:

- Princesses and Pirates describes a play that a group of four-year-olds created and acted out many times over the course of six months. The educator, Kim, used the drama as a jumping-off point to extend children's learning and explore their understandings of dominant gender discourses, among other things.
- The Tiara was created as a video; we present a written description of it here to highlight an example of a child's disruption of heteronormativity.
- Becoming Rapunzel highlights an activity Fikile created in her centre when an Asian-African child drew a picture of herself with long blonde hair. Fikile wanted to invite the children to explore their views and representations of themselves and others in a social context.
- Entangled Bodies is a series of three pedagogical narrations that Christine created to challenge the discursive-material meanings that were commonplace in her centre regarding children with special rights.
- Building a Fort is an instance of how children's learning emerges in unplanned and unexpected ways. It is rich with examples of concepts we discuss throughout the book, as are all of the pedagogical narrations in this section.

Please feel free to read these stories in any order. After most, we've included a text box that will refer you to places in the book where we work with the narration. Please note that in all of the examples, the children's names have been changed to protect their privacy.

Princesses and Pirates
by Kim Atkinson

The following story was dictated to me by four 4-year-old girls in my preschool class:

> One day there was an evil stepmother and there was a cottage and four princesses and a castle. The princesses went to their cabinet where they had treasure. And then the evil stepmother tied up the four princesses. And then they escaped deep, deep in the forest. Then the evil stepmother goed in her van and she wanted to get the princesses out of the forest. Then all of the princesses walked home, and then they went in the princess car and drove to the mall. After the princesses went shopping, they catched up with the evil stepmother, and then they got her out of the van and threwed her in the garbage. The evil stepmother got out of the garbage. She pulled the four princesses and took them to their house and tied them up. The princesses got untied and danced with the prince. Then after the ball they throwed the evil stepmother in the garbage again and they lived happily ever after.

Children acting out princesses and pirates stories

I have been hearing stories like this for months, watching as the girls drape themselves in shiny fabric, don lace and high heels, and dramatize princess tales. Princesses are clearly an important, even necessary, part of their play, and I realize I need to listen more closely. I decide to document the princess play through images and words as a way to focus on, observe, and question the girls' interactions. Through the use of documentation, or pedagogical narration, I hope to deepen my understanding of what princesses mean to these girls. I want to broaden our conversation about princesses and find ways to support the children's play.

I suggest to the girls that they dress up and act out their princess story. They enthusiastically agree. One girl takes on the stepmother role and is deliciously evil, while the others are regal princesses. They act out the story in front of the rest of the 4-year-olds. When the performance concludes, Lance and Colin inform me that the story needs pirates. They add to the narrative:

LANCE: *Pirates stole the treasure from the princesses.*
COLIN: *Then the pirates went to a special castle and they hided the treasure. The pirates were watching because they were in the castle. They took the treasure to their boat. They fighted the princesses with a sword.*

Over time, we act out the story again and again. More boys declare themselves pirates, more girls become princesses, until, within a group of 18 children, 15 are now part of the story. It is played out with great vigour, and the roles are clear. Girls are princesses and evil stepmothers who go shopping, dance, and drive vans. Boys are pirates who use swords, ride boats, and steal treasure. Boys are definitely not princes.

As someone who studied feminism in the 1970s, I am puzzled and frustrated by the children's strict adherence to stereotypes. In my training as a primary teacher, I was taught that we merely needed to provide a non-sexist environment and model non-traditional gender roles. Children were assumed to absorb the social environment in which they lived and unquestioningly acquire identity as it was presented to them. So it followed that by changing the physical and social environment, we could reshape how children learned gender. But, as Hughes and MacNaughton (2001) so aptly note, "despite nearly 40 years of such advice, early childhood classroom teachers and families remain perplexed about why so many young children still actively seek and construct traditionally gendered ways of being, despite adults' efforts to offer alternatives" (p. 114).

As the play continues to evolve, I want to challenge the children to see if they understand gender differently than they act it. I gather them together and ask, "What do princesses do? What do pirates do?" According to the children,

Princesses:
- Live in a castle.
- Wear pretty dresses.
- Put on jewellery.
- Ride in carriages.
- Dance with the prince.
- Wear pretty shoes.
- Put on makeup.
- Walk daintily.
- Wear crowns.

Pirates:
- Steal money.
- Fight.
- Live on a pirate boat.
- No! They live under the ship and have creaky doors.
- Wear ugly shoes and belts.
- Run faster than anything.
- Have swords.
- Wear torn clothes.

I want to give voice to alternative ways of being, open up new possibilities, make room for the Other. I ask the children, "Are princesses always good? What about pirates? Are they good or bad?" The children respond:

> *Princesses are always good.*
> *Pirates are good and sometimes bad.*
> *Actually, real pirates live on the ocean and every one is bad.*
> *They're only bad, but if they're not bad, then they're good.*
> *The nice ones help the princesses. And boys and girls.*
> *No they don't!*
> *Nice pirates don't yell.*
> Pirates fight princesses.
> Kim: Do princesses fight?

Princesses are never mean.
Sometimes princesses fight, when the dragon comes.
Sometimes princesses fight, but not always. Sometimes they
    have swords.
They fight pirates and dragons only. *(The children disagree on
    this point; some maintain that princesses never fight.)*

Our conversations are filled with contradicting views and opinions. The identities of princesses and pirates are clearly complex, far more complex than how the roles are acted in the play. The children view the evil stepmother with some compassion; they see reasons for her evilness. Pirates may have a good side, and princesses may, in fact, fight. But the children share an implicit understanding that pirates are male and that girl pirates are imposters. The children are fusing their understanding of good/evil and of princesses/pirates with understandings of their own experiences. Social complexities on the playground, in their families, and in their worlds influence and inform their views of gendered images. It does appear that children understand gender differently than they act it.

Kim's Reflections

In the sections below, Kim reflects on the events in her classroom through email correspondence with her colleagues in the IQ Project.

The Play Continues

I continue to be surprised that the children have not finished with the Princesses and Pirates play. New ideas are added, characters shift, children try different roles, others remain firm in their initial choice. I am learning that the more space I give for children's ideas, the more ideas they articulate. In other words, the more I listen to them, the more they are willing to share.

The role of the evil stepmother has been abandoned. All the girls are princesses. When I ask if anyone wants to be the evil stepmother, the response is, "She's invisible," and that seems to satisfy everyone. Then one day Kurtis says that he will take on the evil stepmother role. His costume consists of a pair of high heels. No child comments on his new role, but some family members say things like, "Nice shoes, Kurtis." I wonder if the children notice that some find his choice noteworthy.

Mada, formerly the evil stepmother and then a staunch princess, adds a shark role, plays it ferociously for a while, and then returns to being a princess. However, the addition of the shark creates an opening for the

Princesses

boys. Once Mada is finished with the role, the boys take it over, so the next time we act out the play there are no pirates, just sharks. And thus a space opens up for Felicity to be a pirate. I find the whole process fascinating: The children established a set of dichotomous roles. I tried without success to challenge them to think outside those roles. Then, lo and behold, the children themselves created a space for the Other. Felicity is often a pirate now, though no other girls have tried it out.

A couple of weeks later, Felicity informs me that we need to add a mermaid to the story. We act out the play with the mermaid, and the next time we act it out, all the girls want to be mermaids; there are no princesses. Subsequently, the mermaid/princess ratio has evened out; the same girls switch back and forth. Mermaids seem analogous with princesses. Why? At least princesses dance and go to the mall; mermaids don't seem to do anything.

Are the roles children take on—or, more importantly, don't take on—regulated by themselves, rather than peers? When Felicity and Kurtis took on alternative roles, no child questioned it. There are many books about female pirates, so why the reluctance to take on the role? Is it all right for Kurtis to be an evil stepmother but not a princess? Is it okay for a boy to be evil in any role? The media offer some alternatives to gender stereotypes. There are non-aggressive males and active females. Even some princesses are more complex. Are children rejecting these images? Is attraction to archetypes something more instinctual, more powerful?

Thinking with Family Members about Gender Roles

I offer to present Princesses and Pirates to the families of the children involved. I'm pleased that so many of the family members come early to a meeting to hear about the play. In the ensuing discussion, a couple of themes emerge. The first is the apparent disparity between the children's familial realities and their expressed vision of what is "right." For example, a father told a story about his two children playing with French fries and comparing their lengths. When they determined the longest fry, they labelled it the dad and the shorter fry the mom. In reality, the parents of these children don't fit that image; the mom is significantly taller than the dad. Another mom shared that her daughter also believes Dad is taller than Mom when, in fact, Mom is taller. Parents also recounted how their children are of the firm opinion that dads go to work and moms stay at home, even when that is not the case in their family or the families of their friends. It is remarkable to me that children can be so perceptive of societal norms that they recognize the exceptions as such.

The second theme that emerges from discussions with the children's family members is the difference in their child's dramatic play at home and in public. Some boys seem comfortable wearing dresses and jewellery to dance and play at home, but would flatly deny this if asked. One boy, at age 3, was dressed by his sister as "Princess Clang," complete with makeup and jewels. By 4, he would dress up only as a superhero.

Kim Revisits the Pedagogical Narration

I have been rereading Glenda MacNaughton's (2000) book on rethinking gender, which of course raises more questions than answers. Throughout this experience, I attempted to give voice to all the children, adding story as dictated, keeping all roles open for everyone, hearing those who say less verbally but contribute in other ways. My goal was to limit my voice. I wanted to facilitate the children's stories, explore their ideas on the narrative.

But still I reflect on what I might have done differently. Should I/could I push for more gender provocation? Should I voice my observations to the children? Much as I attempted to limit my voice, I still directed the dialogue; therefore my influence was unavoidable. How did I unwittingly influence the process, the story, and the roles that were taken on?

MacNaughton quotes Gherardi as saying that "we learn identity through several interrelated theatrical processes: telling stories, playing roles, critiquing our performances and being critiqued by others. We reshape our stories and our roles as we interact with others and with ourselves" (MacNaughton, 2000, p. 27).

This leads me to wonder if the medium of the play was an opportunity for the children to take on a role that is commonly understood by them, to try it, explore it, absorb the reactions and dialogue derived from it, test it out. If I were able to have this same group of children next year, how would their story be different? Would they be ready to discard these roles for something new? What did they perceive of themselves in their roles? Perhaps they were gauging their performance and that of their peers, watching, evaluating. I suspect they all carefully observed Felicity's role as a pirate and Kurtis's as evil stepmother, checking to see what the consequences might be of stepping out of the gender pattern. Perhaps these princesses are decidedly empowered and capable, they deal with everything themselves, including disposing of the evil twice. The lone male in the story serves one purpose, to dance. Thus, the story might have interrupted and renegotiated some gender typing.

The Princess and Pirates play has been a fascinating journey. I have recognized that children's understanding of gender is far more nuanced than it appears at first. A simplistic view of learning gender by absorbing the social environment fails to explain the complexities evident in the children's play, and denies children's abilities as agents in their own learning. There are many contradicting messages in the children's worlds, and they negotiate their way with dialogue and interaction, by hearing and being heard. Our job as educators is to facilitate the dialogue, to question, and to listen. We need to challenge our assumptions and the children's, and to help create spaces for the Other.

Using pedagogical narration as a tool for listening, for observing children as they construct knowledge, has led me on a fascinating journey. What began as a story dictated by four girls grew into a play involving 15 children that continued energetically for six months. By reflecting on the children's words and images, by sharing them with families, children, and colleagues, I became more attuned to the children, to how they might be thinking and learning. I was challenged to rethink my own theories of identity and gender and to introduce provocations that would challenge the children's understandings. The thoughtful discussions, the questions, and the learning that took place for all involved were unexpected and gratifying.

I've learned that the more I listen to children, the more they are willing to share. From me they need a loose structure, an organizational hand, and a repository for their ideas. They can do the rest.

USING THE PEDAGOGICAL NARRATION TO COMPLEXIFY PRACTICE

In chapter 3, in our discussion of images of the child, Princesses and Pirates helps us to explore how children's play is embedded in societal discourses of gender.

In chapter 4, we discuss how critically reflecting on Princesses and Pirates in our IQ Project learning circles helps us to unpack dominant discourses.

In chapter 5, we show how viewing Princesses and Pirates from a feminist poststructural perspective provokes many questions and reveals a multiplicity of dynamic, textured meanings in the children's dialogue and play, including their simultaneous adherence and resistance to gendered roles and their performance of heteronormativity.

In chapter 6, we discuss how Kim's attempts to unpack and disrupt gendered discourses in Princesses and Pirates is an ethical act that takes courage because it puts the educator in a vulnerable position when negotiating relationships with the children's family members.

The Tiara[1]
by Christine Chan

It's face painting day at the preschool. A group of five 3- and 4-year-old children is gathered around the table I am sitting at. I have painted a few of the girls' faces already. They have chosen to have tiaras painted on their foreheads so they will look like the pictures of the Disney princesses on their lunchboxes, which are sitting on the table.

---

1 The Tiara was documented in video format. It has been adapted for inclusion in the book.

Kay-sun eagerly awaits his turn on the chair in front of me. He is holding the pink lunchbox that features Cinderella, Belle, and Sleeping Beauty. Hae-young and Margie stand on either side of him.

"What would you like today?" I ask Kay-sun.

He points at the pictures on the lunchbox and smiles up at me. Hae-young and Margie also point at the pictures, as if they are helping Kay-sun explain to me what he wants. Kay-sun is fluent in Korean but speaks very little English. His friend Keem watches curiously from the other side of the table as this dialogue takes place.

I take a few seconds to find my words. "Who is that?" I ask.

Hae-young, Margie, and Kay-sun all answer at the same time: "It's Cinderella, and Belle, and Sleeping Beauty! They have crowns and tiaras! They are princesses!"

I hesitate for a few seconds, then I pull Kay-sun's chair closer to me and ask, "Do you want a crown?"

"Yes!" he answers enthusiastically.

"Why?"

He shrugs his shoulders as if to say, "I don't know."

Keem comes around to our side of the table to find out more about what's going on. He helps Kay-sun answer my questions by pointing at the pictures on the lunchbox.

"Which one do you want?" I ask Kay-sun.

Keem clarifies: "Only one. You have to choose only one."

Kay-sun chooses Belle's tiara.

Margie, Hae-young, Keem, and Kay-sun debate among themselves what colour Kay-sun's tiara should be.

"Do you want red?" I ask. "Blue?"

"He wants pink," Keem says, and leaves the table to continue what he was doing before.

"Are you sure you want pink?" I ask Kay-sun. I place the red paint stick beside the pink one so he can choose.

He points at the pink paint stick.

"Pink," he says.

Kay-sun has shoulder-length hair, and I ask him if I can pin it back as I paint his forehead. He nods again with a smile. For the next few minutes, I paint a tiara on Kay-sun's forehead: pink with purple accents, and yellow for the gold. As I paint, Kay-sun studies the picture on the lunchbox and smiles happily.

Keem comes back a couple of times while I'm painting, almost as if he is checking to see what I am doing. Hae-young and Margie are also making sure that I paint Belle's tiara exactly.

When I finish, I find a mirror so that Kay-sun can see his tiara. Holding his hair back, he inspects his image from different angles.

"Where is the hair?" he asks.

"What hair?"

He points at Belle's long hair and big puffy bun. Margie and Hae-young help him to explain: "Up, up! You need to put his hair up."

"Do you want me to put your hair up with a barrette?" I ask Kay-sun. He nods his head and smiles.

While I go to search for a hair barrette, Kay-sun holds the mirror with both hands, carefully inspecting his tiara from different angles. He moves the mirror up and down and side to side. Hae-young attempts to take the mirror out of his hand, but he quickly pulls it back and strides away.

Kay-sun bursts into song as he walks through the classroom admiring his reflection in the mirror: "I love digga digga ding! I love digga digga ding!"

I come back with the barrette and Kay-sun rushes over and sits on the chair in front of me. As I put his hair up and hold it with the barrette, he actively participates by checking his reflection in the mirror that he holds on his lap. Hae-young and Margie supervise me to ensure that I do exactly what Kay-sun wants.

When I'm finished, Kay-sun gets up from the chair and pats the bun on top of his head. For the next few seconds, it seems as if he is dancing through the classroom like a ballerina, all the while holding the mirror.

"What do you think?" I ask. "Do you like it?"

"Yes!" His smile now seems like a permanent feature of his face.

Keem approaches and pats Kay-sun's hair approvingly.

By now it is time for outside play. As I'm gathering the children to get ready to go outside, Kay-sun runs to the art supply cart. He gets a piece of green construction paper and brings it to me, holding it on top of his head.

"But you already have a tiara, Kay-sun," I explain.

Julie, the other teacher in the room, says to Kay-sun, "I can give you scissors and more paper if you want."

Kay-sun follows her to the art supply cart and selects a large piece of pink construction paper. He cuts a thin strip from the long edge of the construction paper and holds it up to his forehead.

"I need tape," he announces.

Julie finds the tape. Now the long strip of pink paper becomes another component of Kay-sun's tiara as Julie tapes it around his head.

Kay-sun searches for the mirror. He smiles approvingly at the new addition to his tiara. Keem joins him, his face now painted as a lion. But Kay-sun pays little attention to Keem. He continues to enjoy his tiara as he watches himself in the mirror, tilting his head from side to side.

As he moves through the classroom he bursts into song again: "I love digga digga ding! I love digga digga ding!"

Kay-sun is clearly pleased with the reflection he sees in the mirror.

> **USING THE PEDAGOGICAL NARRATION TO COMPLEXIFY PRACTICE**
>
> In chapter 5, we discuss how The Tiara allowed Christine to unpack her reactions to a child's gender explorations. A group of educators in an IQ Project learning circle critically engages in queering early childhood practices by disrupting heteronormativity and dominant gender binaries, just as Kay-sun disrupted them in this pedagogical narration.
>
> Also in chapter 5, we use The Tiara to illustrate how a sociomaterial perspective can be a potent tool for disrupting dominant discourses in the classroom.

Becoming Rapunzel
by Fikile Nxumalo

I am an early childhood educator who runs a family childcare centre. Four-year-old Siviwe and her sister Lindiwe, who is seven, attend the centre. In the photograph below, Siviwe is second from the left.

Recently, Siviwe drew a picture of herself with long blonde hair.

SIVIWE: *I have really long, long hair.*
FIKILE: *Long hair?*
SIVIWE: *Ya—really long. I'm wearing my tiara. My clips are in.*

Children in Rapunzel

This spontaneous drawing surprised me because Siviwe had always coloured in the face with brown when she drew herself. Initially I interpreted the drawing as a contradiction of (my perception of) her positive self-view. I have always thought of Siviwe as being proud of her biracial ethnic identity (Filipina-Swazi or Asian-African). In my practice, I try to nurture a sense of belonging in the children and address equity issues whenever they arise. Siviwe's picture and her comments about it led some doubts to surface about what I was doing to broaden the children's gender perspectives and affirm their connectedness to their diverse racial and ethnic identities. With these doubts came many questions about the possible meanings behind Siviwe's representation and the dominant discourses that inform the children's processes of identity construction.

Self-portrait of an Asian-African child

Fikile's Reflections

I wondered if Siwiwe was inserting herself into the prevailing princess identity as a form of imaginative play, and perhaps inadvertently reproducing the typically gendered and racialized narratives that are a part of this identity. I wondered if the drawing held a negative connotation in terms of Siviwe's biracial identity—did she feel that long blonde hair was the most desirable look for a princess? From my perspective, her representation appeared to uphold a powerful discourse regarding what is considered ideal beauty. Was Siviwe choosing to identify with this particular discourse in this particular context? This norm appears in direct contradiction to other expressions of Siviwe's identity, such as those informed by her family's values and beliefs (Hughes & MacNaughton, 2001).

Mirror Images

I decided to prepare an activity that I hoped would invite the children to explore (and perhaps question) their views and representations of themselves and others in a social context. I set up some mirrors at a table with drawing paper and black pencil crayons at each seat. I didn't give the children any specific instructions but waited to see how their interests would be provoked. The children engaged with the mirrors and studied themselves, making playful expressions and telling each other about their facial features as they explored their similarities and differences.

SIMON: *I have a lot of freckles on my cheeks! I have about four on my nose.*

LINDIWE: *I don't have any; I have beauty marks by my chin and eyes.*

SIMON: *What's a beauty mark?*

LINDIWE: *It's blackish—it's a beauty spot.*

SIMON: *If you just think about getting freckles, you'll get them, you know.*

MARK: [smiling broadly] *Me have a lot of hair!*

SIMON: *I have sticking down hair on my face.*

SIVIWE: *Mine is in my pom-pom* [ponytail].

LINDIWE: [laughs] *I have a triangle shaped tooth and a line on my face!*

SIVIWE: *Why does everyone have a line on their face?*

LINDIWE: *Well you can't see it sometimes; it's showing where blood is going in your face.*

SIMON: *Yeah, I have lines of blood going down in my arms.*

Child looking at the mirror

   After some time spent studying their faces and making playful expressions, the children started to draw.

   I felt content observing and listening to the children explore and talk about their similarities and distinctive features in a positive way. I didn't discern any negative attitudes about their identities, though I did wonder about the possible meanings of Simon's statement about how one could get freckles.

Children drawing

Once they started drawing, each child appeared very focused and engaged in their individual drawing processes. I wondered, though, how much the drawings were influenced by the other children. It seems that the children were co-constructing and negotiating meaning in that when one child mentioned a certain feature, the attention of one or more of the others was brought to that part of their face; they were curious to see if they shared that facial feature.

At the time, there wasn't a moment where I felt I wanted to join the discussion. In retrospect, Lindiwe's reference to beauty spots could have been used as an entry point to negotiate different perspectives on the (gendered?) meanings of external beauty. From my initial view, she had used the term in a positive way in reference to herself, but without excluding others. I was also struck by her association of something she described as "blackish" with beauty; I thought that perhaps this could be interpreted as a positive view of her racial identities.

I wondered why a direct discussion of their racial differences hadn't come up in the children's narratives. I thought that perhaps they were simply more interested in exploring what they viewed as their most interesting or individual features. I also thought they may have been influenced by the available materials, as I had provided only a black pencil with which to draw.

Drawing of a princess

Going Deeper

In this activity the children appeared to reveal a positive sense of their identities. I wasn't sure, though, whether this positivity reflected their self-views or if the meanings in their drawings were constructed by the particular social context, such as the unspoken influence of an older sibling on the younger. I thought I might gain more insight by asking Siviwe to tell me about some of her other drawings.

It's interesting to me that when we revisited Siviwe's picture with blonde hair, she gave it new meanings by imagining herself in a Rapunzel storyline: "I'm being Rapunzel jumping on the bed! I made the hair fancy." However, I remain unclear about the extent to which I can infer her self-view from her drawings and her shifting interpretations. How significant are these representations to her self-view if they are understood as contextual and imaginative representations of identity? I think her drawings and interpretations bring meanings and show influences that could be seen as maintaining power relations that are socially shaped through popular culture texts. This could negatively influence her self-view. On the other hand, some meanings could be seen to disturb gendered and racialized sociocultural influences, such as in her imaginative representation of herself as a brown-skinned, curly-haired, wand-swinging musketeer. I am hoping

It's me being a musketeer—I have a sword. I'm pretending it's a wand. I swing it, that's how the bad guys just fall down

Drawing of laughter. It's me laughing. I have a pink line on my face.[2] I got a tiara from the store

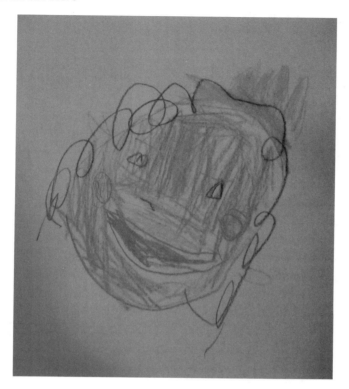

that sharing the documentation and learning more about the process of constructing identities will help me understand how I can begin to challenge those meanings that could be seen as constraining children's self-views.

Building on the Pedagogical Narration

As I deconstructed the children's drawings and conversations in the initial pedagogical narration, I noticed a recurring emphasis on descriptions and depictions of hair, such as in Siviwe's description of herself as Rapunzel: *I made the hair fancy.* I thought the children's curiosities, perceptions, and experiences of their bodily differences needed further exploration. I remained unclear whether the apparent situational contingency of these perceptions lessened the significance of what I saw as Siviwe's association

....

2 This drawing was made soon after the mirror activity where the children had discussed the "lines" (veins) on their faces.

of "fancy" hair with hair that didn't look like hers. I chose to read the children John Kurtz's (2007) version of *Rapunzel*, which tells the original story, but recasts the characters as African-American. Instead of long, silky blond hair, Rapunzel has hair described as "beautiful braids." It is debatable whether this version of Rapunzel can be considered a critical text. It may disrupt racialized images of beauty, but it inserts Rapunzel into the same "powerless but beautiful" female stereotype that is found in many fairy tales. Still, I felt it would be useful to share this book with the children by adopting a social justice framework that could bring forward marginalized or silenced meanings in the text (MacNaughton, 2005).

After reading the book aloud, I opened the dialogue by asking the children what they liked about the story.

SIVIWE: *I liked her clothes. She has puffy sleeves.*
FIKILE: *Anything else?*
SIVIWE: *I liked her hair better when it's the long braids.*
LINDIWE: *It's only so someone can climb it.*
FIKILE: *Does Rapunzel need long hair and pretty clothes?*
LINDIWE: *It's just so the prince rescues her and they marry each other.*
FIKILE: *Siviwe, how do you think Rapunzel could rescue herself?*
SIVIWE: *She can hang her hair on the wall ... but you have to be careful if you use your hair. You can climb down or flip down it, then she'll be down to the ground.*
FIKILE: *What could happen next?*
SIVIWE: *She'll find her mommy and daddy. Will the witch know if she's gone?*
FIKILE: *I don't know but that's a wonderful Rapunzel story. Simon, what did you think about the book?*
SIMON: *The prince looks different. Most boys have normal straight hair.*
SIVIWE: [smiling] *The prince has a pink bow in his hair.*
LINDIWE: *It's because it's braided.*
SIVIWE: *Princes have puffy sleeves and black pants.*
FIKILE: *Why do you think they made this prince look different from other princes?*
SIMON: *To make people buy it because it's a different Rapunzel story.*
LINDIWE: *Because people don't have to be the same.*

Further Reflections

I had not paid much attention at first to the way the male characters were depicted in the story, but the children took up the prince's appearance as a focal point from which to discuss differences. I learned from the children that it is important to deconstruct the ways in which males are drawn and characterized in "female-directed" popular culture texts like fairy tales. The children seemed surprisingly attuned to the ways in which masculinity is typically framed in these stories. I wondered why they focused again on hair ("normal," "straight," "long," "braided," and adorned with a bow) as markers of difference.

I had mixed feelings about my success in opening up the children's negotiations of difference. I felt I was unable to engage Mark's interest; he remained silent in our conversations. Also, while the children brought up some of their understandings about fairy tales, I had doubts about whether we had really critically engaged with the story's messages. For instance, did the story and our discussion about it have any effect in disrupting dominant beauty ideals? While it seemed that Lindiwe disrupted dominant perspectives, Siviwe appeared to both stick to and resist dominant gender and racialized roles. She seemed skeptical of this version of Rapunzel, as expressed in her focus on gendered differences such as the prince's clothing and braided hair. On the other hand, when asked, she created a powerful self-rescuing Rapunzel. This would seem to support the theory that encounters of difference are a site for complex identity negotiations in which contradictory, situational, and contingent perspectives are constructed (Saldanha, 2006).

I think the children's focus on hair supports the idea that children often engage in "politically nuanced interactions" rather than overtly political practices in their everyday negotiations of identity (Skattebol, 2003, p. 160). I am also now wondering if the characters in this book were somehow unintentionally exoticized—such as by having a prince with long braided hair. Could this partially explain the children's responses to the characters' hair and clothes? But then, what are the political effects of associating certain black hairstyles with exoticism/strangeness? I feel this brings us right back to the place we started, with Siviwe's image of herself as a blonde Rapunzel and with unanswered questions regarding its meanings and significance to identity constructions.

One challenge I have is finding the language to critically consider silenced meanings or views in texts such that children don't feel there are "right" answers or that they are being led to completely reject the texts. While I think it is useful to critically examine texts with the children, I wonder if my approach is too leading. I also wonder whether it is possible to know whether these critical explorations have any effect on the children's perceptions of themselves and others.

Entangled Bodies

Christine was interested in challenging dominant ways of thinking about the child. She was troubled by the material-discursive meanings that were commonplace in her centre regarding Stephanie. Stephanie is a child who received specialized support from a special needs educator. She had undergone numerous tests, did not speak, and had very little unguided participation as she was shadowed by an adult in the classroom all the time. After being introduced in the IQ Project learning circles to literature from Reggio Emilia that presented a rich, competent image of the child, Christine wanted to challenge and unpack the ways in which she viewed and worked with children in her classroom.

Below is a series of pedagogical narrations Christine created to experiment with ways of thinking about relationships with Stephanie as a member of the classroom. These narrations are examples of how we might reconceptualize the image of the child in ways that unsettle the deficit or lack that typically accompanies a designation of special needs in the classroom (Goodley, 2013). Hierarchical binary divisions, such as ability/disability, need/competence, normality/difference, independence/ dependence, inclusion/exclusion, and the designation of special needs can all act to create inscriptive and disciplinary effects that compartmentalize and simplify children's identity (Sylvia Kind, personal communication; Goodley & Runswick-Cole, 2012). These binaries and labels can obscure possibilities for opening to the complexities, multiple subjectivities and strengths of children both within and outside of the ways in which their difference matters to their and others' ways of relating with the world (Kind, 2006).

Critical disability theory politicizes dominant special rights practices (Goodley, 2013) and is a useful tool as it provides educators with multiple perspectives that trouble the binaries and deficit-based practices that can accompany encounters with difference in the classroom. Importantly, we see in Christine's narrations how these critical theoretical perspectives come alive in relationship with the possibilities that emerge by the particularities of Stephanie's embodied presence, the materials, Christine's practices, and other social and discursive effects. We invite the reader to consider how the image of Stephanie is entangled and reconceptualized in relation to the sociomaterial particularities of each encounter in the narrations that follow.

Stephanie and the Sticker Moment

Stephanie approaches Sally and reaches for her. She laces her fingers into Sally's petite left hand. With fingers interlocking, hand in hand, a connection is made.

Stephanie leads and Sally follows, although a look of uncertainty is written on her face. My curiosity is piqued as I watch this unlikely pair. Where are they going? What does Stephanie have in mind? I can't believe that Sally is agreeing to follow.

One step, two steps ... STOP.

Abruptly, Stephanie turns toward Sally and peels off the sticker on the front of Sally's sweater.

With a look of slight panic, Sally shoots her gaze up, her eyes saying, "Help me! She took my sticker!"

I am invisible behind the camera; Sally bypasses me and seeks intervention elsewhere. Stephanie studies the sticker, transfixed by the characters of *Madagascar*. I am intrigued by the quick turn of events.

Stephanie carefully places the sticker onto her own shirt and reveals a smile of contentment. Without any intervention, what will Sally do? Will

Stephanie reaching out to friend

Stephanie and Sally holding hands

Stephanie walking with a sticker

she take the sticker back or will she choose to share it? I can tell she is busy thinking. I am curious to see how this unfolds.

Stephanie walks away and steals a few minutes alone with the sticker.

Not far behind, Sally stays close to her treasure from home, still quietly pondering what to do. Suddenly Stephanie approaches Sally with the sticker. Frozen in my step, my body clenched into a tight ball, I am wishing in my head, "Please just give it back!" Like a hamster wheel in my head, my thoughts are running fast.

My balloon of hope makes a loud "POP" as Stephanie pivots and walks in the opposite direction. At this point, grown-up hands gently enter the picture. What is Stephanie going to do? Will she protest loudly? Or has she spent enough time with the animals of *Madagascar* that she is willing now to return the sticker to its rightful owner?

Stephanie pulls the sticker close to her face with both hands and observes it intently. I am still holding my breath. Waiting stops time.

Quiet as can be, Sally stands still and waits. Her patience is astounding.

On her own, Stephanie holds the sticker up to Sally's chest. She pats the sticker down onto Sally's sweater and turns away. Ahhhhhh ... finally. I am breathing again, perhaps for both Sally and me.

Stephanie patting sticker onto Sally's sweater

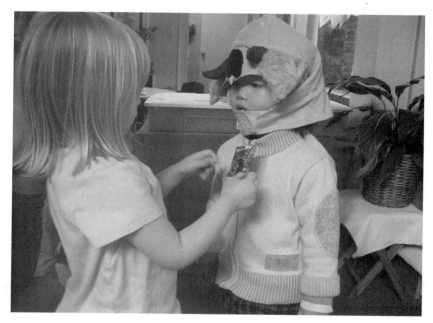

Stephanie comes back one millisecond later to have one … last … look.

Paths may cross many times in one day, especially in our classrooms. What meaning can be made of this particular crossing? An unlikely pair meet up for a short time over their shared interest in a sticker? Did time stand still for patience and generosity to shine through? Was Sally's act of trust and sharing repaid with the return of her beloved object? How will this crossing affect this "unlikely" pair in the future?

USING THE PEDAGOGICAL NARRATION TO COMPLEXIFY PRACTICE: (RE)CONFIGURING THE IMAGE OF STEPHANIE AND SALLY

Let's look at the intra-actions that are enacted in the images of Sally and Stephanie. Christine says: *Where are they going? What does Stephanie have in mind?* Better yet, *I can't believe that Sally is agreeing to follow.* Boundaries around the image of Sally are established in this intra-action and a specific representation of Sally is configured. A material meaning of the image of Sally is articulated and becomes meaningful. The image of the child emerges discursively and materially in this intra-action. But this is not a fixed image because this intra-action is continuously entangled with others. Christine continues: *With a look of slight panic, Sally shoots her gaze up, her eyes saying, "Help me; she took my sticker."* Yet the image of Sally is (re)configured as Christine writes that *her patience is astounding.*

We can't leave behind how these intra-actions also configure images of Stephanie: *Stephanie leads and Sally follows,* Christine says, *although a look of uncertainty is written on her face.* The boundaries placed here are entangled with the boundaries and possibilities that the image of Sally enact in their own intra-actions.

Moreover, the material-discursive intra-actions that Christine embodies are entangled in the configurings and reconfigurings of the image of the child: *Frozen in my step, my body clenched into a tight ball, I am hoping and praying for it; I am intrigued by the quick turn of events; I am curious to see how this unfolds; I'm wishing in my head, "Please just give it back."* Christine's discursive-material practices are agentic in that they also make possible certain meanings about Sally and Stephanie.

The point is not that Christine's thinking about the children is changing over time. The point is not that the meanings of the images of Sally and Stephanie are achieved through Christine's thoughts and actions. Rather, what we want to emphasize is that the dynamics taking place are "what matters in the ongoing materializing of different spacetime topologies" (Barad, 2007, p. 141). Barad (2007) reminds us that the world is in constant rearticulations through processes of relationalities and entanglements. Entities or boundaries, she continues, are created through these processes. So, it's not entities that precede entanglements or relations. The world is agentic, always changing and creating boundaries.

Further analysis of Stephanie and the Sticker Moment can be found in our discussion of the image of the child in chapter 3, where we highlight change as intra-action, and in chapter 6, where we use it to illustrate pedagogical narration as a nomadic ethical act.

Stephanie and the Art Supply Cart

Stephanie surveys the art supply cart, much like she does most days. Standing over the cart, she surveys the assortment of pencil crayons and coloured markers. It is not unusual that she reaches over the clear glass jars and seizes handfuls of markers and pencils. The drawing utensils are held captive in her tightly clenched fists as she walks away from the open art centre.

I pull a chair up to the art supply cart and guide Stephanie into the seat. To my surprise, she settles in with no resistance. I ease the drawing tools out of her fist and place them in front of her on the table, handing one back to her. I simultaneously slip a piece of construction paper in front of her.

Minutes later, Stephanie is freely exploring the art materials. She seems content and peaceful.

Dani approaches the cart and sits down next to Stephanie. I prepare myself for Stephanie to make a move. Will she leave the table if Dani gets too close? Will this closeness irritate her? I speculate and strategize to keep Stephanie at the table if she decides to leave. Will she or won't she?

I hear and see nothing to indicate that Stephanie wants to leave this post I imposed on her. She doesn't seem to mind Dani's presence, and I am ecstatic, though I try to keep my energy calm. Dani needs my assistance to write a love letter to her parents. I am delighted to help but a bit distracted by wanting to absorb Stephanie's experience at the art supply cart.

Stephanie holding markers

Wordlessly, Dani approaches Stephanie and gently pats her shoulder. Stephanie winces slightly, but she doesn't reject the touch.

Next Ella approaches and unexpectedly throws her arms around Stephanie. Just as quickly, she returns to her seat to continue with her own explorations. Stephanie receives the hug by not rejecting it. My heart feels full.

When Ryan replaces Dani and Ella at the table, Stephanie reaches forward and grasps all the markers and coloured pencils. She takes a few steps to the right and places the tools in a wicker basket, then returns to collect more. She picks up the glue stick without its cap. Ryan gets up from his chair and positions his body in front of the wicker basket. He gestures, "Where is the cap?" Was he watching Stephanie the whole time?

Ryan steps away and returns with a cap, which he places on the table in front of Stephanie. Once again, no words are spoken. Ryan's only expression is the glimmer in his eye. I thank him for helping Stephanie to find the missing glue stick cap.

When Stephanie moves on to explore the natural collage materials, Ryan dips his hand into one of the glass bowls and sprinkles a handful of beans on the table.

Children hugging

"Are these for Stephanie?" I ask.

Ryan nods.

What are these children conveying with their silent gestures? Are they simply acts of kindness? Did Dani just want Stephanie to know she was there? And was Ella's hug a gesture of encouragement—"You're doing great, keep up the good work"—? Are the children expressing to Stephanie, "You're wonderful and I enjoy you being here with us"?

Gestures of affection, care, and kindness occur in silence, and only the children know their meaning. All I can do is listen to them with my heart.

USING THE PEDAGOGICAL NARRATION TO COMPLEXIFY PRACTICE: RECONFIGURING THE IMAGE OF THE CHILD

In chapter 3, we highlight how Christine's practices are agentive in that they play a role in producing the very phenomenon (the image of the child) they set out to grasp (Barad, 2007).

In chapter 5, we look at Stephanie and the Art Supply Cart from a sociomaterial perspective.

Stephanie and the Paints

Stephanie stands in front of the easel flashing strokes of yellow and black onto white paper. Faster than lightning, the brushes are back in their jars and Stephanie abruptly leaves the easel.

I tense up, thinking, "Oh no, come back ... come back and paint some more!" My head swivels up in Stephanie's direction. I see Sage and Dani approaching.

Perfect. I call them over.

"Help Stephanie back," I say, as I walk backwards to clear the area.

Without skipping a beat, Sage and Dani gently lead Stephanie back to the easel. I watch in silence, breathing a sigh of relief. I'm so delighted they're holding hands.

No time wasted, Dani hands Stephanie a brush loaded with orange paint.

With the physical encouragement of the brush from Dani and the soft gentle guiding of Sage's hand on her back, what will Stephanie do?

She accepts the brush, and paints over her flashing black strokes.

Dani, on standby, anticipates Stephanie's every move. With another brush ready and waiting, Dani swiftly intercepts by handing another paint-laden brush to Stephanie as she drops the brush back into the glass jar filled with orange paint.

Stephanie accepts the brush again.

Still as can be, I watch from behind the lens. I can hardly contain my mounting excitement.

Sage finds interest elsewhere, while Dani politely observes from the sidelines with another brush waiting in her hand.

"So much black," Dani comments. "Stephanie really loves black!" she declares.

Stephanie steps back from the easel, turning slightly to the right. Is she finished now and ready to go? Or is she waiting for Dani to serve her with another paintbrush?

Whatever the case may be, Dani seems to leave Stephanie with little choice; she eases another brush into her hand while softly supporting her arm.

Stephanie drives the paintbrush into the small glass jar and dunks it into the white paint.

Dani trails behind and directs the brush: up and down, up and down.

Stephanie holds on for the ride.

Dani then shifts her focus onto the blue paint. Is she getting it ready?

Sage returns for a brief moment. Why did he come back? Is he checking up on the girls' progress? Or is he just being his usual self, the caring soul who walks around lighting up everyone around him?

Dani feels for Stephanie's hand with a nurturing touch. Effortlessly she glides another loaded paintbrush into Stephanie's right hand.

With both hands now firmly gripping the paintbrush, Stephanie uses her body and wields the brush across the paper from left to right and back again.

At this point, I notice that Dani is gone. Why did she leave? Did she feel she had done her part? Did she feel she was no longer needed and that Stephanie was well equipped to continue on her own?

Finally, the brush trails slowly and steadily off the paper onto the back of the easel. Stephanie drags her brush along the wooden railing, adding to the mounting dried up paint. Her arm putts along the bottom, much like when the batteries run down in a gadget. When she comes to the end of the easel, she simply returns the brush to its designated jar.

Stephanie shuffles away to one of her favourite spots, the snack basket. Who comes around the corner? The girls meet again.

Dani sees Stephanie and beams with delight. She scoops Stephanie into her arms and affectionately squeezes her, like she's trying to get the last drop of juice out of her.

I melt.

With arms wrapped around each other, the girls share a private moment away from the flashing camera. They reunite in an embrace that emanates warmth, kindness, thoughtfulness, and generosity to the lucky ones who are fortunate enough to witness.

USING THE PEDAGOGICAL NARRATION TO COMPLEXIFY PRACTICE

In chapter 3, we work with Stephanie and the Paints in our discussion of configuring and (re)configuring the image of the child.

In chapter 6, this pedagogical narration helps us to highlight ethics as relational.

Building a Fort
by Kim Atkinson

We Build a Fort

The idea of forts emerged with Thomas suggesting that a clamp could be attached to the windowsill and rope could go across the room and then be attached to the grid on the other side.

Jack tried over and over again to attach a clamp to the windowsill, but he couldn't get it to stay.

Jack attaching clamp

Attached clamp

I suggested hammering a nail into the wall.

Jack worked hard to tie the rope to the clamp and then to fit the clamp to the nail.

Then began the task of stringing the rope across the room and attaching it to the grid on the other side.

But the rope wasn't long enough!

Jack saw that another rope was needed and suggested clamping two ropes together.

A hook was spotted on the ceiling so I stood on a stool and put the rope through that.

The rope was then pulled to the grid and clamped on. Voila! Now the fabric could be draped over the suspended rope.

Everyone shared a satisfied sense of accomplishment.

Then Some Bad Guys Build a Fort

A group of boys runs to the blocks.

"Let's build a fort!"
"This is my gun."
"But they can also be skis, right?"
"This is a gun. You guys sit here."
"Stop it, this is only my hiding place."
"No, we can hide here."
"Shoot the girls, only the girls. Shoot the teacher!"
"My bullet can shoot through a window."
"If someone's talking, you say 'Yes, Sir!' (saluting) *and you walk 'Huh Huh Huh!'* (marching)
"Yes, Sir!"

What Is a Bad Guy?

I wanted to explore what meanings the children were making in their play, so I asked them some questions.

KIM:	*What is a bad guy?*
CHILDREN:	*Robbers and be rude and steal stuff.*
	Be really bad. They kiss girls!
KIM:	*Are bad guys bad all the time?*
CHILDREN:	*Yes, bad guys are bad all the time.*
	Can be both. Bad guys can be good.
KIM:	*Do your families like this game?*

Twelve children say no; one child says yes.

MARY:	*Sometimes I like to play Batman, I like to play bad guys in Batman. I only play bad guys with a friend or by myself. I could be a mermaid bad guy.*

NINA: *I like to play good guys as long there's no bad guy. Bad guy beavers just fight and eat girls.*

KIM: *Why do they fight?*

THOMAS: *'Cause they eat girl food.*

NINA: *I don't really like that part of the story. Everything Thomas says is about dying.*

FREDDIE: *They do bad stuff like hurt people. Really hurt. I know, I play it.*

KIM: *Is it pretend or real?*

FREDDIE: *Pretend game.*

Kim's Reflections

In the sections below, Kim reflects on the events in her classroom through email correspondence with her colleagues in the IQ Project.

Bad Guys … and Girls

Bad guy play continues daily. I decide to create opportunities to express being "bad" in other ways, so I read Maurice Sendak's *Where the Wild Things Are* and we act it out. The boys choose not to be the "wild things" but to be Max, which surprises me at first until I realize that they have understood Max as the more powerful character.

We also act out *The Three Billy Goats Gruff.* The girls choose to be the billy goats and boys are the troll.

The idea of eating and shooting girls has come up in stories dictated to me:

> *We have dirt for dinner. Chchch. And we eat girls for dinner. Then we go out hunting and get dirt, and we turn them back into girls 'cause they're disguised. We plug in the Christmas tree and it's not dangerous. And then we go to bed. We wake up in the morning and the birds eat the worm, the birds eat the dirt and then bring it to us.*
>
> *We go Cha! And then we eat some wood. This time we eat wood. We are beaver spies. When we see writing—cha cha cha—we want to write too. Cha cha cha. We go and fight people and then we go and get girls and then we turn them into wood and we eat them. Cha cha cha. We eat wood all the time, every night, too. Cha cha cha. Birds come and eat the worms and they bring them to us and we eat them. And then they turn into wood. Then we pooed them out. And we go cheer, cheer, cha cha cha.*
>
> *We eat wood in the soil and every night we eat girls and turn them into wood. And we munch on the wood every night. We go*

to sleep in the morning and we wake up at night. We're nocturnal.
And we go to school at bed. We eat wood every night. We get
ropes and we catch a live fish and eat them. (By all the spy-fighting
beavers.)

The boys act out these stories, but no girls want to be part of them.

The girls voice some thoughts on bad guys. One notes that she would play a bad guy, but she seems to challenge some dominant gender discourses and she hedges, adding that she will only do it by herself or with her own friends, or as a "mermaid bad guy." Another voices her objection to being "girl food"; she observes that the stories all seem to be about dying. But the girls are silent on the topic of the boys' play and how girls are represented in it.

The boys' voices are dominant, making it difficult for the girls to have their voices heard.

I repeatedly ask the girls if they have stories to tell that we could act out, but none respond.

I feel strongly that I need to make a space for the girls' voices, so I write a story. Using characters and themes from stories the girls have told me in the past, I write about Goldilocks, dogs and cats, and a curious girl in a forest. I reference some "bad guys" by incorporating the sound of them "gnashing their terrible teeth," but I kept them hidden in the forest. I read the story to the group and suggest we act it out. The response is positive, and when we are done I ask if any additions or changes are needed. Many suggestions come forward, which I incorporate. Here is the result:

Once upon a time there was a curious girl named Goldilocks who
was walking in the jungle with her jungle cats and jungle dogs. As
they walked, they touched the shiny leaves and vines that hung
from the trees. They listened to the "thud thud thud" of the buffalo
running. It sounded like this:
"Thud thud cha cha cha. Thud thud cha cha cha."
The jungle cats and the jungle dogs did a jungle dance.
Goldilocks and the jungle cats and dogs kept walking. They heard
some jungle birds. They looked up to where the birds were flying
and saw a princess sitting in a tree eating pineapple. Goldilocks said,
"Come on down," so the princess jumped, but she didn't fall because
she had wings and she could fly.
Goldilocks and the jungle cats and dogs and the princess kept
walking together in the jungle. Suddenly they heard a terrible hissing
and gnashing of teeth. It was snakes having a wild rumpus. "Let's

get out of here," said Goldilocks. So the princess and Goldilocks and the jungle cats and the jungle dogs ran and ran. Then they saw a puff of smoke. It was a little dragon. "Hello, my name is Puff,' said the dragon. "Do you want to go to a land named Honalee?" "Yes," answered Goldilocks and the princess. The jungle cats and the jungle dogs did another jungle dance.

"Thud thud cha cha cha. Thud thud cha cha cha."

That meant yes.

So they all got on a boat and crossed the ocean that was full of sharks. They came to a land called Honalee and they went to a house and had some tea and went to sleep.

(Everyone sings "Puff, the Magic Dragon.")

Bad Guys Won't Go Away

Bad guy play continues daily among four boys, with others frequently joining in. The play usually results in conflicts, hitting, pinching, name calling, and anger. Parents express concern and talk to me about their children being fearful and not wanting to come to school. One sends an email:

> *I am writing to you for some advice on how to respond to Maria. She is still worrying about coming to school because of relationships with some of the "bad guy" boys. Yesterday she told me that she needed to have her hair straightened before she went back to school "so Tori won't know it's me." "Or else they will kill me," she added.*
>
> *Of course we know that is not the issue, but I just am at a loss now. I feel like I keep dismissing her problem by saying things like "they are just trying to get your attention/join your game"; "maybe you could just play with some other friends"; "just walk away."... Is there a better way to approach this with her?*

A father expresses concerns about his daughter. She came roaring at him at home, saying that she would "kill him." He is alarmed and wonders what can be done about the language and play among the boys, which he sees as the source of the problem. During our conversation, he notes that he played similar games when he was a child.

In February, Tori, a boy at the centre of the bad-guy play and the conflicts, comes to school one morning very upset. His mom tells me he has been talking all weekend about Stephen and about the conflicts. He has been telling complete strangers about his fear and anger.

At group time, I bring up the topic and a flood of comments erupts.

TORI:	*I'm worried about Stephen hurting me. He's doing it again and again.*
WILL:	*I don't want to be hurt.*
STEPHEN:	*I don't want anyone to hurt me either. Jack slapped me.*
KIM:	*The words that people use can hurt as much as a hit. When you say "I don't like you, you're so stupid," that hurts inside you, in your heart.*
FINN:	*When you say "I don't like you, you're so stupid," that hurts.*
KIM:	*Does it make you sad when people tell you they don't like you?*
STEPHEN:	*Yes.*
KIM:	*There are two ways to hurt people: hit and pinch them, and use words that are unkind.*
TORI:	*People don't like him bugging them.*
FINN:	*I know. We could make Stephen happy by tickling him.*
STEPHEN:	*You don't have to do that. I'll already be nice.*
WILL:	*Sharing to make people feel better.*
COLIN:	*Instead of hurting, you could say "Use your words."*
KIM:	*What if they said no? What can you do when you are angry, instead of hitting or saying something mean?*
CHILDREN:	*Get a grown-up.*
	No name-calling.
	Say "Don't do that."
	Say "I don't want to talk to you anymore."

It seems that voicing the fears and anger defuses the situation. Though conflicts still arise, they are less frequent and are more easily resolved.

But the bad-guy play continues unchanged. It impinges on everyone, even those who have no part in it. John doesn't play the bad-guy game, but he keenly observes it. He tells me two stories that seem to show that he feels the need to equip himself in defence. He draws pictures of the weapons he would use to defend himself, and he makes weapons out of cups and tape that he wears on his hands.

In April, Tori and Colin are running away from Stephen again and telling him they don't want to play. We talk AGAIN about how that makes people feel. They continue to play bad guys and talk of "getting" the girls. I feel like a broken record.

After our parent meeting, a parent takes me aside to tell me about a conversation in the class meeting. It seems most parents are afraid to go into the block room because of the bad-guy play. The few who do venture in feel they can deal with the play; therefore, they feel an obligation to be there. But they also resent not being able to enjoy the more peaceful art room.

In May, I am starting to think progress is being made. Girls are speaking up about their dislike of the play and boys are beginning to hear them. Today, though, four parents take me aside to voice concerns. Three tell me that their child is worried about the bad guys, and one tells me she is very tired of feeling judged as the parent of a bad guy. A parent emails to say she saw my article in *Island Parent*[3] and was relieved to know that she is not alone in struggling with this topic.

USING THE PEDAGOGICAL NARRATION TO COMPLEXIFY PRACTICE

Kim reflects on her experiences of presenting Building a Fort in chapter 4, in the section "Pedagogical Narration as a Discourse of Meaning-Making."

Kim's engagement with parents in relation to bad-guy play is mentioned both in chapter 3 and in chapter 6 in our discussion of ethics as relational.

....

3 Kim's article (Atkinson, 2007) is included in chapter 4 in our discussion of pedagogical narration as a discourse of meaning-making (see pp. 126–128).

THINKING TOGETHER

In this chapter we explore the theories and processes of pedagogical narration and discuss how this tool can be used to make children's learning visible, complexify practice, and keep curriculum alive. We briefly investigate the links of pedagogical narration to approaches in three different contexts: Italy; New Zealand; and Australia. We critique the "McDonaldization" of pedagogical documentation and discuss some concerns with how this revolutionary tool is unfortunately being used as part of an *evolutionary* project in most North American contexts. Using examples from our collaborative work with early childhood educators, we consider pedagogical narration as:

- A discourse of meaning-making.
- A political tool.
- A vehicle for public dialogue.
- A materializing apparatus of knowing.

Pedagogical Narration as a Tool to Complexify Practices

I remember so clearly the day that Erika quietly approached me as I stood mixing paints at the sink. "When did God get alive?" she asked tentatively. I held my breath for a moment, and then I told her I thought she was asking a very important question. I suggested that we take the question back to the other children at our morning meeting. When we gathered together later in the morning, Erika proposed her question. A flurry of ideas poured forth from the children, and I was thankful that I had my tape recorder at hand. Later I shared the transcript with the children's families. This episode sticks so firmly in

my mind as an example of what Malaguzzi[1] talks about—the steady flow of
communication through pedagogical documentation. (Laurie)

Pedagogical narration,[2] simply put, is a way to make children's learning visible as educators make decisions about curriculum development. It can take the form of:

- anecdotal observations of children
- children's works
- photographs that illustrate a process in children's learning
- audio and video recordings of children engaged in learning
- children's voiced ideas

In addition to the children's words and images, educators include their reflections and questions and invite their colleagues, the children, and the children's families to add their thoughts. Pedagogical narration thus provides a focus for concrete, meaningful adult and child reflection on children's learning experiences and processes so that educators can make informed decisions about developing curriculum. Through dialoguing, listening, and reflecting with others, curriculum can be deepened.

At the same time, pedagogical narration is more than this—much more. We see it as a productive space for complexifying early childhood education curriculum. We use it as a tool, both to complexify our curriculum and to make the complexity of our curriculum visible. In our collaborative work with early childhood educators, we use pedagogical narration for reflection, deconstruction, planning, experimentation, and action within a discourse of meaning-making. Further, we use it as a *doing*—as a process rather than an activity that can be accomplished once and for all.

Clearly we're not talking here about simply observing children and displaying the products of our observations. The emphasis is on the *process* of developing curriculum through pedagogical narration rather than on curriculum as *product*.

In pedagogical narration, the educator acts as a researcher, considering multiple theoretical perspectives to interpret children's learning and to plan curriculum, in dialogue with other educators, children, and families, for further pedagogical possibilities. From this perspective, pedagogical narration is not

---

1 Malaguzzi, 1993.
2 Pedagogical narration is a term used in British Columbia. Similar processes are called pedagogical documentation in Sweden and Italy; learning stories in New Zealand; and action research in parts of Australia.

about creating beautiful displays of children's work; it is about creating "a visible trace ... that supports learning and teaching, making them reciprocal because they are visible and shareable" (Rinaldi, 2006, p. 100).

As the pedagogical narrations in this book demonstrate, layer upon layer of meaning can be found in children's encounters with each other, with material-discursive worlds, and with us in our everyday work. It is through pedagogical narrations that we attempt, together, to tease out these (provisional, momentary) layers of meaning. In this chapter we invite you to join us in this meaning-making. Thinking with others helps us to ask new questions and consider multiple perspectives, and you may find meanings we did not see.

Documenting Children's Learning across Three Contexts

As we mentioned in chapter 1, our journey as a critically reflective community involves learning with others. We have been greatly inspired, for example, by the early childhood programs of Reggio Emilia, Italy. In particular, the Reggio understandings of pedagogical documentation[3] have stimulated our work with pedagogical narrations. We have also learned a great deal from pedagogues working in New Zealand and Australia, among other contexts. Here, we briefly touch on these three contexts, which all approach the documentation of children's learning differently, as we note in the following sections. These three perspectives are informed by environment and narratives tied to place; however, similarities can be seen across all three contexts. In each of them, the child is seen as a competent individual with multiple potentials, and in each, children's learning is made visible to educators, their colleagues, the children themselves, their families, and the whole community.

Reggio Emilia: Pedagogical Documentation

The programs of Reggio Emilia have had a profound effect on early childhood education practice. The work of Loris Malaguzzi, the programs' originator, has inspired us as it has inspired many thinkers in other parts of

---

3 For a detailed explanation of the history and philosophical underpinnings of pedagogical documentation in Reggio Emilia, see Dahlberg, Moss, & Pence, 2007; Edwards, Forman, & Gandini, 1998; New, 2007; Giudici, Krechevsky, & Rinaldi, 2001; and Rinaldi, 2006.

the world. Gunilla Dahlberg (Dahlberg, 2000, 2003; Hultqvist & Dahlberg, 2001; Dahlberg, Moss, & Pence, 2007) and Peter Moss (Moss & Pence, 1994; Moss & Petrie, 2002; Brannen & Moss, 2003), as well as many others, have built on Malaguzzi's work.

From early on in the Reggio Emilia educational project, educators recognized the rich potential pedagogical documentation offers to make the learning of children and educators visible within the broader community. The artifacts of photographs, video, and transcribed conversations provide children and educators with a tangible record they can revisit to extend the learning. This documentation serves as a research tool for the educators; it builds curriculum, encourages ongoing evaluation and renews the educational experience. In addition, the detailed information they collect and display for families and other public audiences invites their reactions and support.

Reggio pedagogue Carlina Rinaldi describes pedagogical documentation as "a process of reciprocal learning" (2005). Elsewhere she writes:

> Knowing that each day is not a closed box, pre-packaged, something that has been prepared for you by others (schedules, planning), but rather a time that you construct with the others, children and colleagues—a search for meaning that only the children can help you find—is the wonderful thing that we have found in our work and in which we would like you to share. It is what we call "pedagogical research." And we believe that it is precisely documentation and research that provide the generative force which makes each day a special day. (2006, p. 98)

In the early months of my master's program, I had the opportunity to visit Reggio Emilia's world-famous travelling exhibit of children's work, *The Hundred Languages of Children*. For three whole days, from dawn until dusk, I was immersed in looking closely at every photograph, reading every printed word of the exhibit. I was transfixed. Tears rolled down my cheeks, again and again. My experience is not an uncommon one—I've since spoken with numerous people who have had a similar response. Why is this? Cadwell (2003) suggests that perhaps, in the work from Reggio Emilia, we see our own great potential reflected in everything that we lay our eyes on. It is as if we recognize our deepest selves in the glistening murals and the robust clay figures made by children; in the tile-floored, sun-filled spaces; and in the way the adults and children are alive with respect and knowledge of one another. We immediately sense the extraordinary meaning and beauty of everyday life in a school for the youngest citizens—a school that mirrors both who they truly are and who they will become. (p. 2)

In the exhibit, it was obvious that the Reggio Emilia schools are radiant with stories that trace the search for meaning by children and adults. The documentation joyfully portrays the educational journey. The exhibit bears witness to what I had always believed possible but had yet to experience. The educators, parents, community, and young children of Reggio Emilia live the possible. My tears were provoked, perhaps, because I felt a fervent hope that school, as I have dreamt it, and what I thought it could be, might be transported toward the possible. (Kocher, 2008)

The image of the child (see chapter 3) is integral to how pedagogues in Reggio Emilia think about and use pedagogical documentation. The Reggio educators do not formulate specific goals for the children's projects or activities in advance. Their objectives are flexible and adapted to the children's interests. Children's participation is emphasized. Children are understood—and treated—as capable of autonomously making meaning from their daily life experiences.

Likewise, the image of the educator (see chapter 3) is interwoven in how pedagogical documentation is presented. The early childhood educators see themselves as observers and researchers, and the pedagogical documentation as a component of their research. As Malaguzzi (1993) explains, through their documentation educators "try to capture the right moments, and then find the right approaches, for bringing together, into a fruitful dialogue, their meanings and interpretations with those of the children" (p. 81). Educators use pedagogical documentation to better understand what is going on in their practices and to inform their planning. They also use it to support and sustain both the children's learning and their own, thus building curriculum.

The research project *Making Learning Visible* [4] describes the Reggio Emilia approach to documentation as "visible listening." Its key processes include:

- conducting careful observations
- developing questions and tentative answers about how and what children are learning
- collecting evidence of individual and group learning
- interpreting observations and evidence in relation to your question(s)
- inviting others' interpretations
- using the information to guide future teaching
- starting all over again (Project Zero, 2006)

In our own projects with educators, the emphasis on starting all over again is a significant aspect of our journeys toward complexifying practices. As Anahi, an educator in the IQ Project, noted when sharing her pedagogical narrations with us: "I am willing to rewrite, enhance, or bridge any gaps within my learning process." This willingness to recognize one's work as incomplete, provisional, and momentary is key to the way we conceptualize pedagogical narration.

Iris Berger (2010, 2013) has written extensively about the connections between pedagogical narration (a practice developed in British Columbia, Canada) and pedagogical documentation. As Berger says, pedagogical narration has its roots in pedagogical documentation and the writings of researchers in Reggio Emilia. Berger (2013) describes pedagogical narration through the work of political theorist Hannah Arendt on storytelling (or narrativity as she called it):

Arendt's notion of storytelling stands in sharp contrast with conventional ways of thinking about narrative as defining meaning, giving an authentic account of events, or providing explanation and information.... For Arendt telling a story was not about capturing the "truth"; stories are told *"to stir people to think about what they are doing"* ... From this perspective, the practice of pedagogical narration can be seen as a practice by which early childhood educators invite their communities to first *think* and then engage in *collective judgment* about events that

4 http://www.mlvpz.org

invoke questions and puzzlement. Constructing pedagogical narration affords reflective judgment because it entails a kind of interpersonal visiting where diverse viewpoints (of children, teachers, consultants, parents, and community members) are made visible and become an opportunity to encounter the standpoint of others. (pp. 71, 74)

New Zealand: Learning Stories

The New Zealand approach to documenting children's learning is called "learning stories." The premise behind the approach, which is part of the relationship-based focus of New Zealand's national early childhood education curriculum Te Whariki (Government of New Zealand, 1996), is that when we notice, recognize, and respond to children, we are alive to their possibilities.[5]

In the Te Whariki curriculum, as Smith and May (2006) explain, educators are to notice children and observe what they are interested in and how they are learning. In other words, they are to pay attention. Paying attention to another person, they write, is not always comfortable: The words *attend* and *tension* share a common root, *tendere*, which means "to stretch." To really attend to another or to pay attention to another person involves stretching ourselves, straining to listen, to see, to feel.

As part of this complex process of paying attention, early childhood educators *recognize* (Smith and May note that the root of the word *recognize* means to learn again, to know again) what children are up to, what are they trying to do, what are they interested in. They do not impose their ideas on the children, but truly recognize the children and their work. It is a challenge, they write, to really observe and get to know a child, to resist preconceived ideas of who that child is. In the Te Whariki approach, it is only after taking the time to notice and recognize children that educators can respond to them effectively, building on the children's interests, skills, and abilities.

As is the case with pedagogical documentation, practice grounded in the Te Whariki approach considers the perspectives, hopes, rights, and voices of children, their families, and their communities. Margaret Carr notes that learning stories look very different from performance goals that measure school readiness. They involve "collaboration with families, high expectations of confidence in the children, and multiple opportunities for children to tell their stories" (Carr, 2001, p. 205).

....

5 For a detailed description of New Zealand's early childhood bicultural programs and to access the Te Whariki, please see http://www.educate.ece.govt.nz/learning/curriculumAndLearning/TeWhariki.aspx.

Australia: Collaborative Critical Reflection and Activism

Glenda MacNaughton (2003, 2005) works in the Australian context. MacNaughton doesn't necessarily speak of pedagogical documentation or learning stories. Still, her work with educators using poststructural and feminist analyses has been a source of inspiration for how we approach pedagogical narration.

In her work with educators, MacNaughton challenges top-down approaches embedded in the idea of theoretical applications to practice (e.g., developmentally appropriate practice). She invites educators to engage with the economic, political, and social contexts in which children live and educators practise. She proposes to create spaces for early childhood educators to act in the name of social justice and to work within spaces of difference that do not conform to uniformity. *Doing Foucault in Early Childhood Studies: Applying Poststructural Ideas* (MacNaughton, 2005) is an innovative example of how early childhood educators transform practices by emphasizing postfoundational knowledge and social change. MacNaughton (2003) plays back and forth in a fluid way between theory and practice and encourages educators to be active participants in constructing and deconstructing their practices and the knowledge that underpins them.

MacNaughton (2005) proposes creating "critically knowing early childhood communities" where early childhood educators find spaces that "honour ethical engagement with children, respect diverse and multiple childhoods and embed quality in all that they do" (p. 189).

We invite you to look for traces of MacNaughton's approaches in the pedagogical narrations we have included in this book.

The McDonaldization of Pedagogical Documentation

Pedagogical documentation takes time. We think of it in terms of the Slow Food movement as compared to a fast food approach. Significant amounts of time are required to document the children's learning, and more time is needed to study and engage with the documentation. Tools are required—cameras, tape recorders, video cameras, computers. Space is needed to display the children's ideas. (Laurie)

As we discussed at the beginning of this chapter, we use pedagogical documentation (though we call it pedagogical narration) as a tool to both complexify our practices and to make visible the layers of complexity in those practices and in children's learning. Pedagogical documentation has become widespread because the Reggio Emilia philosophy has gained international recognition. We were eager to embrace the approach when we began our work with educators, but we were concerned—and we continue to be concerned—about a tendency toward a superficial, oversimplified approach to documenting children's learning—what Ritzer (1993) calls "McDonaldization."[6]

We are also concerned that awareness of the Reggio philosophy has been interpreted by some in the North American context as an incremental step in the growing body of early childhood education knowledge. Early childhood educators who take up the approach are seen as having developed ever more sophisticated understandings of children and their development and appropriate care. This view is consistent with the **modernist** view of "progress." Therefore, we want to think carefully about how we approach pedagogical documentation. Our use of pedagogical narration, instead of pedagogical documentation, is in part a response to resist the North American tendency to "consume" Reggio Emilia ideas. By using pedagogical narration we attempt to ensure that we stay close to Reggio Emilia's "original" idea of documentation as a political tool that allows us to live authentically alongside children, families, and communities. In that way our understanding of pedagogical narration is close to the work of reconceptualist thinkers (e.g., Dahlberg & Moss, 2005).

Reconceptualist thinkers understand the significance of the Reggio philosophy quite differently from those who support developmental theory (Dahlberg, Moss, & Pence, 2007). Ideas from Reggio Emilia can stimulate a rethinking of early childhood education practices and an examination of their underlying assumptions—and indeed they have. Reggio Emilia is the first early childhood approach broadly accessible in North America that could stimulate a discussion of early childhood education in the postmodern era. Unfortunately, it is rarely used in this way in North America. Ideas from Reggio Emilia have the potential to enable the deconstruction of North American early childhood education, but this potential is still unrealized. The early childhood education field in North America is far from embracing either Reggio Emilia or the discourse of meaning-making that is so much a part of the Reggio experience. The field is still dominated by discussions of quality childcare centres from a managerial perspective, and these discussions are closely tied to DAP discourses. This relationship between DAP and quality is important to note because developmentally appropriate practices and classrooms have become understood as synonymous with quality.

....

6 Also see Johnson, 2000, and Grieshaber and Hatch, 2003, for a discussion of the McDonaldization of pedagogical documentation and the Reggio Emilia project.

Pedagogical narration is closely tied to Reggio Emilia's pedagogical documentation as a political project. Reggio Emilia arose out of the devastation of post–World War II Italy, where pedagogue Loris Malaguzzi and a group of parents began a school to promote the ideas of tolerance and respect, experiential learning, relationships, and a myriad of ways to discover the world. The aim at the time was to disrupt the fascist discourses that had decimated understandings of education, with devastating consequences for individuals and places. Education in Reggio Emilia was, and we think still is today, approached as a *political* project that engages with the particular social, cultural, political, and ethical contexts of the time.

When Carla Rinaldi (2006) speaks of pedagogical documentation, she is somehow challenging a fascist education. For us, pedagogical documentation speaks directly to the political project that the citizens of Reggio Emilia were trying to challenge, the fascist discourses that had created injustice and intolerance of difference. We think that sometimes, in early childhood education, we reduce pedagogical documentation to a romanticized version of learning that we don't believe is the project of Reggio Emilia. We would like to reclaim a different approach—a *political* pedagogical documentation—through our use of pedagogical narration.

We believe, as Dahlberg, Moss, and Pence (2007) have argued, that the work accomplished in early childhood by people in Reggio Emilia has been (mis)interpreted by many in the North American context as an evolutionary project—one that builds on existing **positivist** ideas. The Reggio programs and the ideas behind them are not evolutionary; they are *revolutionary*, reconceptualist, and postfoundational in nature. Developmental theories are only one of many influences on Reggio, and at times they have been critically viewed (Rinaldi, 2006). Reggio leaders have understood that no theory is the absolute truth, and that every theory is just a starting point for further investigation and discussion.

With these cautionary notes in mind, we proceed now to explore how we complexify pedagogical narration—and complexify our practices through using pedagogical narration—in our context in British Columbia. In the next four sections, we use examples of pedagogical narrations created by the educators in our projects to highlight this revolutionary tool's potential as a discourse of meaning-making, as a political tool, as a vehicle for public dialogue, and as a materializing apparatus of knowing. As specified at the beginning of this chapter, we see pedagogical narration as being intimately connected with curriculum development. However, our discussion below focuses specifically on educators' processes of complexifying practices through pedagogical narrations. We encourage you to use these processes of complexifying practices as a step toward developing your curriculum.

Pedagogical Documentation as a Discourse of Meaning-Making[7]

When we began our collaborative work with pedagogical narrations, we not only had to learn new ideas; we also had to unlearn *concepts and ways of doing our practices. In particular, we had to unlearn how we observe young children. (Enid)*

Observation Is a Beginning, Not an End

Child observation plays an integral part in early childhood training and practice. Typically, the goal of observing children is to assess them in relation to developmental standards (Dahlberg, Moss, & Pence, 2007). As such, observation can be understood as a means to assess children's psychological development in accordance with predetermined stages of a "normal" child. Understood from a modernist perspective, child observation is based on the assumption that an objective, external truth can be recorded and represented accurately. We remember learning, in our own training as educators, how to detach our emotions and feelings from what we were observing. We, as educators, did not matter in our observations. As scientist and philosopher Donna Haraway (1991) might note, we were asked to take an objective and innocent stance, distanced from everything and everyone, when observing what children were engaged in.

In pedagogical narration, on the other hand, observation is contextual and subjective; it involves children in a process of co-construction with educators (Dahlberg, Moss, & Pence, 2007). Adopting a poststructural perspective in our work with pedagogical narrations, we do not claim that what is documented is a true account of what has happened. Rather, we recognize that narrations can in no way exist apart from our own involvement in the process. We are active subjects and participants as we co-construct and co-produce the documentation. From this perspective, documentation is understood as a narrative of **reflexivity** and **diffractive engagement**. Being aware that we are not

---

7 We introduced the concept of a discourse of meaning-making in chapter 1.

representing reality "makes it easier to critically analyze the constructed character of our documentation and to find methods to counteract and resist the dominant regimes" (Dahlberg, Moss, & Pence, 2007, p. 147). As the pedagogical narrations we include in this book demonstrate, adopting an objective perspective in our observations would reproduce injustices that we are not willing to overlook. Pedagogical narration, then, is not to be confused with observation. Pedagogical narration doesn't stop at observation; observation is always only a beginning point.

Making Meaning

In the practice of pedagogical narration, educators continuously critically reflect on the ways in which meanings and knowledge are conditionally constructed in relation to social, political, and other systemic and discursive conditions. Educators also critically reflect on how they themselves engage with the ideas embedded in pedagogical narrations to create certain subjective accounts, interpretations, and conceptualizations. In other words, in making meaning with pedagogical narrations, educators are creating and enacting new theories as they interact with children's, families', and colleagues' words and actions in the narration. This is a radical disruption of the idea that an objective singular account of knowledge can be produced.

In our work with pedagogical narration, we embrace multiple perspectives and subjectivities, complexifying practice in ways that would be limited within a modernist discourse of objectivity and neutrality. Following the work of Peter Moss and Gunilla Dahlberg (2008), we use pedagogical narration as a dialogic process of collective interpretation, as a powerful tool for disrupting dominant conceptions of quality and moving toward a discourse of meaning-making, where taken-for-granted assumptions and knowledges are deconstructed and reconstructed and where multiple perspectives are embraced.

Berger (2013) pays attention to the *narratives* included in pedagogical narration. She says,

> The pedagogical narratives can act as a constant reminder that pedagogical relationships are fraught with ethical and political choices that necessitate a critically engaged public. When the pedagogical narratives are shared, the educator takes further responsibility in narrating the collective version of the story by being attentive to how others' perspectives might have changed the initial narrative. (p. 15)

In pedagogical narration what is *narrated* is not necessarily a true account of what happened in a particular event. Rather, the *narrated* material of "children's words and experiences is viewed as an occasion for dialogue" through which educators, children, and families "share and negotiate their different perspectives and understandings" about the *narrated* event (Berger, 2013, p. 14). In this way, each of the perspectives shared enriches, challenges, and broadens the possibilities for interpretation and, more importantly, for future pedagogical response and action in curriculum.

We expand on the idea of opening to multiple perspectives in chapter 5. Now we'd like to turn to the pedagogical narration Building a Fort. Please take some time to reread Kim's narration on pp. 105–12 and then her reflections below.

Building a Fort/Building Meanings

Kim presented Building a Fort many times (in our learning circles, to families, in conference presentations), and it always generated dialogue. The subject matter—including gun play, bombs, and boys shooting girls and teachers—raises visceral, emotional responses ranging from recognition that gun play can be a place from which to begin a dialogue with children, to anger and heated debate about whether gun play and its inherent gendered violence, as related above, should ever be tolerated. Kim wrote the following reflections after presenting Building a Fort at the IQ Project sharing circle.[8]

> *Yesterday I presented my narration at the sharing circle. It was an emotional and intense time. I purposefully included the most challenging and difficult moments I had experienced with the children to illustrate the theme our group had chosen: ethical identities of children and educators. We wanted to highlight the silences, the places where we are frozen. So I brought out all the bad bits.*
>
> *As I progressed through the presentation, I could feel the tension in the room elevate. There was no dialogue yet, but I sensed the emotional temperature rising. I felt it within me as well, my voice cracking or shaking. I felt I was being judged as an educator.*
>
> *The dialogue that took place after my presentation was emotional. It included the influence of media and video games, violence in our world, how our own histories inform how we react to the play, how gender works in children's play, what I was trying to achieve by not shutting down the play, ethical choices educators make, and wondering when and how to intervene— among many other topics.*

....

8 As noted in chapter 1, the IQ Project learning circles consist of small groups of educators who meet monthly, while the sharing circles bring the groups together periodically to learn from each other. Educators share their pedagogical narrations in their learning circles first. Some narrations are also presented again at the sharing circle.

> *At times, I felt that some educators believed I was misguided and*
> *irresponsible. But others saw the value of opening this "crack," as Enid puts*
> *it (following Leonard Cohen's reference): the crack is how the light gets in.*
> *(Kim)*

Kim wrote these reflections in the midst of the tensions she was living as she attempted to make multiple meanings of circumstances that unfolded in her preschool classroom. Kim understands that gender, racialization, and violence (difficult topics to deal with in a classroom with young children) are shaped by, and shape, the discourses of her preschool. In our conversations with Kim, we could see how she struggled, and continues to struggle, with these aspects of her practice. These are not exemplary moments for Kim or us, but they are moments that bring conflict, inequality, and violence to the forefront of practice; therefore, they need to be addressed and challenged, not ignored or made invisible.

Later, Kim wrote the following piece for a local parenting magazine. We include it because it shows how Kim stayed with the problems and tensions of the encounter and thought about them in different ways. It illustrates, in our view, how we can engage in meaning-making through pedagogical narration.

GOOD GUYS AND BAD GUYS[9]

In my line of work I meet a lot of bad guys. They carry guns, swords, sabres and fantastical weapons full of levers with complicated capabilities. These bad guys go by many names and have powers to fly, transform, and disappear and reappear at will. They are all very mean.

I meet good guys as well. The good guys seem to have a comparable arsenal of weaponry and powers with the added skill of making traps to catch the bad guys, which is often their sole occupation. Often the good guys appear just as mean as the bad guys.

I am an early childhood educator and I work among the good guys and bad guys every day. The names change according to current trends or the players' imagination, but the themes never change. There is fighting, sneaking, stealing, capture, and rescue. Barricades are built, hideouts are constructed, roles are determined. There is killing, though no one seems to die. Identities shift seamlessly as Batman morphs into The Joker, who becomes The Captain. Witches and princesses rub shoulders with Darth

....
9 This piece is a shortened version of Atkinson, 2007.

Vader and Spiderman. Ferocious monsters growl at equally ferocious kittens. I stand in their midst, wondering why.

Consider this dialogue among a group of 4-year-olds:

> *"This is a gun. You guys sit here."*
> *"Shoot the girls, only the girls. Shoot the teacher!"*
> *"My bullet can shoot through a window."*
> *"What power does your gun shoot?"*
> *"168 metres."*
> *"Mine shoots fire."*
> *"Mine shoots pistols."*

As parents we are alarmed, even horrified to hear our child talking about weapons, shooting, and killing. The intensity, the language, and the appearance of aggression is disturbing. Often it seems this play emerges suddenly. One day our child is playing teddy bear picnic, the next they are shooting the teacher. We are taken by surprise, with no idea how to respond.

Early childhood educators are often just as unsure how to respond. I have spent hours discussing weapon play and bad guys with colleagues and this much we agree on: It's there in every group of preschool-age children and we can never really make it go away. We can insist on "no weapons" all we want, but the children are too clever for us and make things that are not really guns at all, just things that look like guns and shoot goo and slime. We all know toast can be chewed into a gun.

We are conflicted. We don't really like gun play, but we know we are in a losing battle to change it. We know most parents don't like gun play, either, and they are looking to us to see how we deal with it.

The fact that gun play elicits such strong emotions and uncertainty among adults is not surprising. Our image of childhood is that it is a time of innocence, that children have a purity that we can protect. Aggression and violence are not part of our image, thus we are shocked when we see it.

We also might be fearful of where this kind of play will lead. Will a child who talks of shooting the teacher become a violent teenager? Are we raising unfeeling, uncaring children?

As I sit among the bad guys voicing my objections to being shot, I watch and listen carefully. I don't see unfeeling children; I see a complex drama with powerful characters. I see heroic deeds and negotiation. I see identities explored within the themes of good and evil.

Brian Edmiston (2008) writes in *Forming Ethical Identities in Early Childhood Play* that children explore their ethical identity within the context of the mythic play of good guys and bad guys. As children try on these roles, they can evaluate the perspective of that role and experience that identity. The adult role, Edmiston says, is to create dialogue about the issues of good and evil, caring, empathy, and power.

As the children continue to shoot one another, I ask them some questions about guns. Their answers reveal that being rude is as bad as stealing and that bad guys can be good sometimes. But most revealing to me is that the children fully agree that they are playing a pretend game. The bad guys "really hurt people" and Freddie knows it because he "plays" it. Really hurting in pretend play … the children are not confused by this finessing of real and pretend. I think it is we adults who are confused by it.

When we are alarmed by the aggression and violence of bad-guy play, maybe we are missing something. Maybe we are failing to give children credit for their understanding of "pretend." We see the intensity of the play and conclude that we are seeing aggression and violence. What we are more likely seeing is pretend aggression and violence. How does that make a difference? It makes a huge difference to the children playing it. They know they are acting out roles, trying out characters. They know they can "really hurt people"—but in play.

In conclusion … I really have no conclusion. Bad guys still roam freely in my preschool and I still don't like being shot at. I sometimes have an emotional reaction to what I see and hear and sometimes I wish it would just go away. But I am also asking questions, asking for explanations, asking for stories and drawings and trying to really listen. And I am making space for the play even when it's hard to, because, as teacher and author Vivian Gussin Paley (2005, p. 25) puts it, "When play is curtailed, how are children to confront their fantasy villains?"

Keeping Curriculum Alive

Why do we observe children's learning? Why do we attempt to make meanings from our observations? Why do we narrate classroom events? Pedagogical narration is an important tool for educators to create curriculum. Educators work with pedagogical narration not just to narrate classroom events or to make children's learning visible "after the event." Our observations and narrations become part of the curriculum planning process, enabling our work with children to move over time. In other words, processes such as observations, making meaning on our own and with others, and developing rich narratives allow educators to keep the curriculum alive. Rinaldi (2006) reminds us of this when she says:

For the teacher, being able to reflect on how the learning is proceeding means that she can base her teaching not on what she wants to teach, but on what the child wants to learn. And in this way she learns how to teach, and teacher and children search together for the best way to proceed. (p. 101)

The goal here is to keep the curriculum open, not "to close down the event" (Olsson, 2009). In Becoming Rapunzel (see pp. 86–95), Fikile engages with ideas that the children are bringing to the classroom, and asks questions and develops curriculum to keep the ideas going. She creates new problems for the children, not solutions. The children don't necessarily respond in predetermined ways. But it is precisely these unpredictable responses and turns that keep the curriculum alive.

We hope these reflections have illustrated our view, as we discussed in chapter 1, that a discourse of meaning-making:

- requires an active, engaged early childhood educator.
- accommodates diversity, complexity, and multiple perspectives.
- encourages individual judgements and uncertainty.
- views consensus and unanimity as neither necessary nor desirable.
- requires individuals to make ethical philosophical choices and judgements.
- draws on concrete experience.
- involves critical, reflexive thinking about pedagogies.
- contextualizes everyday practices within a particular social location and time.
- produces meaning in dialogue with others.
- keeps curriculum open and alive.

Now that we have explored pedagogical narration as a discourse of meaning-making, let's take a look at how this tool can be used toward political ends.

Pedagogical Narration as a Political Tool

We discussed in chapter 2 that critical reflection, which is central to our approach to pedagogical narration, is grounded in political intent. Many of the educators in our projects, when they begin, do not think of their work with children as political. Often, educators describe themselves as enhancers of children's development, reflecting a kind of innocence in their work.

Educators do not see themselves as engaged in gender work, anti-racism work, and so on. This is due in part to the decontextualization and individualization emphasized in child development theories (see chapter 2). As we explained in chapter 2, we instead see early childhood practices as always embedded in political, social, cultural, and economic contexts. So, what does this mean for pedagogical narration?

Critical reflection requires a deep engagement with the ways in which knowledge is socially and politically constructed and with the power effects of that knowledge. How we make meanings of the observations we collect through the process of pedagogical narration holds immense potential for educators and researchers to become aware of, and disrupt, **hegemonies** of knowledge such as binary thinking, racisms, gendered discourses, **heteronormativity**, and so on. In our work, it is through this process of interpretation that we often come to interrogate the universal developmental theories of early childhood. Educators become aware of some of their implicit assumptions about children by expanding their own perspectives, by seeing the many meanings that are embedded in one moment of practice. Through these awakenings, educators come to consider hidden assumptions, and to act to interrupt injustices. One way that we find pedagogical narration to be a transformative political tool, both in research and in practice, is in unpacking, destabilizing, and interrogating binary thinking.

Disrupting Binary Thinking

> *The boy said, "You can't be the mother; you're not pretty."... What really struck me was how he was defining mother and also how motherhood was defined in opposition to fatherhood—that there needed to be both—so those are the heterosexual norms. Which also makes me think about racialization, class, and any other social construction of identity—they are interrelated and we can't really separate them from each other. (Scarlett)*

Euro-Western thought frames oppositions, such as:

- rational/irrational
- ordered/unordered
- objective/subjective

In early childhood education, we also discuss the distinction between included and excluded, empowered and disempowered, and voiced and voiceless as if they were natural opposites (MacNaughton, 2005). MacNaughton (2005) notes, however, that the significance of binary oppositions and their "other" is that the "other" is not equal to the main part of the pair.... The pairs are always ranked, so one part of the pair always has a higher value in the ranking and is privileged over the "other." (p. 83)

Binaries are packed with certainties that disempower children and make early childhood educators expert knowledge holders. Binaries bring practices and research to a halt, a standstill space in which possibilities for encountering other ways of seeing and relating are closed (Dahlberg & Moss, 2005; MacNaughton, 2005).

Binaries of "Race" and Gender

In our collaborative critical reflections with educators, we frequently encounter binaries relating to gender and "race," and we work to disrupt the inequities through our deconstructive discussions. In the following example, an IQ Project participant who worked in an inner-city setting in Vancouver's Downtown Eastside wrote observations from her everyday practice in a journal she kept to make children's understandings of racialization visible. The dialogue below motivated the centre's educators to engage in an ongoing inquiry among themselves to better understand how children make meaning of processes of racialization.

The poorly funded centre is located in a decaying building surrounded by a high, wired fence along a busy street. Two weeks before the children's conversation took place, the group had taken a walk around the neighbourhood during which they had encountered a homeless man. At the time, the children showed little interest in the man.

The participants in the conversation are Kai (5), Rashond (6), Tyronne (5½), Jamal (6), Jahrul (5), Rita (educator), and Maya (educator). The educators and children were setting up a beach scene in the centre's garden area when the following dialogue took place.

"NO CHINESE-FACE HOMELESS"

KAI: *There no Chinese-face homeless.*
TYRONNE: *Yes, there is.*
KAI: *No homeless Chinese face, I say.*
JAMAL: *Of course there is. People don't live somewhere everywhere.*
KAI: [becoming loud and angry] *No homeless Chinese face!*
MAYA: *Kai, calm down, buddy.*

KAI: *I not buddy.*

MAYA: *Okay, okay. Please calm down, Kai.*

KAI: *No Chinese-face homeless.*

TYRONNE: *He's crazy!*

KAI: *I not crazy, African face.*

TYRONNE: *I'm Native, stupid. Brown.*

KAI: *You have face like Rashond. He African face.*

JAMAL: *Black face come in many shades.*

RITA: *Kai, why do you think no Chinese people are homeless?*

KAI: *Home in China.*

TYRONNE: *Stupid, stupid, stupid.*

JAMAL: *Hush.*

> Rashond and Jahrul, attracted by the loud voices,
> move closer to the group.

JAHRUL: *What's up, man?*

TYRONNE: *Kai is crazy.*

JAHRUL: *All Chinese people crazy man. My Chinese uncle is crazy.*

TYRONNE: *You got a Chinese uncle?*

JAHRUL: *Yea.*

JAMAL: *Hush! So what, you have a black uncle. Kai got a black uncle.
            You got a white mama. Hush.*

> Kai is following this exchange
> with clear confusion.

RITA: *Kai, my friend, I'm sorry you're sad. Would you like some
            water?*

> Twenty minutes later ...

JAMAL: *Kai, some people don't have place to live 'cause the prime
            minister is bad.*

KAI: *Yes, bad. He hurting me.*

JAMAL: [Surprised] *He is?*

KAI: *Yes. Tyronne and Rashond they laughing at me.*

JAMAL: *Oh. Well, people from everywhere can sleep on the streets.*

KAI: *I no see no Chinese face.*

JAMAL: *Chinese people are homeless, African people, Native people,
            white people, Spanish, black people, every people.*

KAI: *No Chinese face.*

JAMAL: *We ask your mom. She's got a Chinese face.*

KAI: *My mom no like you African face.*

JAMAL: [laughing] *Not true, your mom loves my African face.*

> Later that afternoon, Kai was observed sitting in
> amongst the props used for the beach activity.
> He had covered himself with a piece of cardboard.
> I asked him what he was doing.

KAI: *Chinese-face homeless.*

This dialogue powerfully illustrates the use of pedagogical narration as a political tool. In thinking about it together with others, we came to view the children's actions as creative attempts to resist the limitations of their racialized subjectivities by using their conversations as sites of political struggle (Parr, 2005). We wondered if these children were making visible the subjectification that positions them as "less than" within the binaries of racial identity.

Foregrounding issues of social justice and activism in our interpretations of this pedagogical narration allows us to resist viewing the children's actions "through hierarchical systems of signification ('barbaric' culture or via the unified notion of 'the oppressed')" (Parr, 2005, p. 289). Instead, through these dialogues we see the children complexifying the interplay of racisms, debating the conflicting ways in which racisms work. We can therefore move beyond the idea that the children were being racist and view their actions as invitations for us (educators, researchers) to complicate the concept of "race" by making visible the paradoxes and multiplicities of racialization. The children's actions can be considered as both a struggle and a transformation (Parr, 2005). Our collaborative analysis led us to see children's powerful experiences of racisms and their capacity to make meaning of them in thoughtful and justifiably reactive ways.

Through engagement with pedagogical narrations, children's expressions, thoughts, feelings, and discussions can be seen within the context of a long history of socially constructed ideas that contribute to the injustices of racialization and marginalization. Educators can collaborate with children to create spaces of social justice. Building early years settings as sites for political struggle means recognizing co-workers, families, and children as creative, competent subjects who can question and challenge dominant discourses (see chapter 5) and disrupt the hierarchical binaries that assign fixed and marginalizing meanings, such as what it means to be "Chinese," "African," or "First Nations." Critically exploring and considering multiple interpretations and possibilities through pedagogical narration can pave the way for new possibilities for children, families, and educators to step beyond their prescribed roles and assumed limitations to reveal surprising capabilities to mobilize sociopolitical change (Pacini-Ketchabaw & Berikoff, 2008).

While pedagogical narration offers transformative potential in working toward social justice, we also want to suggest that a critical dialogue around contextualizing pedagogical narration within Eurocentric perspectives is required in early childhood education. We ask ourselves how pedagogical narration can become more than a Eurocentric critique of Eurocentrism. While the example we have provided here explores how educators can more explicitly address the coloniality of power in their multicultural communities (see also Pacini-Ketchabaw & Berikoff, 2008; Pacini-Ketchabaw & Nxumalo, 2010), continued serious thinking about this question is needed. We are only beginning to open the dialogue of pedagogical narration as a means to make other types of knowledge possible. Pedagogical narration, then, cannot be seen as *the* tool that will solve the challenges presented by binary and hegemonic thinking. Rather, pedagogical narration becomes a possibility that is always to be revisited, revised, and challenged. It is a practice for questioning assumptions that involves questioning its own assumptions.

Pedagogical Narration as a Vehicle for Public Dialogue

Documentation in all its different forms ... represents an extraordinary tool for dialogue, for exchange, for sharing.... It means the possibility to discuss and to dialogue "everything with everyone." (Hoyuelos, 2004, in Moss, 2007, pp. 19–20)

As Reggio leader Loris Malaguzzi's biographer, Alfredo Hoyuelos, suggests above, pedagogical narration acts as a potent political tool in making the everyday learning experiences and practices of the early childhood classroom visible and open to engagement, contestation, and co-construction by families and the wider community. Hoyuelos describes the ideological and ethical concept of a transparent school and transparent education—a concept from which "a political idea also emerges, which is that what schools do must have public visibility" (quoted in Moss, 2007, pp. 19–20).

Public visibility creates early childhood education spaces as public arenas for collaborative dialogue and engagement. In this way, pedagogical narration can be seen to be a form of democratic practice where "sharing the documentation means participation in a true act of democracy, sustaining the culture and visibility of childhood, both inside and outside the school" (Rinaldi, 2006, p. 44)

Pedagogical narration can also disrupt a powerful binary in early childhood education that separates home from school. Through families' and other community members' participation in pedagogical narration, the child and the early learning classroom are situated in relationship to the community and are viewed as contributing to local knowledges (Kocher, 2010; Moss, 2007).

When pedagogical narration is situated in the public sphere, a shared understanding of the child as strong, competent, and capable can be foregrounded that further disrupts a singular "truth" of the child. At the same time, it can be recognized that this image of the child is a political choice that is continually recreated through the openness to dialogue with multiple perspectives and theories of children and childhood, "where the political is enacted through the appearance of a plurality of ideas and perspectives" (Berger, 2010, p. 60).

Pedagogical narration thus serves an important advocacy role in communicating that children are respected citizens and that early learning spaces are places where something of importance is taking place (Moss, 2007; New, 2007). Stories are told that reveal children in creative, unexpected, and unprecedented ways. In addition, making stories about children's actions and learning processes visible to the public entails constructions of children that are not abstract. Through these stories, children are released from their anonymity; they gain a multiplicity of identities and become the focus of dialogue and interest. The narrations can be offered as a collection of stories that tell about early childhood from many vantage points and thus enlarge our shared understanding of what early childhood education is and can be. These stories are not offered as the "truth" or as an example of "best practice"; instead they suggest ways of seeing children that invite conversation and inevitably change the public dialogue about early childhood education.

Through encountering and engaging with pedagogical narration, community members can see that early childhood educators are not simply observers and guides, caretakers and technicians. Not only are children's ideas and theories made visible, so are educators' complex practices with children, families, and colleagues as they research, document, critically reflect, share their contextualized understandings, and consider new provocations and resources to build on the children's questions, learning, and interests (Rinaldi, 2001).

The Images of Learning Project (Davis & Atkinson, n.d.), described below, is an inspiring example of using pedagogical narration as a tool to invite curiosity and "create and sustain a public sphere of engagement with questions concerning young children's education" (Berger, 2010, p. 64). The project was created by IQ Project participant educators Danielle Davis and Kim Atkinson. By highlighting educators' questioning, wondering, and celebrations as they work with theory in practice, Danielle and Kim are using pedagogical narration as an activist tool. They have created a travelling exhibit that invites the public to interpret and interrogate children's and educators' meaning-making from many perspectives. In this way, families and others in the community participate in and engage with children's learning.

IMAGES OF LEARNING PROJECT: MAKING VISIBLE CHILDREN'S COMPETENCIES AND EARLY CHILDHOOD EDUCATORS' WORK

The Exhibit

FIGURE 4.1: Photo from Images of Learning Project showing children working with light projector

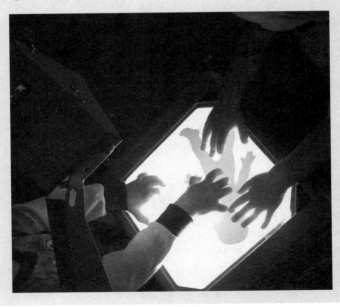

FIGURE 4.2: Photo from Images of Learning Project showing shadows projected by light projector

The exhibit includes a series of life-sized free-standing panels designed to call attention to children as protagonists in their own learning, capable of expressing themselves in myriad ways. The panels display photos, dialogue, and reflections that tell stories of learning. "Storybooks" attached to the display offer more images of children's intelligences. Educators' reflections and collaborations weave throughout, questioning, wondering about, and celebrating each story. Viewers are invited to contribute their understandings by leaving "traces" on an interactive art instalment. Opportunities are provided to investigate "the child's views."

The Images of Learning Project is being showcased in a variety of public settings across British Columbia. It invites parents, early childhood educators, policy-makers, school boards, teachers, licensing officers, academics, and the interested public to build professional relationships and to showcase both the important work of early childhood educators and the competencies of young children.

Our Beliefs

The people behind the Images of Learning Project believe that children are creative communicators in continuous dialogue with their world. Through art, sculpture, language, drama, and stories, children demonstrate the depth of their existing knowledge and their continuous search for new knowledge. When you look at a child, we want you to stop and listen deeply to:

- the many ways children communicate.
- what children know.
- how children research what they do not know.
- how children integrate that research into new learning.

The Images of Learning Project builds on the work of community awareness modelled by Reggio Emilia's *One Hundred Languages of Children* exhibit, which has travelled the world making visible children's competencies and early childhood educators' work.

Pedagogical Narration as a Materializing Apparatus of Knowing

> *This idea of creation, this ability to form with [materials] … the materials are not passive. It's a very powerful experience because there is constant motion. The materials are alive and there is constant intra-action between how the children are creating and how the materials are answering back, and how that can change at any moment and lead to a new exploration. (Nadia)*

The discourses that individuals engage in demonstrate through language how they understand the world; discourses are transmitted through verbal

exchanges, news stories, classroom discussions, books, websites, policy documents, and countless other avenues. Discourses also operate through images,
such as those we see in the media.

As we discussed in chapters 2 and 3, sociomaterial perspectives allow us
to move beyond discourse to consider how materials actively shape learning
and how subjectivity emerges as bodies—and their actions, perceptions, and
emotions—interact with objects, spaces, and discursive elements.

Following Lenz Taguchi (2008b), we see pedagogical narrations as tempo-
rarily capturing an intra-active event; in the narration's materialization, "it
becomes a territory for further intra-activity and processes of new learning"
(p. 8). Pedagogical narration, then, can be understood as a *materializing apparatus of knowing* (p. 9) that produces multiple interpretations of an event or
pedagogical encounter. These interpretations are limited and shaped by the
discursive borders of our understanding and by the material or physical participants in the event the narration captures.

Like Lenz Taguchi (2009), we see in pedagogical narrations how

> learning is a collaborative process of meaning-making that takes place
> between human subjects, their bodies and things, in specific places and
> spaces around questions and problems arising in the moment or event
> of investigation, constituting important turning-points in the event.
> This makes the teacher change the material conditions of her practice,
> sometimes in the midst of the process, and sometimes after having read
> and analyzed the documentation afterwards. (p. 90)

We illustrate these complex ideas with ordinary moments from practice
that educators bring to the IQ Project learning circles. During our discussions,
we are interested in questions of materiality and sociomaterial **intra-actions**
in children's learning. Like Lenz Taguchi (2009), we wonder what the consequences might be of viewing pedagogical practices from a perspective in
which "learning and knowing occurs in the interconnections that take place
in-between different forms of matter making themselves intelligible to each
other" (p. xv).

As we take up this question in our discussions of pedagogical narrations,
comments like the following arise:

> *These photos speak to me of the agency of the material, the intra-action
> between those materials that we might have thought of as static and fixed,
> as being in movement and doing something to each other. The materials are
> becoming, as they connect with each other. (Jenny)*

This is a good example of where, if you hadn't captured the moment with photos and reflection … [and] taken time to write about it, to think about it, to portray the moment, to share the teacher's thinking, it would be easy for somebody—parents or whoever—to think, "Oh, they're just mucking about." Not to value it in the same way. (Rita)

The following pedagogical narration illustrates how a multitude of linguistic and discursive elements come together to create a materializing apparatus of knowing.

JACOB'S ENCOUNTER

Heather enjoys creating on the melting tray, and every day she asks me to warm it up. One day Jacob, who is new to the centre, comes over. After watching Heather for a brief moment, without taking his eyes off the tray, he says, "I want to do that."

Heather responds: "I show you."

Jacob begins cautiously, commenting that the tray is hot. As his hand moves back and forth with the little pieces of green and then orange wax crayons, he speaks about "the furnace" being hot. Then he notices a little puddle forming where he left the tiny piece of green crayon. He stops and looks straight at it. Heather leaves with her creation; Jacob continues his project, moving his hand over the paper in strong circles and talking to me about the puddles that are forming and the colours that are spreading and changing.

"The furnace makes puddles … a little puddle."

Then he begins to drop crayon pieces onto the paper. He leans over closer to watch the crayons turn to puddles.

"I'm watching the puddles."

(Nadia)

NADIA'S REFLECTION

Jacob referred to the melting tray as "the furnace." His understanding was being stretched. The tray is hot, but he is not getting burned; instead, puddles are forming. He noticed that the little leftover bits of crayon that he couldn't move around anymore were changing. It fascinated him. He repeated the process and noticed that he got the same results. He then placed pieces of crayon on the paper and watched them melt. He used large pieces of crayon to move the puddles around, and he watched the crayon colour spread into the puddle colour and transform into other colours.

Sylvia Kind (2010) writes about "a medium for negotiating and interacting with ... a partner in the creative process, an object of encounter" (p. 125). Jacob was interacting with the puddles, the heat, and the colours. I was watching this "new experience 'talk back' through the process and progress of making art" (p. 125). It unsettled and provoked him. Jacob's knowledge was expanding as his interactions with the materials continued.

In this pedagogical narration, we can see how discursive and linguistic elements—the educators' interpretations of the child's understanding, the spoken invitation from Heather, Jacob's verbal expression of interest in the activity—*and* the material conditions of the encounter (the crayons, the heat of the child's finger, the light in the room, the smells of the melting crayons, the intermingling colours of the melting crayons as they move across the white paper) *and* the time the children have to explore the materials all come together to create what is captured in the pedagogical narration.

We see the production of Jacob's subjectivity as a curious, competent learner making multiple meanings, for example, in his connection of heat with a furnace. Through the pedagogical narration, Jacob's subjectivity emerges in this temporary moment as an effect of multiple intra-active relations of the discursive and the material environments—including discursive norms, things, bodies, and the classroom space (Lenz Taguchi, 2009).

The pedagogical narration is only a partial account of the encounter from the educators' and others' viewpoints and interpretations. Many other human and non-human bodies that we cannot capture in this pedagogical narration were part of this intra-action. When we view pedagogical narration as a materializing practice, we can begin to see how "existence is not an individual affair" (Barad, 2007, p. ix).

Next, in chapter 5, we discuss processes we have engaged in as we reconceptualize the image of the child and complexify early childhood education practices, specifically through putting postfoundational ideas to work in interpreting pedagogical narrations.

CHAPTER 5
....

OPENING TO POSSIBILITIES

In this chapter we introduce the processes we use to analyze, deconstruct, and make meaning of pedagogical narration. Here we put to work the postfoundational theories we presented in chapters 1 and 2 and the ideas on pedagogical narration that we explored in chapter 4. We discuss how pedagogical narration makes dominant discourses visible and suggest why it is important to expand our lenses beyond a modernist view of child development. Then, to encourage readers to open to multiple perspectives, we consider some examples of pedagogical narration through lenses of:

- Postmodernism.
- Rhizoanalysis.
- Social justice perspectives, including anti-racist and postcolonial perspectives, feminist poststructural perspectives, queer theories, and critical disability theory.
- Sociomaterial perspectives.

For clarity's sake, in this chapter we discuss the different theoretical lenses one at a time. We want to highlight, however, that these orientations are not singular approaches; they can work together to enrich our understandings of practices and allow us to envision multiple possibilities for ethical and equitable pedagogies. None of these perspectives is more valid or important than another. Each engenders different ideas, and in that way, they complexify practice. If the theories included in this chapter are new to you, we encourage you to refer to Understanding our Language: A Glossary (pp. 195–216) to help you navigate the ideas presented below.

Engaging with Pedagogical Narrations
through Multiple Lenses

> *One day there was an evil stepmother and there was a cottage and there was*
> *four princesses and there was a castle.... All of the princesses walked home*
> *and then they went in the princess car and drove to the mall. And then the*
> *princesses ... went shopping.*
>
> *Pirates stole the treasure from the princesses.... They took the treasure to*
> *their boat. They fighted the princesses with a sword. (excerpt from Princesses*
> *and Pirates, pp. 76–83)*

Children reflect the ideas and words of the people around them, and they try to make sense of them in light of their own experiences. When we document children's learning and play, we can ask ourselves what assumptions the children are making or what questions they are asking.

In this chapter we draw from examples from practice that educators have brought to the IQ Project learning circles, revisiting some we discussed above and introducing some new ones, to illustrate how we put alternative perspectives to work as we critically reflect on pedagogical narrations. In choosing how to approach the pedagogical narrations we create and work with, we consider that what we see and how we see are not absolute truths. We consider our interpretations to be perspectival, contextual, situational, and provisional (Dahlberg, Moss, & Pence, 2007). We consider the meanings that emerge from

FIGURE 5.1: Princesses and Pirates

our collaborative dialogues about the narrations as neither fixed nor final, but as **nomadic**[1] practices that embrace uncertainty, nonlinearity, and the subjectivity and politics of knowledge (Deleuze & Guattari, 1987). This approach has opened up routes in our practice and reflective dialogues that counter and confront normalized ways of thinking and acting, leading us always to ask more questions instead of seeking final truths or answers.

A key element of these processes is to challenge ourselves to think differently about our own assumptions and explore how a **deconstructive analysis** can open up spaces of equity and social justice (MacNaughton, 2005). Through these processes we invite educators to construct themselves as critical pedagogues who question their previous knowledge about the child, themselves, children's families, and the learning context.

Making Dominant Discourses Visible

To interpret pedagogical narrations, we refer to theories and construct our own theories to explain what we observe. Developmental approaches are the most readily available theories we have to understand pedagogical narrations (see discussion on observation in chapter 4). These ideas, which rest on the concept of normality among all children and families, are part of a **modernist** intellectual tradition. Modernist thought assumes that one can arrive at something called the truth through a rational process of thought and scientific investigation. According to developmental psychology, which is rooted in the **positivist** science of the modern era, individuals are thought to be fully realized when they become mature, independent adults using faculties of reason.

Developmental psychology has a strong hold in the early childhood education field, particularly in North America. Evidence of this hold can be seen in the enduring influence of the concept of developmentally appropriate practice (DAP), definitions of quality, and theories of child development that assume universal laws and norms. In fact, these ideas have such a strong hold that they constitute a **dominant discourse**.

We use the term *dominant discourse* to describe the way things are named, spoken of, and written that comes to be experienced as objective and true. Dominant discourses function as "regimes of truth" (Foucault, 1977) that hold power over individual and societal ways of understanding the world. They influence our thoughts, ideas, and actions.

In early childhood education, discourses about child development have become taken-for-granted "truths" that influence how individuals think and act within early childhood contexts; they determine "correct" ways of thinking

....
1 We use the term *nomadic* here to signify movement and multiplicity.

and acting. It is important to keep in mind, however, that discourses that are taken up and perceived as the truth are only perspectives or interpretations of the world. By bringing forward other perspectives, we can challenge dominant discourses that construct and constrain childhood identities.

Our intent is not to dismiss developmental perspectives as wrong. Rather, we want to consider how a developmental reading may obscure important issues, such as those relating to social justice and equity. A developmental lens may also oversimplify the complexities of children's meaning-making and their understandings of their social and material worlds. Developmental perspectives often conceal the ambiguities, complexities, and unknowns that emerge in everyday practices.

Examining Dominant Discourses

Let's begin by considering Princesses and Pirates through a developmental reading. Viewed through a lens of developmental psychology, the children in this pedagogical narration could be seen as developing their understandings of (biologically predetermined) gender. Their dialogues could be read from a cognitive development perspective as girls learning to be girls and boys learning to be boys, emphasizing children's age-based progressive socialization of gender differences and roles. These readings, however, fail to notice how the children's enactments reflect (or disrupt) socially constructed gender discourses (MacNaughton, 2000).

As a way to unpack gendered dominant discourses in Princesses and Pirates, in our learning circles we raised several issues for critical reflection. For example, we discussed the children's ideas of what princesses and pirates do. Here is a collection of ways that the children described princesses and pirates in their play and in response to Kim's questions:

> *Princesses: live in a castle ... wear pretty dresses ... put on jewellery ... ride in carriages ... dance with the prince ... wear pretty shoes ... put on makeup ... walk daintily ... wear crowns ... go shopping ... drive vans ... are always good.*
> *Pirates: steal money ... fight ... live on a pirate boat ... live under the ship and have creaky doors ... wear ugly shoes and belts ... run faster than anything ... have swords ... wear torn clothes ... are bad. (However, there are good pirates and bad ones; the nice ones help the princesses and children.)*

When we first discussed this pedagogical narration in our learning circles, we noticed that the children's descriptions contained assumptions about what it means to be a girl and a boy, and who can and cannot be a princess or a pirate. We treated the items in these lists as **gendered**, and not just as part and parcel of how children learn to socialize with others. As seen above, the children constructed princesses and pirates in ways that conform to the dominant social construction of gender in Euro-Western society. To unpack this construction, we asked questions like these:

- What gender discourses are at work in these encounters?
- What other encounters take place during the day that are part of gendered discourses?
- How are dominant discourses, such as what it means to be a boy and what it means to be a girl, normalized in our practices?

We considered the ways we organize our classrooms through the home centre, the building centre, the art centre, and so on, and how this taken-for-granted organization is already potentially gendered. We also started to wonder about the kinds of costumes we make available in the classroom, and how these too provide gendered messages to children.

By asking these questions and bringing these ideas forward, our hope is to disrupt and interrupt the dominant discourses that we tend to perpetuate in our practices. Our intention is never to accuse educators (or families), but rather to see how power relations work—and how we can become more ethical and more intentional in our work for social justice.

Unpacking dominant discourses, then, allows us to engage with issues of power: how power circulates; how it regulates what counts as knowledge; how it shapes, through language, what is seen as desirable; how it shapes subjectivities (MacNaughton, 2005). Engaging with issues of power, politics, and knowledge can be seen as an act of political activism that simultaneously complexifies practice and disrupts modernist notions of a singular objective truth. Engaging with dominant discourses allows us to take into account children's active participation or agency in constructing (gendered, racialized) subjectivities that they view as powerful and desirable in particular contexts (MacNaughton, 2000, 2005).

Postfoundational Perspectives

On one hand, as participants in collaborative critical reflective thinking, we realize we are immersed in disrupting a developmental psychology body of knowledge that is a logical and familiar discourse for us. We realize that we have been subjects of study under this lens and have also been subjects that reproduce the same dominant discourse when we interact with and interpret children's subjectivities and discourses. On the other hand, we become aware that familiarity with this dominant discourse—its linearity and universality—has restricted the possibilities of multiple readings when examining and interpreting our images of the child, the educator, and the learning community. (Alejandra)

As we have seen above, a developmental perspective is one possible interpretation we can bring to pedagogical narration. A developmental lens is limited, however, by its affinity for a singular reading of the children's encounters. If we use *only* this lens, other possibilities for interpretation, such as the nuanced interactions, negotiations, and complexities in the children's dialogues, would remain hidden, as would possibilities to challenge inequities within the dominant gender discourses that are expressed in children's daily encounters.

Postfoundational interpretations would begin to address these complexities. In the sections that follow, we explore how we use postfoundational theories to interpret pedagogical narrations.

Postmodernism

Postmodernism is an approach that recognizes diversity among individuals in terms of class, gender, "race," sexuality, ethnicity, places of origin, abilities, and other characteristics. (Note that we use quotation marks for the term "race" to emphasize that race is a socially constructed phenomenon with no biological basis. Anti-racist theories depart from the assumption that racism can be understood merely in relation to race. Rather, race is viewed as intersecting or interlocking with other systems of inequality such as gender, nationality, migration, class, sexuality, ability, language, and so on. Furthermore, anti-racist scholars use the terms "racialization" and "racialized" as a way of moving away from reinforcing problematic concepts such as race and ethnicity. The term racialization requires us to move from an unexamined conception of race as an essential category toward an analytical view of assumptions about race and how these are fundamental to our understanding of people and their cultures.)

From a postmodern perspective, no universal, absolute knowledge or reality exists: Knowledge (just like "race") is socially constructed. Key elements of postmodernism include:

- an absence of certainty, control, and predictability.
- openness to the presence of many voices and views.
- a need to engage with other views and explore a world that is profoundly diverse.

Postmodernism is based on the premise that many interpretations of the world are possible. An important aspect of postmodernist theories, which we embrace in our critical collaborative engagements with pedagogical narration, is the potential they hold for multiple, dynamic views of a single event.

In our work, we find that transformation of thought occurs when we encounter and get familiar with the proposals, language, tools, and strategies of postmodern perspectives. For example, in reading Princesses and Pirates through a postmodern lens, we can consider questions like these:

- What possibilities emerge for curriculum that might deepen children's explorations of gender?
- What provocations could we provide to blur gender binaries and transgress their normativity?

In the sections below we explore other perspectives that deepen the complexities postmodernism brings to light.

Rhizoanalysis

In **rhizoanalysis**, children's documented encounters are read by placing them alongside other diverse texts, including those outside of early childhood (e.g., from child development texts, news media, popular culture, feminist texts) to create multiple meanings and understandings of children and to link, for example, negotiations of gender and "race" in the early childhood classroom—all with the deliberate political intent of practicing for social justice (MacNaughton, 2005). MacNaughton (2005) demonstrates how a tactic of rhizoanalysis can be a potent way to build complex pictures—of the child, of observation, of research—so as to "deconstruct and reconstruct meanings and, in doing so ... map other possibilities and other ways of knowing, while remaining open to rewriting them" (p. 144).

To take a rhizoanalytic approach to Princesses and Pirates, as a beginning, we could juxtapose this pedagogical narration with Bronwyn Davies' (1989) findings that young children often strongly adhere to gender binaries. Davies finds, for example, that many children reject feminist characterizations of girls in popular-culture texts like *The Paper Bag Princess* (Munsch, 1980). We see in Princesses and Pirates that children maintain a dualistic model of male and female as they negotiate these roles in their play and storytelling. Despite Kim's attempts to disrupt these meanings, the children are committed to "doing gender right" (Butler, 1990) among their peers.

KIM: *Are princesses always good? What about pirates?*
CHILDREN: *Princesses are always good.*
            Pirates are bad.
            There are good [pirates] and bad ones!
            The nice ones help the princesses. And boys and girls.
            No, they don't!
            Nice pirates don't yell.
            Pirates fight princesses.

Taking a rhizoanalytic approach, we might also consider the text below, which illustrates that children do not just affirm dominant gender discourses; they resist and negotiate them. Here we see a child negotiating gender as she describes how she transformed her Disney Princess Mulan doll into a super-hero with a cape:

> She's really a princess, but I'm pretending she's a super hero. Her powers make her fly. She can make tornadoes. She can use power from her hands to make fire. Sometimes she makes the bad guy dead with her fire. This is how they make her weak: They make a stronger power—wind— and they blow her over to the door. My mom got her for me when I got back home from Disney World. That's not her natural clothes; her natural clothes—but I got this—this is my other Barbie's thing—this is her—my Barbie's cheerleading skirt.... I want her to talk in there. [Lowering pitch of her voice and bending close to the digital voice recorder.] I have super powers and I am a superhero and I can't have a lot of powers and I can make tornadoes. (Wohlwend, 2009, p. 75)

In this example, the child both disrupts gender norms (e.g., by making "power from her hands") and conforms to them ("I can't have a lot of powers"). By reading Princesses and Pirates against this text, we are able to see that the children's maintenance and reproduction of gendered discourses is not totally static. Instead, there is a fluidity through which children constantly negotiate with discourses. Unlike developmental understandings of gender that assume that children passively learn gender (e.g., by watching and listening to others), feminist poststructural theories emphasize that children play an active role in negotiating gendered discourses (Blaise, 2005). Children are not just marked by gender discourses; they *do gender.*

Here is a snapshot of a moment when the children in Princesses and Pirates are actively doing gender. Note that they both comply with and challenge gendered discourses. They "stretch" these discourses to fit the context in which they are positioned by Kim, and they find new ways to position themselves.

KIM: *Do princesses fight?*
CHILDREN: *Princesses are never mean.*
             Sometimes princesses fight, when the dragon comes.
             Sometimes princesses fight, but not always. Sometimes they have swords.
             Princesses never fight.
             They fight pirates and dragons only.
KIM: *Do pirates dance?*
             NO!
             Only to pirate music.
KIM: *Do pirates wear jewellery?*
             Pirates only put on ugly earrings.

Through these texts, and through others we might draw from, we can complexify children's gendered meaning-making and our own understandings and positioning within dominant discourses.

Next, we further complexify our readings of pedagogical narrations by expanding our lenses to include social justice perspectives.

Social Justice Perspectives

Social justice perspectives identify relations of power and knowledge that contribute to and sustain inequities related to "race," class, gender, sexuality, disability, and age, among other sources. We reiterate that all of the perspectives we discuss in this chapter can work together to open multiple ways of seeing. For example, although our emphasis above was on gendered discourses, racialized discourses are also embedded in Princesses and Pirates. We invite readers to unpack how gendered and racialized discourses intersect in the children's dialogue.

In this section, we look at anti-racist and postcolonial perspectives, followed by feminist poststructural perspectives and queer theories.

To illustrate how anti-racist and postcolonial lenses might work to complexify our understandings of children's meaning-making, we introduce a dialogue between a group of young boys and two educators, Kaya and Susan, at an inner-city childcare centre in Vancouver, BC. The children in the centre were primarily of African, Aboriginal, Latin American, or East Indian heritage. Of the children in this dialogue, only Winston was identified as white.

STAND UP²

WINSTON: *My grandmother says that black people are stupid and Native people are more stupid.*

TYRONNE: *You need to shut the fuck up.*

WINSTON: *Kaya! Jahrul and Tyronne want to beat me up.*

KAYA: *Why?*

JAHRUL: *Because him says we're stupid and more stupid.*

KAYA: *Can you talk about it?*

JAHRUL: *Yeah, but we like to beat him up.*

Jahrul and Tyronne give each
other perfect high fives.

KAYA: *I think you should use your words.*

TYRONNE: *What words? Funny. Really funny.*

KAYA: *Thoughtful words.*

JAHRUL: *OK, tell your grandmother we beat her up too.*

KAYA: *Jahrul, your mother wouldn't like that. She wants you to grow up to be a gentleman.*

JAHRUL: *Susan wants me to be a strong man, a true man, a great man.*

TYRONNE: *A rich man.*

WINSTON: *I just said my grandmother says you are stupid. I don't believe that, and my mother says it's wrong and unkind.*

KAYA: *What did your grandmother say?*

WINSTON: *That black people were stupid and that Native people were stupid.*

KAYA: *Tell your grandmother that Susan needs to speak with her.*

Jahrul and Tyronne are overjoyed.

TYRONNE: *Tell your grandmother that Susan beat her up.*

This dialogue provoked much discomfort when we discussed it in our learning circles. Initially, we were disturbed by the language the children were using and the harassment we read in the educator's positions. Through collaborative reflection, we interrogated how children negotiate belonging, identity, and power from several perspectives, including anti-racist and post-colonial lenses.

....
2 This dialogue was first published in Pacini-Ketchabaw and Berikoff, 2008, pp.257–258.

Anti-racist Perspectives

An anti-racist perspective complicates and interrogates "**race**." It can help to make visible the effects of **racialization**, which we understand as a possible effect of encounters with "racial" difference. Racialization refers to the discursive and material processes by which social significance is attached to categories of difference in ways that are potentially divisive and discriminatory (Crutcher & Zook, 2009; Pacini-Ketchabaw, White, & Armstrong de Almeida, 2006). These categories include differences in skin and hair colour, language and accent, clothing, religious markers, citizenship status, performance and intelligence measures, and inferred "personality" traits, among others (de Finney, 2010, p. 485).

As with all of the perspectives we discuss in this chapter, we would not use an anti-racist lens in isolation nor look to it to provide definite answers. However, for interpreting a dialogue like Stand Up, an anti-racist perspective allows us to examine the multiplicities, complexities, and contradictions of "race" and racialization that are visible in the children's dialogues. For instance, we might view Tyronne and Jahrul's use of language and threats of violence as enactments of prevalent stereotypes of black masculinity. The children's words could also be viewed as an act of resistance against the oppressions of the racialized power enacted in the dialogue (whereby "Natives" and "blacks" are categorized as stupid). By naming the force of "race" and racisms as mattering in these children's lived experiences, we can begin to consider possibilities for pedagogies that challenge inequities, and move away from assigning individual blame to any of the children involved. We can consider how social and systemic forces act to construct, perpetuate, and magnify the **othered** positioning of racialized males in relation to the dominant group (Escayg, 2010).

Numerous intersecting and potentially oppressive influences come together to charge the encounter in the Stand Up dialogue, including the influences of gender and class. An in-depth examination of the nuances and complexities of racial formations of black males in North American contexts, including popular culture that young children often have access to, is beyond the scope of this book. However, by adopting an anti-racist perspective, we can look beyond the children's enactments of violent racialized discourses as isolated individual encounters and consider them instead within a critical analysis of hegemonic power relations that are embedded within the fabric of the racial and cultural diversity of North American society and that regulate and fix racial hierarchies, identities, and categories (Escayg, 2010).

In using an anti-racist perspective to read pedagogical narrations, we see transformative potentials to make interrupting racisms (Pacini-Ketchabaw &

Berikoff, 2008; Pacini-Ketchabaw & Nxumalo, 2010)—by this we mean challenging their presence and hold in a context in which they are masked by official state discourses of multiculturalism. In Canada, this official state discourse is reflected throughout the educational system, including early childhood education; we pride ourselves on "celebrating diversity." However, while differences are acknowledged in early childhood practice and theories, they are based on normative understandings of cultural differences and they assume universality and homogeneity for all children.

Early years theories/practices that define minoritized and racialized children against dominant discourses fail to problematize inequities within social structures—and consequently they position some children as other than normal.

FIGURE 5.2: Self-portrait of an Asian-African child

For example, in a report entitled "The Quality of Life of Aboriginal People in Canada," Daniel Salée (2006) argues that the "macrostructural dimensions such as the dominant pattern of power relations ... of the Canadian political economy" go largely unnoticed as the cause of social injustice and inequity within Aboriginal communities, thus "implying that the source of the problem is the community itself" (p. 24). Similarly, in some of our discussions of the children's dialogue in Stand Up, some educators viewed the children's behaviour as representative of children in inner-city childcare settings.

In our work, we critique multicultural discourses (Pacini-Ketchabaw & Berikoff, 2008; Pacini-Ketchabaw, White, & Armstrong de Almeida, 2006) and anti-bias curriculum (Pacini-Ketchabaw & Bernhard, 2012). We believe that as a structure of national governance under which cultural pluralism is emphasized but systemic inequities and exclusions on the basis of "race," class, and language are depoliticized, minimized, or silenced, multiculturalism contributes to the persistence of racism (de Finney, 2010; Pacini-Ketchabaw, White, & Armstrong de Almeida, 2006). The boundaries created around cultural groups act as a medium for racialization by identifying difference with culture (Dirlik, 2008). Within the discourses of acceptance and "fitting in," racialization in early childhood typically remains unaddressed (Pacini-Ketchabaw, 2007).

Further, multicultural approaches in early childhood education are framed within essentialist and fixed views of culture, ignoring constitutive social relations of power (Pacini-Ketchabaw, 2007, p. 224). The anti-bias approach (Derman-Sparks & A.B.C. Task Force, 1989; Derman-Sparks, Ramsey, & Edwards, 2006) has been recognized for its consideration of power relations. The analysis of power relations, however, requires further elaboration. For example, the guidelines proposed for educators tend to be somewhat individually focused. In other words, the children's attitudes are the main focus of intervention, instead of the micro-interactions, complexities, and contradictions of power dynamics.

Postcolonial Perspectives

Postcolonial theories enable critical inquiry into the effects of colonization in the present day. They provide a framework from which to understand the lingering impact of Western colonialisms in terms of persistent social inequities that are divided along racial and ethnic lines (MacNaughton, 2005). As Bhabha (1994) notes, colonialism is both a "regime of truth" and a "form of **governmentality**" (p. 101).

Colonial discourses are powerfully enacted through the expression of racial categories, hierarchies, and stereotypes. In the dialogue above, the construction of "blacks" and "Natives" as Other relies on repeating stereotypes that are essentialized and inferior points of difference from whiteness.

By using a postcolonial lens, we can expand our understandings of children who come from diverse sociocultural backgrounds. This perspective provides a means to challenge the colonizing discourses and practices of modernist universal "truths" that construct children as different from adults; it allows us to create "new and different possibilities and avenues for children" (MacNaughton, 2005, p. 19). A postcolonial lens helps us to see "leakages" from colonial pasts in present social discourses.

Viewing the children's dialogue from a postcolonial perspective, we can take an activist stance aimed at confronting and undoing the assimilative forces of colonialism (De Lissovoy, 2010). We can ask questions that may take us in different directions to those we might take if we viewed the dialogue from a developmental perspective, for example. In a developmental reading, the historical, political, and systemic factors that create exclusion and marginalization might be rendered invisible, and the focus might be on viewing individual children or marginalized minoritized groups as being "at risk" (Pacini-Ketchabaw & Berikoff, 2008).

In drawing from postcolonial perspectives to critically reflect on the dialogue, we can move away from judging children as "problem children" and their words as good or bad. We can take a decolonial perspective that seeks "the Otherwise" (MacNaughton, 2005, p. 146) by disrupting the power of colonial discourse and engaging politically with this encounter. Some questions we might critically reflect on during this process might include ones like these:

- How do colonial histories matter to the children's and educators' situated histories and presents?
- How are stereotypical colonial discourses enacted in this context? For instance, the children's dialogue could be viewed as a re-enactment of powerful colonial discourses that construct racialized hierarchies and position certain groups as inferior to those at the helm of the (neo)colonial order (Jiwani, 2006).
- How have racial and economic hierarchies from colonial pasts carried through to frame the social, political, and material landscapes in which these children live? What do these hierarchies do to these children's subjectivities? How do they charge these encounters and the violence therein?
- What discourses might be at play in the educators' responses to the children in Stand Up ("Can you talk about it?" and "I think you should use your words")?

- How can the physical environment (in this case, a poorly funded centre in an inner-city neighbourhood) be seen as an active manifestation of coloniality?
- What are the effects for social justice and equity when the emphasis of our pedagogical encounters with racialized and immigrant children is on a multicultural pedagogy that focuses on the individual child while masking the effects of racialization in these children's everyday encounters (Pacini-Ketchabaw & Berikoff, 2008)?

In both the political and the relational realms, repetitions of coloniality continue to objectify and pathologize children. In making visible these inequitable colonial discourses and their effects on children and families, we see possibilities to disrupt and reconceptualize colonial legacies. Doing so requires us to be aware and to critically engage with the material, affective, attitudinal, structural, and discursive processes and outcomes of coloniality that are manifest in encounters with those who are subjectified as Other (Swadener & Mutua, 2008, p. 37)—in this encounter, "Natives" or "blacks." By engaging with post-colonial perspectives, we can shine a light on the real, constrictive effects that neocolonialism has on children, families, and communities.

Critical Disability Perspectives

Critical disability theories bring alternative perspectives to the "individual, medical and deficit models [that] continue to dominate thinking *about* disabled people" (Goodley, 2007, p. 319). For instance these theories locate dominant and normative engagements with disability within particular social, economic, political, and cultural constructions. These critical perspectives interrogate the exclusionary and pathologizing effects of dominant sociocultural and political constructions of disability, including normative pedagogies and educational standards as well as other normalizing policies, practices, institutions and material environments that act to exclude children with what are normatively labelled special needs but what we here call special rights from what is considered educational success. Importantly, these theories make visible the taken-for-granted ways in which people with disabilities are marginalized (Goodley, 2007; Goodley & Runswick-Cole, 2012; Heydon, 2005; Oliver, 1990, 1996).

Goodley (2013) poses questions that are useful in critically reflecting on disability or special rights in the classroom from a social justice perspective:

- How are non-disabled bodies made more seemingly viable and desirable than disabled bodies?

- How do societal practices uphold the precarious higher status of non-disabled people through the abjection (rejection) of disabled people?
- In what ways do disabled bodies rearticulate what qualifies as a body that matters? (p. 636)

Bringing a social justice perspective to critically encounter social constructions of disability or special rights can create openings toward undoing the oppressive, yet often taken-for-granted, ways of relating to children with special rights. Importantly, a social justice perspective engages with the complex entanglements between disability, gender, "race," sexuality, class, as politicized categorizations and materializations of bodies (Goodley, 2013).

The pedagogical narrations in Entangled Bodies (pp. 96–105) bring attention to the emergent ethical relationships between Stephanie, the children, and the materials. Through these narrations, Christine troubles a "materialization of the norm" (Butler, 1993, p. 16), while making visible strengths in the ways in which Stephanie encounters the world. The encounters captured in these narrations act to unsettle the disabled/abled binary by highlighting the emergent relationships and connections between Stephanie, the other children, Christine, and the materials—the sticker, paints, and the art supply cart. In addition, rather than a detached, objective observation of what Stephanie can and cannot do, Christine immerses herself as a part of the encounters. She questions her uncertainties and doubts and is a part of the articulation and re-articulation of an image of Stephanie. This is an encounter that does not seek to erase Stephanie's difference, and instead shows ethical praxis (see chapter 6) as emerging in relationship that cannot be captured by the hierarchical and bounded designation of a "special needs" label.

Feminist Poststructural Perspectives

Feminist poststructural perspectives allow us to bring an understanding of difference, political struggle, and inequality to our readings of pedagogical narrations by emphasizing gender in conjunction with "race" and class. Robinson and Jones Diaz (2005) outline the key ideas of feminist poststructuralism as follows:

- Identities and individual subjectivities are constituted within social discourses and are negotiated, shifting, complex, and contradictory.
- Knowledge is partial and is constituted within discourses.
- Power is a process that operates through social discourse and is practised and negotiated by individual subjects at both the macro (institutional) and micro (everyday life) levels in society.

- Individual subjects have agency in their lives; they are not passive, powerless "victims."
- Social inequalities are constituted within, and perpetuated through, the social discourses that are historically and culturally available to individual subjects.
- Childhood is a socially constructed concept that is constituted in the social discourses that are historically and culturally available to individual subjects.
- Individual subjects perpetuate social inequalities through their everyday interactions and practices. (p. 16)

Feminist poststructural perspectives disrupt the idea of an essentialized girlhood or boyhood. Instead, they foreground the complex and paradoxical ways in which "subjectivity is produced in a whole range of temporally and spatially contextualized discursive practices—economic, social and political—the meanings of which are a constant site of struggle over power" (Weedon, 1987, p. 21).

Revisiting Princesses and Pirates (see pp. 76–83) from a feminist poststructural perspective provokes many questions and reveals a multiplicity of dynamic, textured meanings in the children's dialogue and play. We can ask, for example:

- How are the children choosing to position themselves in alignment with dominant understandings or discourses of gender?
- How are the children actively choosing to contradict and/or resist normalized dominant discourses of femininities and hegemonic masculinities? How do they revise and contest normative discourses of femininity?
- What desires are produced for the girls in this play and what desires may be marginalized?
- How do dominant images from popular culture, such as Disney, intersect with children's gendered performances?
- How are Disney storylines taken up by the children in ways that maintain, resist, or transform normative gender binaries?
- How do the children interact with each other to adhere to, regulate and disrupt the gendered norms?
- How is power enacted by drawing on hegemonic gender discourses in the children's dialogue?
- How do contemporary discourses of neoliberal capitalism intersect with Western middle-class gender norms in the princess play?

- How does the notion of gender as performance (Butler, 1990) help in interpreting these narratives? How do children enact gendered performances through their bodies?

Feminist poststructural analyses of children's gendered identity negotiations can make us differently aware of the role of dominant gender discourses in children's lives and of how children conform to and resist these discourses (Davies, 1989; MacNaughton, 2001; Walkerdine, 1990).

Queer Theory

Another idea important to social justice perspectives is that of "queering" our practices to disrupt taken-for-granted **heteronormativity**. Queering early childhood practices further complexifies our feminist poststructural analyses. Mindy Blaise (2005) explains that, "by recognizing and questioning concepts of normalization and privilege found within heterosexual culture, **queer theory** helps deepen understandings of the social construction of gender" (p. 20). Queering our practices

> provides an alternative perspective that is helpful for challenging generally accepted notions of gender, specifically for recognizing how heterosexual discourses dominate in the classroom and how they play an integral part in creating what children consider to be normal and right behaviours. Most importantly, teaching queerly is about exploring and then disrupting assumptions about diversity, identities, teaching, learning, and young children. (Blaise, 2005, p.185)

Heteronormativity remains invisible in developmentally appropriate practice (DAP)—and, indeed, in any dominant and in many non-dominant discourses of childhood in the North American context. The singular way of knowing children defined by DAP leaves little space for engaging with pedagogical narrations in ways that disrupt normalized gender identities and sexualities. Children's negotiations with gender, with queer identities (of which many variations exist), and with other non-normative identities may be marginalized by early childhood practices and pedagogies. In bringing this perspective to our interpretations of pedagogical narrations, we can consider how we treat heterosexual norms in our daily practices. Blaise (2005) notes that,

> for instance, when teachers read stories during group time, they rarely question whether the adult female and male characters in the stories are married. Rather, it is simply assumed that they are. Heterosexual

behaviours are reinforced as teachers observe from the sidelines when children are playing "princess" at the dramatic play area and simply smile or laugh when commenting how cute the girls are as they get ready to go out dancing with the prince. (p. 22)

Princesses and Pirates is an example of how heteronormativity creeps into our classrooms. In this pedagogical narration, the children are situated in a "heterosexual matrix" (Butler, 1990) in which the boys emphasize masculinity (by engaging in rough and violent behaviours) and the girls emphasize femininity (by concerning themselves with looking beautiful and running away from the boys).

The Tiara (pp. 83–86) provides an example of an educator who was motivated to examine her reaction to a child's "gender bending." Christine, the educator who created The Tiara, explains her impetus:

> My videotaping of this moment began with an intention: I was interested in understanding more about Kay-sun's interest in princesses. This moment wasn't out of the ordinary. Kay-sun had asked me to paint his face as a princess in a previous face-painting session. This time, I chose to videotape the moment because it challenges me as an educator.
>
> Several times Kay-sun has come to the preschool with his hair done up, or with curls, or with a hairpiece on his hair—with fake hair. One of the Korean moms told me that it's very common for Korean families to dress their little boy in dresses and to do their hair. I've been taken by surprise when Kay-sun comes in with his hair done. The first time it happened, I think he may have noticed my reaction because he didn't keep his hair like that for very long.

Christine felt she needed to examine her reaction to Kay-sun's behaviour in the classroom. She also realized that she didn't have enough information or knowledge to engage in thinking about Kay-sun's expressions of gender. When she brought The Tiara to an IQ Project learning circle to reflect on it within our collaborative critically reflective community, Christine provided some background information:

> Kay-sun loves pink. Any time we ask the children to make a colour choice, he chooses pink. There is a group of girls who always bring princesses into the classroom—on their backpacks, t-shirts, lunchboxes, and in books. When I read the books about princesses to the girls, Kay-sun runs to hear the stories.
>
> Another interesting piece about this boy is that he speaks very little English. He and two other children in the classroom—Hae-young and Keem—are fluent in Korean. These three children speak Korean to each other in the classroom.

After watching her pedagogical narration, which was in the form of a video, some of Christine's colleagues offered their thoughts.

DOREEN: *When I was watching the video I wondered what the child's question was—to look and look and look in the mirror—what is he asking? There is something that is fascinating him. I wonder how, as a teacher, you can find out what is fascinating a child and respond to it?*

ALEJANDRA: *Perhaps he wants to confirm his plan of becoming this princess ... trying to confirm the image he wanted to become. His discursive assumption seems to be "I don't have any prejudice to borrow my character from this princess and see how I feel ... how it feels on myself." This process of becoming different is without any hesitation.*

GALE: *I think we can't discount children's awareness of gender, because many girls had the tiara painted and there wasn't a group being drawn to it— it was when a boy decided to do it [that the children became interested in what was going on].*

Most of the learning circle participants were familiar with developmental understandings of gender, and those were the only lenses they had to think about how children "do" gender. At our next learning circle, we read a few pieces from Mindy Blaise (2005) and Affrica Taylor (2007) on queer theory and feminist poststructuralism as a means to engage in learning about gender and how it can be thought about from different perspectives. As we critically examined our understandings of gender, we became aware that we could think about Kay-sun's explorations as part of gender negotiations rather than viewing his behaviour as a "problem." We also began to think about gender and racialization and the intersection of these social constructions.

Our engagement with The Tiara provides an example of how we critically engage in queering early childhood practices in our work with early childhood educators. Our dialogue was intended to disrupt dominant gender binaries, just as Kay-sun disrupted them.

The children in this narration are creating and recreating gender. Kay-sun is performing different ways of being a boy, and so are the girls who are playing with him. This process demonstrates the fluidity of doing gender that we spoke about in the section above on feminist poststructural analyses. These children are actively producing and disrupting gendered positions of what it means to be a girl and a boy.

Queering our readings of pedagogical narrations allows us to complexify our practices by asking more questions. For example, we might ask:

- How do we challenge and disrupt discourses that emerge in our classrooms: the "girly-girl," the "cool" girl, "boys will be boys," and others?
- How do we queer the organization of our classrooms in ways that would allow us to "invent gender equity strategies" (Blaise, 2005, p. 30) which can confront and change the social order we are immersed in?
- How do we shift our perspectives and understandings of gender? For example, how do we avoid blaming the children, or television programs, or movies, or video games for the social inequities of our classrooms and engage instead in disrupting the dominant discourses of gender and heteronormativity that are always present in our classrooms?

Heteronormativity can be a difficult topic to engage with, but as we saw with our examples, it's a normative discourse that needs to be recognized and challenged in early childhood education. We cannot pretend that heteronormativity does not inhabit the classroom, just as we cannot pretend that different kinds of racism do not enter the room, or that colonialism is a thing of the past.

We believe that incorporating feminist poststructural, postcolonial, anti-racist, and queer perspectives as an intrinsic part of early childhood pedagogies can act as a potent force toward social justice.

Sociomaterial Perspectives

So far, through our analyses in this chapter, we have highlighted understandings of the social/discursive construction of knowledge as central in our processes of engaging with pedagogical narrations. Next, we turn to matter—the physical substance that occupies space and possesses mass; in other words, the bodies and things in the classroom. Like meaning, Barad (2007) notes, matter is not a static entity;

> it is not little bits of nature, or a blank slate, or a site passively awaiting signification; nor is it an uncontested ground for scientific, feminist, or economic theories. Matter is not immutable or passive. Nor is it fixed support, location, referent, or source of sustainability for discourse. It does not require the mark of an eternal force like culture or history to complete it. Matter is always already an ongoing historicity. (pp. 150–151)

When we looked at the pedagogical narrations that educators in our projects worked on, we were struck by the prominent role that materials played, both for children and for educators (Pacini-Ketchabaw, Kocher, Sanchez, & Chan,

2009). Following Barad's suggestion above, we became interested in looking at the multiplicity of human and non-human forces that come together in pedagogical encounters, and in considering how such a sociomaterial perspective might further complexify our interpretations of pedagogical narration and open pedagogical possibilities. In our work with educators, we work with sociomaterial perspectives, particularly through images, to decentre an anthropocentric view and to complexify our understandings of how children negotiate racialization, gender, and sexuality in their processes of subject formation.

We introduced the idea of sociomaterial perspectives in chapters 2 and 3, and in chapter 4 we explored how a sociomaterial perspective allows us to engage with pedagogical narration as a materializing apparatus of knowing. Here we return to the idea that discourse and matter are inextricably entangled in an emergent intra-active relationship (Barad, 2007). In this view, discourse is not superior to matter since matter itself is seen as exerting a force or agency of its own and actively participating in the production of knowledge (Lenz Taguchi, 2009).

The concept of **diffraction**, which we introduced in chapter 2, helps us to think through a sociomaterial lens. As M'charek (2010) explains, both human and non-human agents "interfere" with one another, and they both emerge differently from the effects of their encounter. Thus we can focus not only on what an encounter represents, but on how it emerges differently through our very engagement with it. Through this thinking, we can consider how diffraction

> incites us to attend to practices, to juxtapose them, so as to unravel what objects are made to be in them. This method suggests that objects or subjects do not have an essence, but are ... effects of our interaction with the world. This does not make them less "natural" or "biological," but rather differently natural and biological. Nature (and the biological) is not a singular entity out there, but rather a node elsewhere. Objects are made in a normatively charged field of action. In addition, objects are not one or singular, but rather, as Annemarie Mol (2002) has taught us, multiple. (M'charek, 2010, p. 308)

Let's consider how we might work with Stephanie and the Art Supply Cart (see pp. 101–103) using a sociomaterial theoretical lens. To begin, we might ask: How do the materials—the art supply cart, the pencils, the paper, the markers—become entangled in the configuration and reconfiguration of the image of the child?[3]

----

3 See chapter 3 for further discussion of the image of the child from a sociomaterial perspective.

Certainly we have to look at these materials as being discursive. Discourses operate through them; art materials are historically and culturally specific practices (Kind, 2008). Art materials are not passive. They are enmeshed in early childhood histories as well as other kinds of histories (Kind, 2010). Knowing this, we might ask how art materials have become an important tool in every early childhood classroom. Here is what our colleague and former learning circle facilitator, artist Sylvia Kind, noted to us in our conversations about materiality:

> Sullivan (2005) describes how artists think about art materials. Different media don't just feel or act differently or have different properties or produce different forms and images; they also provoke different ways of thinking as the artist engages and works with them. A camera, for instance, is not just a tool for recording information; it evokes a particular way of thinking, processing ideas, and making meaning that is profoundly different from the way one works with wool, dyes, found objects, or drawing. In drawing the human figure or in using a camera to create a particular image of a person, the subject may be similar, yet engagement with the different media and processes constructs unique perceptions and ways of thinking through the subject. The meaning is not in the technologies, materials or processes. Rather, these invite interactions, evoke certain possibilities, frame ways of seeing, and give particular structure to the ideas being explored. Meaning is not fixed in specific materials, images, processes or artworks; they are generated in their use and in their interaction. (2010, pp. 123–124)

Sylvia explains that this means that how we think about art processes and materials shapes what is possible.

> For example, if we think of clay as a sculptural material that is used for making objects, then it suggests certain engagements. We may set out individual clay slabs or balls on the table and give directions or support in how to create particular objects. We might talk about form, texture, structure, and balance. We may subtly or directly encourage individual sculptural objects. What we think clay is for shapes our experience with it, and the language we use to talk about the experience constructs particular meanings. If, on the other hand, we think about movement, place, impermanence, and relationality, then we may consider the

possibility of moving toward and away from the clay, attending to the
relationship of clay to its surroundings, and inviting interaction with
others. These concepts give structure to and shape our investigations
with the medium. And so we may set the clay out in other ways:
as a big block in the center of a large mat on the floor, as several
blocks stacked so they echo a child's height, in a space with several
overhead projectors to facilitate a complex play of shadow, bodies,
movement, and constructions. These various ways of setting out the
clay do not just invite different interactions. They also shape what
and how we see and the meanings we construct of the experience.
(2010, p. 124)

In Stephanie and the Art Supply Cart, the materials in the encounter matter
to Christine's configuration and reconfiguration of the image of Stephanie.
The art materials intra-act with Stephanie, with Christine, and with the other
children. Further, they are active agents in the intra-activity that constitutes
a phenomenon (in this case, the image of the child); thus they are productive
of the image of the child.

As Sylvia notes above, the art materials in Stephanie's cart can also be seen
to be reinvented through intra-actions. The materials and the activity that we
observe in this pedagogical narration are important aspects of Christine's and
our configuration of the image of the child. The materials and the activity are
both active agents and part of the image of the child that becomes configured.
Therefore, they are also always open to rearrangements, rearticulations, and
reworkings. In short, the image of the child that becomes intelligible in the
pedagogical narration is entangled in intra-activity that involves Christine's
and the children's constant becomings, but also the materials' constant
rearrangements (Pacini-Ketchabaw et al., 2009).

Decentring an Anthropocentric View

In our collaborative critical reflections, we have found it challenging to shift
our perspectives from an "**anthropocentric** gaze" (Hultman & Lenz Taguchi,
2010, p. 526) to one that acknowledges the idea of things and children/educa-
tors being in a complementary relationality and in constant flux. This struggle
can be seen in the dialogue below, where we reflect on a pedagogical narration titled The Pool. Despite the difficulty of making this shift, we and the
educators in our projects continue to engage with these concepts and attend
to the agency and transformative possibilities of materials in our interpretations of pedagogical narrations.

A sociomaterial perspective foregrounds the immense complexity of the world—and, by extension, of our practice. In particular, when we disrupt the view of the world as something "out there" to be discovered and represented by us, it becomes clear that we cannot know with any certainty all the multiple and shifting relations that are at work in any given pedagogical encounter.

In what follows, we invite you to consider some of our reflections on The Pool (see pp. 42–44), which we introduced in chapter 2 as an example of diffractive reading.

As we discussed The Pool in our learning circles, we were interested in considering the role of the materials in relation to other materials and the children (as a way of decentring an anthropocentric view). We asked ourselves:

- How are the materials active agents in the encounter between the children, the pool, and the sand?
- What are materials capable of in this encounter?
- How does the relationality of materials with the social/cultural/discursive aspects of our classrooms reconceptualize our understandings of learning in early childhood education?

We invite you to see what possibilities, questions, and struggles emerge for you when you consider the agency of both human and non-human matter in this encounter.

FIGURE 5.3: Child creating pool in sandbox

Leila created the pool. She began by pouring water into the corner of the sandbox. As the water ran away, Leila screamed and called out, "It's leaking!" Some children helped her to build the pool up; some policed the leaking; some replaced the water that leaked; some caused the leaks.

In the IQ Project learning circles, we discussed these encounters between children and materials. Some of our comments follow.

LAURIE: *The emphasis is much more on the materials and how they speak back ... talking about sand as a "partner."*

CAILEIGH: *It's almost as if there is a spirit of generosity in the sense that they identify Leila as the builder; possibly that created generosity on her part to include them, the fact that they honoured her as the builder. A magnanimity on her part. I don't know; that's a speculation.*

LAURIE: *That last photo shows that intimate connection with the sand and the water, the wet and the dry, the pooling and the dissipating.*

VERONICA: *If you look at the little boy's hands in the sand, I think that, visually, it's an interesting representation of the intra-action. When I look at the photo, I even have that sensation ... it affects me—what the sand feels like in my hand. Even looking at his face—I think something is happening there, for both the sand and the boy.*

BARBARA: *I was thinking the same, thinking of what it feels like. There's a connection between the earth and the hands.*

VERONICA: *The photo speaks to me of the agency of the material. The intra-action between the sand and the water, those two materials that we might have thought of as static, or fixed, are actually in movement and doing something to each other. The water is changing the sand, but the sand is changing the course and the movement of the water, too. They are becoming as they connect with each other.*

JENNY: *It's not passive; the water is pushing back. It's a very powerful experience because it is alive and there's this constant intra-action between how the materials are creating and are answering back to what the children do and how that can change at any moment and lead to a new exploration.*

VERONICA: *Instead of thinking of the children, I wonder about writing from the perspective of the sand. It's not like we know the child's perspective any more than we know the sand's perspective, right? We're just making guesses as we write from the child's perspective. It might be interesting to write from the point of view of the sand. What's happening for the sand?*

Materials, objects, and physical (non-human) elements have been important components of early childhood educational practices since programs for young children were developed. This materiality, however, has been invisible

and under-theorized in developmentally appropriate early childhood practices. We find that using sociomaterial perspectives to "read" pedagogical
narrations, specifically through images, pushes us to complexify our (anthropocentric) views.

Sociomaterial Perspectives on Gender and Sexuality

A sociomaterial perspective can be a potent tool for disrupting dominant
discourses in the classroom. Consider, for example, how a multitude of human
and non-human, discursive and material elements come together in moments
like the one in which Kay-sun is transformed into a princess in The Tiara
(pp. 83–86). The marks on the children's faces, the pink colour of the paint,
the mirror and the child's reflection in the mirror, the images of Disney
princesses on the lunchboxes, the educators' responses to Kay-sun's request,
the arrangements of the children's bodies as they gather wordlessly around
Kay-sun—all of these and many other forces intra-act in this moment to
create an ethical encounter with difference, a new enactment and exploration of gender and sexual identity.

How do these forces create new subjectivities for the children in the
classroom? What kinds of subjectivities emerge as the pink marker is applied
to the children's foreheads? What kinds of forces do the Disney images exert
on us, on the children, as these images are coupled with a multitude of other
forces? How do materials in the classroom invite heteronormativity to be
performed and/or disrupted?

Sociomaterial Perspectives on Racialization

Similar questions can be asked about materials' transformative intra-actions with
racialization. Let's return for a moment to the dialogue Stand Up (p. 152) that
we discussed earlier in the chapter.

A sociomaterial perspective allows us to consider not only the ways in
which racisms are present in the children's encounter through ideological, systemic, and discursive dependencies, marginalizations, and exclusions
(Pacini-Ketchabaw & Berikoff, 2008). We can also consider how racisms and
racialization *emerge* in the intense relationalities of an encounter. In other words,
racial differences are not only socially constructed; they are also *enacted* in
encounters between bodies, things, and places (M'charek, 2010; Saldanha, 2006).

When racialization is conceptualized as everyday **assemblages** (of discourse,
materials, bodies, space, time), an encounter can be seen as a relational event
made in connections between these elements. In this particular encounter, we
could focus on the assemblage of the crumbling walls of the childcare centre;
the children's memories of conversations with their families; remnants and

rearrangements of colonialism, multiculturalism, law, language, and migration; the predominantly brown bodies in the space; the clothes the children are wearing; aromas; the sense of tragedy evoked by the approaching sound of a police siren; a certain facial expression; and much more. All of these forces come together in the assemblage to charge racialization as an event, as cultural theorist Saldanha (2006) puts it. In the particular moments of this dialogue, the effect is a violent conflict, a sedimentation of physical and material divisions between bodies. This encounter could be seen to have a dampening effect in its divisive potentialities and in the circulation of negative affects (expressed and enacted as anger and producing **the Other** as a fearsome subject [Zembylas, 2009]).

Encounters such as these are repeated and aggregated to create racialization as a force in everyday life. However, in the intense sociomaterial relationalities of encounters with difference, the potential always exists for racialization to be assembled *differently*. We can envision possibilities for ethical encounters with difference as contexts, perceptions, and a multitude of human and non-human forces come together differently. In this view, racialization proliferates in rhizomatic, "constantly morphing" ways, some of which may solidify, reinforce, or create racisms, while others may disrupt or disregard racial divisions (Saldanha, 2006, p. 20).

Within the context of early childhood education, this sociomaterial conceptualization of how racialized differences come to matter provides a pedagogical space from which to describe, interpret, and create new trajectories in the negotiations of racialization in early childhood settings. This conceptualization of racialization also allows us to ask questions that focus on what racialization does and how it functions in the children's encounters, in addition to how it is discursively represented. We can ask, for example:

- What particular arrangements and connections between bodies, discourse, and material elements can be interpreted as a part of children's negotiations of racialization?
- What does racialization do in this particular encounter?
- What kinds of encounters are possible?
- What new elements can "race" be linked to and, as a result, transformed into something new?

Drawing on the concept of diffraction, we can also ask how the encounter transforms us and the children as parts of the assemblage (Pacini-Ketchabaw & Nxumalo, 2010).

Engaging with racialization as sociomaterial encounters suggests "understanding the world from within and as part of it" (Barad, 2007, p. 88). This understanding brings the possibility for us to engage with each event or encounter as it emerges. In other words, we can work toward pedagogies that enable educators and young children to experience new encounters with difference, for example, through creative experiences with each other, nature, art, movement, stories, and so on. This possibility suggests a nomadic and creative approach to early childhood education practices that extends and expands our practices to that which is not yet known (Hultman & Lenz Taguchi, 2010, p. 540).

Such an open and unknown gesture toward practice is often difficult for many educators to think about. However, we believe it is a gesture that we as educators are ethically obliged to consider.

Opening to Multiple Perspectives Complexifies the Learning Journey

In this chapter we have illustrated how using multiple perspectives and immersing ourselves in pedagogical narration can lead us to ask different questions and explore other understandings. Critically reflecting on such questions and understandings with colleagues, children, and families has profound implications for our practice. In our work as educator-researchers, we can act with political intent and foreground issues of social justice; we can ask whose voices are silenced or marginalized. We can look at our assumptions about children and their families and consider their validity, relevance, and usefulness in our work. If we look carefully, closely, and deeply, we may become aware that, in contributing our perspectives on pedagogical narrations, we transform the stories that are told—and we are transformed by our engagement with them.

In the journeys that we take when we engage with children and others through pedagogical narrations, we are guided by our ethics. Here we refer not to ethics that are provided by public policies and regulations (e.g., codes of ethics or standards of practice), but to those that underlie our approach to our practices. These ethics are the topic of our next chapter.

CHAPTER 6

OPENING TO ETHICS

In this chapter we explore the ethical challenges that confront us in our daily work with young children and families. We describe how we foreground an ethical approach, particularly in the spaces of uncertainty, discomfort, and complexity in which we often find ourselves in early childhood pedagogy.

We discuss:

- Our understanding of an ethical approach.
- Ethics as relational.
- Ethical praxis.
- Ethics as political action.
- Ethical difficulties of working with pedagogical narrations.
- Pedagogical narration as a nomadic ethical act.
- Centring ethical potentials in our practice.

An important focus of our work with educators is confronting ethical dilemmas like those we see in many of the pedagogical narrations we deconstruct and critically reflect on in this book (e.g., Building a Fort, pp. 105–112; No Chinese-Face Homeless, pp. 131–133; Stand Up, p. 152). Accordingly, we return to some of these narrations in this chapter to explore some of the complexities that emerge as we navigate the spaces of discomfort they provoke.

Inviting an Ethical Approach into Our Practice

Hillevi Lenz Taguchi (2005) says that once we revise what we "know" about how children think and learn, we often have to change what we do with them. She points out that when we gain new understandings, we can't continue with our old practices; ethically we are obligated to examine our practices. I've certainly found this to be true in my work with early childhood educators. For instance, I've been engaging in ongoing collaborative, critically reflective dialogues with a group of educators that trouble fixed routines and schedules. These educators have begun to ask important questions about the role of routines in their practice. For instance, they wonder who benefits from fixed schedules. What theories emphasize the importance of routines? What perspectives are marginalized by a developmental perspective on the role of routines? How does the clock act to interrupt and limit children's explorations? Why are educators and children so frustrated and stressed during transition times? All of these questions and more have been raised, and practice-as-usual has been cracked open. (Fikile)

What Do We Mean by an Ethical Approach?

In our work with educators, we embrace postfoundational perspectives that view the work of early childhood education as imbued with political and ethical questions. In these perspectives, ethics are conceptualized from a relational standpoint; accompanying actions are situated, contingent, and often marked by uncertainty (Dahlberg & Moss, 2005). This means that we understand ethics to take into account whom we are working with at a specific time in a specific place. Each moment of practice is unique and demands that we approach it as such.

In this conception, ethics are never fixed or final, nor can they be predefined in terms of specific rules or ethical codes (Braidotti, 2006a). This lack of universal guidance makes ethical practice anything but straightforward.

We explore some of the ethical complexities we encounter in our work later in this chapter. First we want to introduce how we work with the idea of ethics as relational, as praxis, as political action. These framings of ethics are central to our work with educators, as the practice examples throughout the book have illustrated.

Ethics as Relational

An early childhood community consists of educators, children, their families— and everyone's histories and aspirations. To this complex web of relationships, children bring their understandings, impressions, and experiences of the world and people. Families, in entrusting their child to a new situation, bring their beliefs, values, and expectations. Educators bring—among many other things— their knowledge and understandings of how children learn and grow. These interwoven layers of hopes, fears, desires, and expectations often have competing pulls. Educators must be aware of these pulls; they have to balance their understanding of individual children and families with their concerns and hopes for the group and with their own beliefs. (Enid)

Within each early childhood community, the educator is in a pivotal position to create an environment of trust and a feeling of safety. A code of ethics can guide us, but codes don't speak to the small acts and words we exchange every day. We believe that at times we need to interrogate preset codes of ethics for their colonial legacies—as they are usually founded on oppressive colonial practices.

Educators constantly make decisions that affect children and their families. How they reach a given decision will depend on the understanding and knowledge they have gained within their relationships. This practice calls for more than just a code of ethics; it calls for total engagement of heart, mind, and spirit in intensely relational encounters.

We enter into dialogues with our colleagues and with children and families, listening to layers of meaning and responding carefully. Each relationship is unique and requires "its own conversation" (Bowden, 1997, pp. 3–4). An ethical approach can help build a bridge of trust.

Thinking with sociomaterial perspectives, we can also extend a relational ethics to include our intrinsic co-implicative entanglements with and responsibilities for the non-human (Barad, 2007; Haraway, 2003). For instance, the materials we use in our centres and the multispecies places and spaces we inhabit and encounter all invite consideration of other ethical relations. For a while now, some of us have been contemplating some of these ethical implications (see Common World Childhoods Collective, 2014).

Relationships with Colleagues

When we think about relationships in early childhood education practice, we tend to think first about our relationships with children and families. However, some of our richest and most productive relationships are with our colleagues—other educators. In our view, sharing knowledge and responsibility with colleagues through collaborative practice is part of an ethical approach to early childhood education practice.

In our collaborative work with educators, pedagogical narration provides spaces for us to think together about practice, to challenge common practices, to reflect on our relationships with specific children and families, and to wonder about learning. Documenting a moment in a child's day can lead to deep discussions of what was seen and experienced. A pedagogical narration, whether it is shared through photos, video, or written text, is a documented fragment of children's learning that spurs thought, curiosity, and understanding.

These discussions require us to engage carefully and ethically with our colleagues. In our learning circles, as we engage in critically reflecting on pedagogical narrations, we take seriously the relationships we are building and sustaining among ourselves. We approach a narration with thoughtfulness, wondering what we are seeing and hearing. We look closely at assumptions that may block our understanding. Any number of thoughts, questions, and musings are raised in these discussions, and we strive to look at them from several perspectives. Sometimes our discussions are emotionally charged (see, for example, Kim's account of presenting Building a Fort at the sharing circle, pp. 105–112). The relationships we have built together over time allow us to share our questions and musings in an atmosphere of trust.

Relationships with Children

When we are caught up in the details and everyday routines of our practice, we can neglect to see and hear the child before us. This was the dilemma in which Christine found herself in relation to Stephanie (see the series of pedagogical narrations titled Entangled Bodies, pp. 96–105). Christine was concerned that she only knew Stephanie as a child with special rights, and she wanted to listen to her in other ways. By approaching Stephanie from only one perspective, Christine felt she was overlooking opportunities for deeper understandings both of Stephanie and of other children. We believe that the kind of practice Christine engaged in brings her closer to being in genuine relationship with children.

As Christine shows us, observation and reflection can promote clearer understandings of children and how they live in relationship with others. Watching closely to note children's interests, listening deeply to uncover some of their thinking, and asking children about their play can provide us with insights about their concerns and difficulties. These actions allow us to enter into the kind of dialogue with children in which thinking is transformed.

Children's play, questions, and ideas are rich and complicated. Pedagogical narration cannot begin to capture all the nuances of children's thinking or understanding. Still, while remaining aware that we are merely capturing fragments, we can listen for what resonates with us, what causes us to stop and wonder. Exploring these fragments with our colleagues, children, and families deepens our understandings and keeps them dynamic.

Relationships with Families

As we noted in chapter 3, working with families is not an easy task, especially as we attempt to hold families as competent and full of potential. No ethical code exists to make our work with families straightforward. How, then, do we build and sustain ethical relationships with families? Let's situate our question in an example.

A young family arrives at the centre with their three-month-old baby. During the intake interview, it is explained to them that the program provides the children's food as soon as they begin to eat solid foods, but families are asked to provide formula or breast milk. The program doesn't have enough funding to cover the costs of baby formula. The father is adamant that their baby drinks apple juice and only has two bottles of milk, one in the morning on waking and one at night before bed. The educator is concerned for the baby's health and nutrition.

Several approaches are possible in this situation. One approach might be to tell the parents that the babies must drink formula, not juice, during their time in the program, with an explanation of why juice is not a healthy choice for a baby. Another approach might be to wait and see what happens, while supplementing the baby's juice bottles with some bottles of formula. Another might be to accept the family's request, develop a relationship, and hope to move the family toward a different choice for their child. There is no right approach; each choice will set in motion different thoughts, emotions, and relationships with the family within the program and will be the basis of other choices.

Rules and policies can certainly make our day-to-day routines much simpler. However, policies often bypass places of difficulty and impose solutions. Instead of the educator negotiating a decision within a unique relationship with a particular family, the rule becomes responsible for a decision. Rules of "no gun play here" or "no toys brought from home," for instance, may seem to simplify some issues in a preschool setting, but they also may prevent opportunities for deeper understanding within a relationship or a community. In Building a Fort (see pp. 105–112) we can see how Kim negotiated a difficult terrain—and how doing so required a willingness on Kim's part to take risks in her relationships with the children's families.

No rules or policies cover all situations. No templates exist for our interactions with families and children. Each relationship is different, and each family and child calls us to respond carefully and thoughtfully.

Ethical Praxis

Our words, silences, gestures, actions, or lack of actions affect others. They respond to us, we are affected by them, and so it goes. We don't always know how we affect each other. Within this tension we try to operate sensitively and responsively, but we can never know for sure that we are acting ethically. (Laurie)

Ethics are often presented as a comprehensible system that offers solutions to all situations. Codes of ethics are written to guide educators in their work with children and families. While these codes are well meaning and care-fully thought out, they are written in an abstract format that is divorced from context and people. A code's impersonal nature claims an authority to cover all situations, but our daily interactions with children and families are unique and particular, filled with words and gestures that affect individual children, families, and educators.

For example, a program with a highly organized schedule that values effi-ciency may tend to treat a baby as a diaper to be changed or a bottle to be given. Toys must be cleaned or counters washed, so a child may be answered impatiently. In such an atmosphere, the child may stop asking questions; the baby may become passive. Neither of these interactions is unethical when viewed through the lens of a code of ethics, yet they are questionable if we look at the messages they convey to children.

"No legal definition can free us from the need to bring one another into being." (Bateson, 1994, p. 63)

A code of ethics may limit our thinking and prevent us from approaching each situation, dialogue, and person with a willingness to be both responsive and answerable. In contrast to a code of ethics, we are encouraged by the *ethical praxis* that Heydon (2005) devel-oped: "It is the interplay between theories and practices within the context of teachers' work that we as educators can best understand how the structures of theories and practices guide our eyes, encourage particular brands of thought, and make possible what can and cannot be expressed, and understood" (p. 392).

Rachel Heydon (2005) describes the five features of an ethical praxis:

- incorporates and juxtaposes different theories and practices.
- challenges the limitations of developmental theories.
- demands a critical approach to the histories of early childhood education.
- incorporates a social justice and activist perspective.
- refuses an authoritative discourse by not claiming to privilege one theory or practice over another.

In combination with an ethical praxis, *an ethics of care* (Dahlberg & Moss, 2005) and a *pedagogy of listening* (Rinaldi, 2006) provide us with an ethical compass with which to navigate the tricky waters of our practice, as we describe in the sections below.

Working with an Ethics of Care

The feminist and postmodern notion of an "ethics of care" (Noddings, 1984) was introduced in early childhood education by Dahlberg and Moss (2005), who emphasize care, creativity, relationship, and responsibility. This approach to ethical decision making considers contexts informed by class, culture, "race," and gender, for example. We draw from this approach to ethics in our work with educators by critically thinking about, challenging, and disrupting experts' discourses. For example, we critically reflect on the discourse of early childhood development based on scientific knowledge. As we discuss throughout this book, developmental psychology is a powerful discourse that has "settled so firmly into the fabric of early childhood studies that its familiarity makes it just seem 'right,' 'best' and 'ethical'" (MacNaughton, 2005, p. 1). However, developmental knowledge can have marginalizing effects for children and families who sit outside the norm. In our view, creating spaces for dialogue about alternatives to this dominant discourse is an enactment of ethics.

An ethics of care invokes actions rather than a list of rules. It is not imposed by experts, but achieved collaboratively by early childhood educators, children, families, community members, and others. It comprises enactments of relationships, caring, responsibility, leadership, and activism, and it requires us to take responsibility for ethical choices even when they are complicated by ambiguities. Each decision we make is particular to a relationship and a context. A particular question in one relationship with a child or family will not yield the same response in another relationship. We are responsible to each family and each child to listen and respond as best we can. Olsson (2009) reminds us that "instead of a universalized ethics ... that is easily reduced to a technical practice, there seems to be the need for an ethics that can stand to live in the moment" (p. 83).

Staying in the moment requires our full attention. As one example, asking a baby, no matter how young, for permission to pick her up is part of an ethical approach in some cultural contexts. A 3-month-old infant who is accustomed to being asked, or to being told ahead of time what is to happen, will respond. Babies often can tell you when they are ready to be picked up, but you must pay attention and notice the movements that indicate a readiness and willingness to join you.

Paying attention to another person is not always comfortable. To really attend to another we must stretch ourselves, we must strain to listen, to see, to feel (Smith & May, 2006). It is not a casual process. This attentive presence is an important part of working ethically.

A Pedagogy of Listening

Paying attention demands that we listen, and listening isn't easy, as Carlina Rinaldi (2006) explains:

> [Listening] requires a deep awareness and at the same time a suspension of our judgments and above all our prejudices; it requires openness to change. It demands that we have clearly in mind the value of the unknown and that we are able to overcome the sense of emptiness and precariousness that we experience whenever our certainties are questioned. (p. 65)

In one of our learning circles, we discussed an ethical dilemma that Danielle, an educator, presented about trying to really pay attention to the children's interests and not get carried away with her own enthusiasm. Enid wondered,

> *What is the line here? How can we balance the relationship(s) we have with the children? What does our enthusiasm add or detract from a project or the children's interest? We bring our expertise or knowledge to the relationship—it would be silly to not bring some of our knowledge or interests to this enterprise. But what are the ethics of listening or paying attention?*

Paying attention, observing closely, and listening well require skill gained from experience and understanding. Juggling different relationships includes remaining open to difference and to others' points of view while establishing trust; this can create tensions and uncertainty.

Moreover, a pedagogy of listening does more than make visible the intense relationality of early childhood pedagogies. It also recognizes that listening comes with risks. As we discuss in more detail below, everything we do in our practices is embedded in relations of power, including inequities between educators and children and those that can emerge between children in early childhood settings (Moss, 2005). Therefore, when we simply listen to children without confronting, disrupting, and deconstructing the discourses that create inequities in the classroom, the listening becomes "another colonizing apparatus" that solidifies unjust power relations (Cannella & Viruru, 2004, pp. 146–147). In Princesses and Pirates (pp. 76–83) and Building a Fort (pp. 105–112), Kim attempts to unpack and disrupt gendered discourses. Through this disruption, she tests relationships and puts herself in a vulnerable position as she negotiates the difficult terrain of power relations. As she stretches relationships with others and with ideas, she actually builds and grows relationships into complexity.

Moss (2005) cautions that listening can be used as a tool to "know" and "govern" children and their behaviour according to prespecified goals and outcomes. We therefore remain aware of the potential both for listening and for pedagogical narration to be misused in what we see as unethical ways. For example, as we critically reflected on Stand Up (p. 152) in the IQ Project learning circles, we had to work hard to avoid the need to "know" Winston or, more importantly, to govern his actions. We attempted instead to see this difficult moment in relation to histories of colonialism and racialization. We situated this event within historical forces and current circumstances of the country in which we live. We tried to avoid thinking about this event with prespecified goals, such as those found in developmental guidelines.

We agree with Rinaldi that "listening is not only a technique, and a didactic methodology. It is *a way of thinking and seeing ourselves in relationship with others and the world*" (Rinaldi, personal communication, cited in Moss, 2006b, p. 21; emphasis added). Dahlberg and Moss (2005) situate this complexified view of listening within the *ethics of an encounter*. Drawing from the philosopher Emmanuel Levinas (1985), they emphasize the importance of being open to and engaging with the Other without trying to "grasp" the Other—meaning that we do not attempt to make the Other into the Same by assuming that we can fully know them and understand them according to our perspectives and world views. This perspective counters the taken-for-granted approach to encountering difference and diversity, which is to normalize difference to dominant ways of understanding (Moss, 2006b). For example, as we noted above, the dominant reliance in early childhood education on developmental understandings of children and the accompanying focus on universal ages and stages often leads to assimilating and normalizing children (thus making them into the Same).

Ethics as Political Action

Isn't it amazing how power crops up over and over in our discussions? Whoever is seen to have the most power makes the rules. So who decides? We are extremely powerful in our settings. What do the power relations look like within our centres, across and between children, caregivers, parents, and other professionals? How does equity fit in with this? (Rita)

As we critically reflect on our practice and on children's meaning-making, complexities emerge when we recognize, as Rita does above, that early childhood education practices are embedded in power relations. As Rita's comments highlight, these "practices of power" (MacNaughton, 2005, p. 30) often privilege certain perspectives, such as those of educators over those of children or families.

Dominant discourses solidify inequitable power relations by exerting both political and ethical forces. Confronting these inequities requires ethical choices. As Lenz Taguchi (2005) reminds us, once we make dominant discourses visible and engage with power inequities, we cannot continue with "practice as usual." An ethical stance requires that we continually resist dominant discourses and seek ways to disrupt "taken-for-granted, universalistic, and normalizing ideas and practices" (Lenz Taguchi, 2008a, p. 271).

Early Childhood Spaces as Sites of Minor Politics

Policies related to children, families, and early childhood education settings are shaped by major and minor politics. Major politics include traditional or mainstream politics, institutions, and processes that operate at international, national, provincial, and regional levels (e.g., codes of ethics that are written for early childhood educators). Through the mechanism of government, major politics determine public policies that affect early childhood settings and the lives of children and families. Government decision making and actions are based on traditions, values, and rationalities prescribed by dominant discourses and ideologies (Dahlberg, Moss, & Pence, 2007).

Minor politics, on the other hand, are small spaces where people (e.g., early childhood educators, families, and children, individually or together) negotiate power/knowledge relations, consider alternate discourses, and think about creative possibilities. Minor politics create opportunities for ethical practice through critical and collaborative thinking and exploring other perspectives while questioning, contesting, and disrupting widely held "truths." Minor politics can make visible and disrupt hidden assumptions, discourses, and values that are embedded in early childhood practices and policies. We can see minor politics in action in many of the pedagogical narrations included in this book. For example, in Building a Fort (pp. 105–112), Kim, the children, and the children's families are suspended in a web of unknowns and difficult questions as power relations are reproduced and simultaneously resisted.

Drawing from reconceptualist scholars, we see early childhood settings as spaces that require engagement with issues that affect the everyday lives of young children and families within diverse socio-economic and cultural contexts—that is, we see early childhood settings as sites for minor politics. Minor politics provide a space to contest oppression and social injustices by generating other knowledge, creative possibilities, and solutions that can be realized through advocacy and leadership roles.

The collaborative critical reflections that emerged from discussions with educators about the pedagogical narration Stand Up (p. 152) can also be seen as a site of minor politics. In our engagements with the children's dialogue, we created a political space by embracing multiple perspectives beyond developmental discourse for understanding the children's negotiations. These perspectives included postcolonial, poststructural, and anti-racist feminist perspectives. We view our discussions as ethical encounters with difference because they make visible the power relations embedded within racialized discourses of difference and diversity in early childhood settings. By creating spaces for engaging with and reflecting on the effects of racialized discourses— and on how racialization can be mobilized in sociomaterial[1] encounters with difference—Stand Up is itself a site of minor politics.

Pedagogical narration thus emerges as an intensely ethical act through which we can continually invent new ways to open up both children's and educators' potentialities and build new relationships with others. This ethical approach, as enacted through pedagogical narration and its deconstruction and critical reflection, helps to create a shift away from fixed representations of identity (e.g., gendered and racialized identities, identities defined by social class, age, ethnicity, and so on) toward experimentation and multiple subjectivities. New affective potentials emerge in each encounter. In Christine's pedagogical narrations (see Entangled Bodies, pp. 96–105) we can see ways in which educators' identities, as well as images of children, are reinvented as dominant discourses are challenged. So are children's identities rethought through the discussions in the learning circles about Stand Up and other pedagogical narrations.

Critical readings of how power operates in Stand Up, and how it transforms—and reforms—social relations, can be seen as ethical acts. By moving away from judging individual children and engaging instead with the effects of dominant discourses, such as how they close down possibilities for children's ethical relations with difference, we can begin to question and resist inequity.

Some questions that help us to attend to ethics in relation to Stand Up include these ones, drawn from Glenda MacNaughton (2005):

- What power relations have the children in this dialogue formed?
- Through what discourses do the children understand racialization?
- How do racialized, gendered discourses implicate children and their understandings of themselves and others?
- How does power circulate through children's dialogues and what implications does it have for the possibility for social justice in the early childhood classroom?

Because ethics and politics are entangled, they require action in the everyday, including the everyday practices of early childhood education. This suggests

----

1 See discussions of sociomaterial perspectives in chapters 4 and 5.

that taking an ethical approach to early childhood education practice "is not about a master theory, but rather about multiple micro-political modes of daily activism" (Braidotti, 2006b, p. 134). It is essential, Braidotti writes, "to put the 'active' back into activism" (p. 134).

Ethical action involves being present in every relationship without following obvious or comfortable answers. Being present involves much more than being physically present; it requires us to acknowledge and respond to power injustices, both historical and ongoing. For example, in Entangled Bodies (pp. 96–105) Christine observes that Stephanie is often disengaged from the other children and their activities. Christine is troubled by the discursive-material meanings that are commonplace in her centre regarding children with special rights, and she takes ethical action to challenge and unpack them.

Ethical action can also be seen in many of the other pedagogical narrations we have shared in the book.

Let's now move to considering some of the ethical difficulties of working with pedagogical narration.

Ethical Difficulties of Working with Pedagogical Narration

What is our response and responsibility as educators when faced with places of discomfort; what is an "ethical" response? Are we child centred when we dismiss children's interest in superhero play or weapons? What does child centred mean? What is our role, our ethical role in this dilemma? What type of questions and issues are children struggling with when they explore these and other issues? (Enid)

As Enid's questions illustrate, critically reflecting on pedagogical narrations together opens up places of uncertainty filled with difficulty and tension. We often find cracks in our practice. The complicated questions that emerge in our discussions highlight early childhood pedagogies as "inherently relational, emergent, and nonlinear process[es] that ... [are] unpredictable and therefore unknowable in advance" (Sellar, 2009, p. 351).

Multiple layers are present when educators think about and discuss narrations, dilemmas, and quandaries of practice. In our projects, facilitating a group of educators who are willing to take a deep look at their practice means venturing into unknown territory and hoping that the way will become clear. Sometimes, what seems to be a straight, unambiguous path turns into a treacherous byway.

Within our learning circles we struggle with many ethical difficulties that we encounter in practice. Negotiating relationships with others, carrying on dialogues with families, connecting with babies, collaborating with co-workers, and learning with young children can be frustrating, confusing, enlightening, boring, dangerous, and exhilarating. Early childhood practice means responding to children and families and societal issues where complexity, ambiguity, and uncertainty abound. Negotiating these spaces requires an attentive presence, an attitude of thoughtfulness, and, as we discussed earlier in this chapter, an ethics of care.

Places of Tension and Difficulty

Throughout this book, we have highlighted how issues of racism, violence, gender, sexuality, and so on raise complex questions with no easy answers. Children exploring these issues often do so in an atmosphere of engagement, connection, and curiosity. Within a pedagogy of uncertainty (Britzman, 2009) there is a call at times for an ethical presence, an ethical response. Acknowledging the uncertainties inherent in our practices does not suggest inaction; rather, we have a responsibility to seek out and construct ethical responses, even as we see our responses as "fraught with complexity, with contradiction and contingency, and risk" (Green, 2010, p. 12).

It is also important to consider that, as we struggle with our ethical responses, children are also engaged in struggles to understand and negotiate their ethical responsibilities in the world. Edmiston writes, "To be able to answer, and to create spaces for children to address one another, we must be in radical dialogue with children" (2008, p. 174).

For us, that radical dialogue begins in our learning circles as we help each other to question and to think. By engaging with poststructural ideas, we can consider how children's subjectivities or identities are created within larger contexts. For instance, we can consider how hegemonic masculinities and the individualist focus of neoliberal societies come together to shape children's desires, such as in their repetitions of gun play (see Hunters, Good Guys, and Bad Guys, pp. 37–38; Building a Fort, pp. 105–112).

Chocolate and Vanilla, which we introduced in chapter 1 and discussed again in chapter 2, illustrates how we engage in spaces of tension and uncertainty through a nomadic ethical approach. This narration led to months of thorny discussions in the IQ Project learning circles. During these discussions, educators remained open to *multiple* possibilities for interpretation, positioning, and ethical responses. We discussed, for instance, possible reasons why the children appeared quite comfortable calling each other Chocolate and Vanilla and remained good friends while the adults—the families and the educator—felt uncomfortable. Our conversations raised emotions about racialization and underscored our own discomfort with discussing it. What were the ethics in this situation? Were the children truly comfortable? What did their names for each other reflect? What was our role?

We found that, to engage with this narration, we needed to understand more about how other educators felt and how this encounter charged them. We were careful not to condemn certain perspectives. At the same time, we embraced our own moments of not-knowing. No solutions emerged, only wonderings for further exploration.

Nomadic Thinking and Uncertainty

A common conception among early childhood educators is that we have to have all the answers and that practice needs to be simple (as opposed to theory, which is often conceptualized as more complex). But with Chocolate and Vanilla (pp. 19–20 and pp. 31–32), these assumptions are re-evaluated. We found that we could not ethically engage with this pedagogical narration without further theoretical insights and without extending it through additional moments of practice. This is something we have learned from the idea of nomadic thinking.

Importantly, these dialogues open up a space for us to confront and critically reflect on our own entangled subjectivities and assumptions. Each of us provided a different perspective that opened up more questions and more possibilities for rethinking "race" and its emergence in the classroom. Collectively, we identified many potential directions toward equitable pedagogies. Chocolate and Vanilla can therefore be seen as a nomadic act in that the dialogues it sparked did not assign fixed meanings to the children's racialized encounters; instead, it opened up pathways to engage the children in new encounters, multiple possibilities for becoming, and transformations of "race" beyond fixed notions of identity (Pacini-Ketchabaw & Nxumalo, 2012).

Gathering among ourselves to discuss issues raised in our practice with children and families allows for deep questioning and reflection. Creating a group to discuss and explore children's learning leads to unearthing values and challenging assumptions. It can be a deeply unsettling experience. Issues of "race," gender, sexuality, and violence are not easy to discuss, and they are not often part of early childhood education conversations. As we noted in this book's first chapter, however, curriculum requires complex conversations. We hope our readers are inspired to engage in complicated dialogues like those we have described in this book.

....

Pedagogical Narration as a Nomadic Ethical Act

....

Pedagogical narration promotes a profound understanding of pedagogical traditions and practices, and opens possibilities for ethical, political, and social justice choices of practising teaching and learning. (Alejandra)

We borrow the term *nomadic* from Deleuze and Guattari (1987) to refer to the creation of spaces and ways of thinking that open new routes in practice and resist normalized ways of being and acting. In a nomadic act, we would not necessarily follow pre-existing guidelines that define good practice; we would act toward creating new ways of ethically engaging in practice (Colebrook, 2002). In their "Treatise on Nomadology—The War Machine," Deleuze and Guattari (1987) make a useful distinction between reproducing and following that helps us to think of a nomadic ethical act:

> Reproducing implies the permanence of a fixed point of view that is external to what is reproduced: watching the flow from the bank. But following is something different from the ideal of reproduction. Not better, just different. One is obliged to follow when one is in search of the "singularities" of a matter, or rather of a material, and not out to discover a form ... when one ceases to contemplate the course of a laminar flow in a determinate direction ... when one engages in a continuous variation of variables, instead of extracting constants from them, etc. (p. 372)

Done carefully and thoughtfully, a pedagogical narration provides opportunities for exploration and reflection, a stimulus for questioning and wondering. However, the very process of creating a pedagogical narration is dangerous. A pedagogical narration contains "fragments of a memory" (Rinaldi, 2001, p. 84), providing only partial visibility, an echo. We must be careful not to take the narration to be an objective depiction of an event. These moments are taken from a larger context. When we isolate a moment in time and capture it in photos or text, we necessarily leave details out. There is always another figure or object just beyond the picture frame; other words always follow and precede a text. When we capture these moments of a child's day, we must treat them as fragments and not as representations of a child.

Olsson (2009) argues that pedagogical documentation (or pedagogical narration, as we have been calling it) is a complex, open-ended event in movement. Documentation, she notes, allows for new activations; it allows us to move and experiment to avoid static thinking and the essentialization of children's meanings. We see this creation of movement as an ethical act in its disruption of stabilizing understandings of the child. Similarly, Lenz Taguchi (2009) suggests that the observations we generate in the form of photographs, film, or field notes are not fixed materials that mean something specific; rather they are "substance in a process of intra-active performances and becoming" (p. 63). They are a *doing, a nomadic ethical act*: pedagogical narration "becomes what it actively *does and performs* in relation to the pedagogical practice where it is produced" (p. 64).

Following flows, creating new territories, and allowing thoughts to wander brings nomadic acts, nomadic approaches, nomadic thinking, nomadic orientations, nomadic practices (and so on) to life (Pacini-Ketchabaw & Nxumalo, 2010). A nomadic approach "is not rooted in an ordered space and time, does not comprise a fixed identity, but instead rides difference … knows no boundaries and wanders across diverse spaces. … This circumstance challenges the unitary, binary, and totalizing models of identity in modernist thought" (Zembylas & Vrasidas, 2005, p. 63).

In conceptualizing pedagogical narration as a nomadic ethical act, the focus is on ensuring that the event depicted in the narration maintains its open-endedness and continual movement. A nomadic orientation to pedagogical narration thereby helps to create a shift away from fixed representations toward seeking new affective potentials in each encounter.

Stephanie and the Sticker Moment

We can illustrate these complex ideas with Stephanie and the Sticker Moment (pp. 97–101). Thinking about this pedagogical narration as a nomadic ethical act, we can consider how it disrupts the focus on discovering predefined answers about practices and/or children. While certain boundaries around the image of children are established and specific representations of Sally and Stephanie are configured (e.g., Christine says, *I can't believe Sally is agreeing to follow*), at the same time, this is not a fixed, normalizing image. Through the pedagogical narration we see a transient, emergent reality. For instance, Christine writes: *With a look of slight panic, Sally shoots her gaze up, her eyes saying, "Help me; she took my sticker."* The image of Sally is (re)configured as Christine writes that *her patience is astounding.* As we see in this example, pedagogical narration as a nomadic ethical practice does not take any specific interpretation as permanent; rather, each interpretation becomes a moment of rest in a continuous journey (Braidotti, 1994; St. Pierre, 1997).

We can also consider how the narration stays open through Christine's questions, such as *Where are they going? What does Stephanie have in mind?* Christine's material-discursive practices are nomadic; they make possible multiple, shifting meanings about the encounter between Sally, Stephanie, the sticker, and the other human and non-human forces that act to shape this encounter. Making visible the complexity and richness of children and their encounters is an ethical act. This pedagogical narration allows Christine, the children, and their surroundings to be open to different possibilities, to embrace a "pedagogy of uncertainty" (Britzman, 2009) that, as Olsson describes below, does not seek solutions but engages with processes and events:

> Do not look for solutions; look for and engage in the construction of problems and how this relates to the sense under production. Do not look for knowledge, look at learning processes, that is, look for and construct how the involved bodies join in a problematic field. Do not look for methods, look for and construct how the entire culture surrounding the entering of a problematic field proceeds; take into account thoughts, speech, actions, but also material and environments. (2009, p. 119)

As a nomadic ethical act, pedagogical narration is linked with the idea of *becoming* rather than being. While the idea of *being* concerns itself with the organized state of things—their unity, identity, essence, structure, discreteness—an approach that embraces *becoming* attends to plurality, dissonance, change, transience, and disparity (Chia, 1995). In this way, pedagogical narration disrupts the unitary, coherent subject of modernity, embracing "a dynamic, time-bound, embodied and embedded subject in process: a nomadic ... subjectivity" that includes the material and discursive forces through which the subject is produced (Braidotti, 2008, p. 27). Multiple and fluid subjectivities of the children emerge discursively and materially through the pedagogical narration. For example, Christine says, *Stephanie leads and Sally follows*, yet she also notes, *although a look of uncertainty is written on her face.* This engagement with multiplicity is ethical in its "political resistance to hegemonic and exclusionary views of subjectivity" (Braidotti, 1994, p. 23).

Moreover, Christine is herself diffractively entangled in nomadic configurings and reconfigurings of the image of the child. She says: *Frozen in my step, my body clenched into a tight ball, I am hoping and praying for it; I am intrigued by the quick turn of events; I am curious to see how this unfolds; I'm wishing in my head, "please just give it back."* These practices, made visible through the pedagogical narration, are also intensely ethical through their unspoken connectivity/relationality with the children.

Stephanie and the Sticker Moment can also be seen as an example of a pedagogy of listening that complexifies practices by embracing uncertainty and subjective interpretations. Importantly, Christine does not seek fixed or final answers of who these children are—she generates questions, leaving the moment open to interpretation, to further change by asking *What meaning can be made of this particular crossing? An unlikely pair meet up for a short time over their shared interest in a sticker? Did time stand still for patience and generosity to shine through? Was an act of sharing repaid with trust that a beloved object would return? How will this crossing affect this "unlikely" pair in the future?*

An Ethics of an Encounter

We can also consider Christine's encounter with Stephanie and Sally as an example of an *ethics of an encounter*. As we discussed earlier in the chapter, Levinas has suggested that when we seek to know or "grasp" the Other, we create the Other as the same as us (Moss, 2006b). Christine does not attempt to grasp the children; instead she creates a space for multiple possibilities as she wonders: *Without any intervention, what will Sally do? Will she take the sticker back herself or will she choose to share it?* We can also view Christine's meaning-making of this ordinary moment between the children as illuminating the ethics of an encounter in that it creates more questions than answers. Further, Christine does not seek to judge; she is emotionally engaged in the encounter (e.g., her fervent hope of *please give it back* while at the same time waiting to see what unfolds). Her engagement in the encounter shows a respect for the Other (e.g., she notices that *Sally's patience is astounding*) without seeking to normalize the Other (e.g., she wonders, *What does Stephanie have in mind?*).

Through this pedagogical narration, Christine teaches us that, while it is not easy, we can foreground an ethical stance in our practices where

> The Other is infinitely beyond [our] grasp and slips away whenever [we] try to reduce it to a concept in an attempt to master or capture it. Thus, our responsibility to the Other is infinite precisely because our capacity to learn from the Other has no limits. The focus, then, should not be on knowing the Other but on working toward a radical openness ... and attending to the (unknowable) particularity of the Other ... an ethical relation that welcomes the Other and does not reduce him or her to sameness. (Zembylas & Vrasidas, 2005, pp. 67–72)

Next, we consider the idea of centring ethical potentials in our practice.

Centring Ethical Potentials in Our Practice

There is nothing simple about ethical and political practice. No generalizations can be made as to how we practice, what we do, how we respond. Each pedagogical encounter requires a different kind of attention. There are no shortcuts for any of us. We just need to figure out, together in dialogue, how we want to respond—or, more precisely, how we are able to respond. (Veronica)

In considering how we might respond to children, we centre the ethical potentials in each encounter. Ethics as relational potentialities are put to work in the actual moments of practice and in collaborative critical reflection processes. This is ethics as action. Reconceptualizing ethics as action in this way embraces "openness and risk, attention to ambiguity and to what we cannot know beforehand" (Springgay, 2008, para. 22). Our focus is on active, creative, continual responsiveness. We become curious about and look for the ethical possibilities of an encounter while recognizing that the process is filled with uncertainty and subjectivity.

Conceptualizing practice as creatively emerging from each encounter is challenging because it doesn't offer a prescribed way of practising ethical pedagogies with children. Rather, it suggests that we respond and act in ways that open up to children's potentialities for action, which can never be known in advance (Olsson, 2009). This process requires close attention to the consequences of our responses (Springgay, 2008) and to building and enhancing ethical relations in our practices.

The pedagogical narrations we have shared with our readers come from a place of curiosity. More importantly, they spring from a place of discomfort and of hope that something different can be created of an event. The educators we work with embrace collaborative experimentation, and thereby disrupt a narrow view of "pedagogical work as being exclusively about trying to get children, students and teachers to reach preset goals of preset learning contents as in contemporary developmentally appropriate practices" (Lenz Taguchi, 2009, p. 177). We do this work, this experimentation, not knowing where to go, but knowing that, wherever we go, we will get there through challenging ourselves to stay with the demanding task of ethical practice.

Stand Up ... Again

We close this chapter by returning to the dialogue Stand Up (p. 152) to see what possibilities emerge for social justice when we centre the potentials for ethical relations in our practice. You may recall that Winston sparked this dialogue when he announced *My grandmother says that black people are stupid and Native people are more stupid*. This statement led to a heated exchange among several children.

In this pedagogical narration we see children negotiating their racialized and gendered subjectivities within dominant discourses. As we see in their words, dominant discourses sediment and make inequitable relations proliferate.

They separate the children, leading to the racisms they enact in the dialogue: avoidance, suspicion, and negative judgment of the Other.

The same encounter, however, also holds *potential* to connect the children, the educators, and their surroundings through ethical relations across difference. By looking beyond predefined conceptions of "race" and gender and their repetitions through dominant discourses, we can create ethical potentialities. We can engage with this encounter as emergent, holding potential for seeing the world—and acting in it—differently (Braidotti, 2008).

Centring the potentials for ethical relations in our practice allows us to ask, Why not see this dialogue as a space to make ourselves aware of the devastating effects of colonization? Better still, why not see this encounter as a possibility to engage in the ethics of decolonization?

Centring ethical potentials, then, suggests a creative approach to pedagogies for social justice that engage with each event or encounter as it emerges. These are pedagogies that are always becoming, that open up connections between ideas to continually seek new ethical meanings for social justice that collapse the boundary between theory and practice. Importantly, these pedagogies continually seek creative ways to expand both children's and educators' engagements with difficult issues (Goodley, 2007). Hultman and Lenz Taguchi describe this focus on relational potentialities as

> taking notice of the differences and transformations that emerge in specific events ... [so that] ... we do not look for what a child "is" but we look for the virtual potentialities of a child or an event. (2010, p. 540)

Revisiting Stand Up from these perspectives focuses our attention on how encounters with difference emerge and how they bring with them varying potentialities. In practising for social justice, we must prepare for the unexpected because encounters with difference can emerge in infinite ways. As MacNaughton and Davis (2009) note, acts of injustice—racisms, gender bias, and the like—can be subtle; they emerge without warning, morph unpredictably, and take up unexpected lines of flight. Therefore, in ethical practices that centre social justice and equity, we need tools that allow us to generate ways to combat injustices when they arise. We need tools that unpack the social, political, and material aspects of social injustices (MacNaughton & Davis, 2009). We hope this book has provided you with some tools.

STAYING IN MOTION

Our experiences in our collaborative journeys with educators have taught us that creating space for sharing doubts and uncertainties about practice means enabling a welcoming, respectful dialogue that cherishes each moment as something new, with the potential for something else yet to come. Our wonderings and wanderings into various theoretical positions through pedagogical narration lead us to propose that the mobility and multiplicity of practices call for a nomadic approach to early childhood education. We propose pedagogical practices that are always becoming, that open up connections between ideas to continually seek new ethical ways of thinking and acting, that constantly expand engagements with social justice. In this kind of pedagogy, educators do not necessarily follow pre-existing guidelines that define good practice. Instead, we try to create new ways of confronting dominant ways of being, knowing, and doing. We move toward seeking new potentials, asking, for example: Where else could this go? What kinds of new encounters are possible? What new practices can be linked and, as a result, rearranged and transformed into something new?

In our journeys to complexify practice, we seek to stay in constant motion. We continue to push ourselves toward new thought and to open ourselves to the complexities of practice. We continue to challenge ourselves to pay close attention to specificities in practice, and, more importantly, to avoid closing the meanings we make of these practices. Our discussions around issues such as gun play, princess play, good guys and bad guys (and the gendered, racialized, classed, and sexualized discourses these events involve) come to no definitive answers through this text. But we hope that readers of this book will never look at these events in the same way again.

We have treated the pedagogical narrations in this book as openings for our own thinking and doing. As we write this afterword, we are already working on extending the conversations we began in this book. We hope that readers can use the narrations included here to put into motion and explore new conversations about social justice.

May all of your journeys in early childhood education practice be tentative, transformative, exhilarating, and complex!

UNDERSTANDING OUR LANGUAGE: A GLOSSARY

As you read this book, you may encounter terms you are not familiar with. We explain our understanding of these concepts here and hope that as you encounter them throughout the book your familiarity with them will increase, particularly as we illustrate them with examples from practice.

Anthropocentrism

Anthropocentrism is the view that humans are the central or most important element of existence. **Sociomaterial perspectives** question and disrupt this view.

Assemblage

We use Deleuze and Guattari's (1987) concept of *assemblage* to describe the coming together of material and discursive forces (see **sociomaterial perspectives**) to shape an encounter and, importantly, how we come to understand that encounter. For us, the term highlights the multiplicity and contradictions that characterize connections between the shifting social, economic, political, and material forces that come together in the emergence of knowledge, disrupting the **modernist** conception of knowledge as fixed and objective. The elements and effects of particular arrangements and locations of an assemblage are *emergent*; that is, they arise and exist only as a phenomenon of independent parts working together, and are not predictable on the basis of their properties. Mar and Anderson (2010) explain this further:

> Assemblages are not completed or stable constructions.... They are better conceived as temporary and provisional connective arrangements whose elements could be detached from it and

plugged into different assemblages in which their interactions are different.... [In this view] possibilities always exist, not only for the failure of elements to come into alignment, but for the formation of other assemblages. (p. 37)

Construction/constructs

Also see **deconstruction** below.

A *construct* is an idea or theory containing various conceptual elements; it is typically considered to be subjective rather than based on empirical evidence.

When we talk in this book about *construction*, we are referring to theories about social constructionism that emphasize the importance of culture and context in understanding what occurs in society (Kim, 2001). Social constructionism assumes that reality is constructed through human activity. That is, members of a society together invent the properties of the world (Kukla, 2000, cited in Kim, 2001). For the social constructionist, reality cannot be discovered; it does not exist prior to its social invention. Similarly, knowledge is socially and culturally constructed; individuals create meaning through their interactions with each other and the environment.

Central to this book is the understanding that childhood is socially constructed. From this understanding it is then possible "to explore the social forces that shape the construction; to appreciate the diversity of human systems; to examine the complex interactions of policy, program, community and family systems; and to take an approach to understanding that is not fundamentally reductionist in nature" (Pence & Hix-Small, 2009, pp. 77–78). **Reconceptualist** scholars have brought forward concepts of social constructionism to rethink the role of children in society and in early childhood institutions. Through social constructionism, children can be rethought as human beings with rights, strengths, and multiple identities. This fluid approach disrupts the developmental psychology perspective of the universal vulnerable child and allows for multiplicity and diversity in how we understand children.

Critical reflection

A key concept used in this book is that of *critical reflection* on our practices. By this we mean questioning the beliefs, assumptions, and understandings that frame how we view and respond to children and that shape the learning experiences we make available for them. We emphasize that reflection is not inherently critical, and that reflection without a critical orientation may not be productive and may not hold the potential for transformation. Chapter 2 is devoted to exploring this concept in depth.

Deconstruction

Following Lenz Taguchi (2007), we understand *deconstruction* to be about disrupting, destabilizing, and challenging taken-for-granted notions, values, practices, and "pedagogy as usual." We use these tactics of deconstruction in our collaborative **critical reflection** processes with educators to bring forward, from pedagogical narrations, multiple possibilities for our views of children and families and to question the reasons for, and consequences of, particular ways of understanding our practices.

Diffraction

In physics, *diffraction* is the process by which a beam of light or other system of waves is spread out as a result of passing through a narrow aperture or across an edge. Feminist physicists like Haraway and Barad use this term in relation to reflection, noting that diffraction "does not produce 'the same' displaced, as reflection and refraction do" (Haraway, 1992, p. 300, cited in Barad, 2003, p. 803), but emphasizes the mutual transformation and material entanglements that are a part of **critical reflection**. Diffraction disrupts the **construction** of emotion and intention as fixed concepts to be excavated from one's interior by reflection.

Diffraction thus resists the notion that reflection can be performed separately from practice; it also resists the idea that one's reflections can be represented objectively, where the educator relates a story of her inner thoughts and stands outside of the pedagogical encounter she is reflecting on.

We expand on the concept of diffraction and discuss how we use it to complexify our practices in chapter 2.

Diffractive engagement

The term *diffractive engagement* refers to Hultman and Lenz Taguchi's (2010) observation that "we can never reflect upon something on our own; to reflect means to inter-connect with something … reflection is always done in the midst of a complex network" (p. 536). Diffractive engagement brings together the discursive, material, and linguistic elements that form pedagogical encounters. These elements are in interconnected and interrelated emergent relationship with each other—and with the educator and her thoughts or reflections.

Diffractive visualization

We use the term *diffractive visualization* as an extension of the concept of diffraction (see above). To look at an event or pedagogical encounter diffractively means recognizing that a multitude of discursive, material,

and linguistic elements form the encounter and are in emergent relationship with each other.

Discourse

We view a *discourse* as a body of social knowledge that both constrains and
enables how we think and talk about a particular social object or practice.
Fiske (1996) maintains that discourses have three levels. First, discourses allow
individuals to interpret a particular situation. In other words, individuals
can only make sense of a situation within a discourse. Second, discourses
constitute both power relations and subjectivity. Individuals' **subjectivity**
is **constructed** by their participation in discourses. We enter discourses
and take a position through which we make sense of a situation. Third,
"each discourse has its own style and employs various words, images and
practices in its own fashion" (Ryan, 1999, p. 66). These statements, words,
and practices are not only related, but are also mutually dependent.

As an example, when we began our work with educators, child development
was a phenomenon that educators both experienced directly and found
central to their missions as practitioners. To make sense of this phenomenon as it affected or was affected by their practices, they needed to position
themselves in historically constructed *discourses* on child development.

A discourse of meaning-making

According to Dahlberg, Moss, and Pence (2007), *a discourse of meaning-making*:

- requires an active, engaged early childhood educator.
- accommodates diversity, complexity, and multiple perspectives.
- encourages individual judgements and uncertainty.
- views consensus and unanimity as neither necessary nor desirable.
- requires individuals to make ethical philosophical choices and judgements.
- draws on concrete experience.
- involves critical, reflexive thinking about pedagogies.
- contextualizes everyday practices within a particular social location
  and time.
- produces meaning in dialogue with others.

We expand on these concepts in chapter 1 and illustrate them with a pedagogical narration in chapter 4.

Discursive

The word *discursive* means of or relating to discourse.

Dominant discourse

We use the term *dominant discourse* to describe the way things are named, spoken of, and written that become experienced as objective and true—what Foucault (1980) called "regimes of truth." As regimes of truth, **discourses** hold power over individual and societal ways of understanding the world; they organize our everyday experience of the world, govern our ideas, thoughts, and actions, and determine "what can be said and not said, what we consider normal or not normal, appropriate or inappropriate" (Moss, 2001, p. 10).

Ethics of resistance

An *ethics of resistance* "refers to conscious acts of thinking deeply about the assumptions and taken-for-granted notions we bring with us (often without awareness) as we engage in our daily work with children. As we practice an ethic of resistance, we deconstruct, or take apart, what we 'know to be true,' to reflect on it, analyze it, criticize it, and resist its seductive powers arising from its familiarity" (Lenz Taguchi, 2006, p. 259).

Gendered

Gendered is an adjective that refers to things that are of, specific to, or biased toward males or females (e.g., gendered occupations, gendered positions, etc.).

Governmentality

Governmentality is a concept developed by the French philosopher Michel Foucault to describe how governments try to produce citizens suited to fulfilling those governments' policies. The term also describes the organized practices (mentalities, rationalities, and techniques) through which subjects are governed (Mayhew, 2004).

Power has been analyzed through the concept of governmentality, which, as Foucault (1991) explains, "is the ensemble formed by the institutions, procedures, analyses and reflections, the calculations and tactics that allow the exercise of this very specific albeit complex form of power, which has as its target population, as its principal form of knowledge political economy, and as its essential technical means apparatuses of security" (p. 102). In the Western world, Miller and Rose (2008) assert, governmentality is part of advanced liberal economies. The concept alludes to the multiple "mechanisms through which the actions and judgements of persons and organizations have been linked to political objectives" (Miller & Rose, 2008, p. 26). In this light, the construction of young children and their positioning within early childhood education can be explained through the concept of governmentality.

Governmentality is concerned with an individual mentality that is docile and
able to be governed (Rose, 1996).

Foucault (1991) related governmentality to disciplinary power, which, he
explained, operates through "technologies of self":

> Discipline produces subjected and practised bodies, "docile" bodies.
> Discipline increases the forces of the body (in economic terms of utility)
> and diminishes these same forces (in political terms of obedience). In
> short it dissociates power from the body; on the one hand, it turns it
> into an "aptitude," a "capacity," which it seeks to increase; on the other
> hand, it reverses the course of the energy, the power that might result
> from it, and turns it into a relation of strict subjection. (Foucault,
> 1977, p. 138)

Subjects become accountable for disciplining the self, thereby releasing the
state from the need to govern directly as individuals become self-governed.
As a consequence, what is "desirable" becomes limited to that which is
useful to governments and institutions.

Hegemony

Antonio Gramsci used the term *cultural hegemony* to describe the domination
of a culturally diverse society by the ruling class who control the society's
culture—the beliefs, explanations, perceptions, values, and mores—to the
extent that it is imposed and accepted as the norm.

Heteronormativity

Heteronormativity refers to the processes and practices through which heterosexuality is normalized. Within heteronormative contexts such as schools
(and most other social institutions), heterosexuality is such a powerfully
universal norm that all mainstream social **discourses** are founded on the
presumption that everyone is always and already heterosexual. In the early
childhood context,

> children's standard heterosexualised play—such as mothers and
> fathers, chase and kiss, and mock weddings—are regarded as so
> natural and normal that they are seldom even considered to be forms
> of sexualised play. Heteronormativity relies upon normative gender
> binaries. In order for heterosexuality to be seen as the only "natural"
> and "normal" sexuality and form of sexual desire, girls and women
> have to behave as "normal" or "real" girls and women, and men and

boys have to behave as "normal" or "real" boys. (Taylor & Blaise, 2007, pp.1-2)

Intra-action

Karen Barad's (2007) framework of *intra-action* helps us understand the entangled processes and inseparability of the material and social (or **discursive**) worlds. Barad provides an innovative way of understanding the physical world. Matter, she argues, cannot be thought of as passive. Rather, matter is agentic (having agency) and in constant intra-action. Further, matter cannot be separated from **discourse**. She refers to discourse-matter; in this book we use the terms **sociomaterial** and **material-discursive**. Barad (2007) speaks about intra-action in contrast to the usual *interaction*, which assumes that separate individual agencies precede interaction. In contrast, the notion of intra-action recognizes that distinct agencies do not precede interaction, but rather emerge through their intra-action.

These ideas help us broaden our understanding of the role that materials play in early childhood pedagogies when they are understood as being in complex relationality with the social/cultural/discursive aspects of early childhood education. When we consider that materials are not passive, but are active and participatory, we can consider educators' and children's relationships and encounters with materials in ways that make possible more dynamic pedagogies.

Lines of flight

The term *lines of flight* was used by Deleuze and Guattari (1987) to refer to ways of thinking and acting that resist the norms and limits of taken-for-granted ways of being in the world. We use the concept to refer to early childhood pedagogies that are always in movement and continually seeking new directions. These innovative possibilities are not known beforehand and do not have a predefined end-point; they intentionally seek to resist constraining forces that place limits or boundaries on what is "appropriate practice," for example, or what the role of the educator can be. When lines of flight are created and activated in everyday practice, the change is not seen as planned and implemented by specific individuals. Rather, from time to time "magical moments" occur where something entirely new and different seems to be coming about (Olsson, 2009, p. 63). Lines of flight have the ability to cross borders and build links between gaps and nodes that are typically separated by categories and orders of segmented thinking, acting, and being. Because lines of flight can take place at any time and lead us in a multiplicity of directions, as educators we must not only allow for them to take place, but also give them the appreciation they deserve by challenging ourselves to think and act in often unconventional ways. It is in this unconventional space where young children could become a fundamental part of curriculum development and where the magic moments described above might take place (Chan, 2010).

Material and discursive effects

Through our analysis of how **discourses** work in practices and through language, we can begin to attend to *material and discursive effects*. For instance, when children in Princesses and Pirates (unconsciously) choose to make themselves **gendered** subjects, educators need to pay attention to the *effects* that these positionings have in the lives of young children. Some of the effects might be that girls are excluded from boys' activities, or vice versa, that the classroom becomes divided into gendered spaces (home corner, block corner, and so on), that girls always choose to wear princess costumes during their play or that boys never choose to wear princess costumes.

For Barad (2007), apparatuses are not passive instruments, "mere static arrangements in the world, but rather apparatuses are dynamic (re)configurings of the world, specific agential practices/intra-actions/performances through which specific exclusionary boundaries are enacted" (p. 116). They "are the material conditions of possibility and impossibility of mattering; they enact what matters and what is excluded from mattering" (Barad, 2007, p. 148). Barad continues: "The materialization of an apparatus is an open (but nonarbitrary) temporal process: apparatuses do not simply change in time; they materialize (through) time. Apparatuses are themselves material-discursive phenomena, materializing in intra-action with other material-discursive apparatuses" (p. 203).

We think of pedagogical narrations as what Barad calls apparatuses, and, in turn, material-discursive phenomena. Barad (2007) explains that, from a sociomaterial position:

- apparatuses are specific material-discursive practices;
- apparatuses produce differences that matter—they are boundary-making practices that are formative of matter and meaning, productive of, and part of, the phenomena produced;
- apparatuses are material configurations/dynamic reconfigurings of the world;
- apparatuses are themselves phenomena (constituted and dynamically reconstituted as part of the ongoing intra-activity of the world);

▪   apparatuses are not located in the world but are material
    configurations or reconfigurings of the world that re(con)figure
    spatiality and temporality as well as ... dynamics (i.e., they do not
    exist as static structures, nor do they merely unfold or evolve in
    space and time). (p. 146)

Here is how Lenz Taguchi (2008b) defines pedagogical documentation as materializing apparatus:

> Pedagogical documentation materializes practice for us and makes it a
> *territory where intra-active phenomena can take place and can be "made*
> *visible" as processes of new becomings.* As such it temporarily "captures" an
> intra-active event that has happened, and in its materialization it becomes
> a territory for further intra-activity and process of new learning.... Any
> form of documentation can be understood as a *materializing apparatus*
> *of knowing* that produces different kinds of knowledge, as phenomena,
> depending on the ontological and/or epistemological perspectives we
> bring with us in our usage of it. Pedagogical documentation is a *material-*
> *discursive apparatus*, to speak with Barad (2007), that offers constraints
> on what is produced as knowledge and produces exclusions, depending
> on both the limits of our discursive understandings, and the limits and
> constraints of the material realities involved. (pp. 8–9)

Modernism/modernist thought/modernity

Modernity refers to both a period of time (beginning in the late seventeenth
    century and lasting until quite recent times) and a project (Dahlberg, Moss, &
    Pence, 2007; Habermas, 1983). It emerged through a set of deep social,
    economic, and intellectual transformations that included the Enlightenment
    and the Industrial Revolution. Modernity provided the basis for structural-
    ism, which was primarily concerned with discovering the rules, principles,
    and laws that guide and shape people's actions. Its goal was to develop an
    objective science and a universal morality that would foster human eman-
    cipation and improve the human condition. Modernity was concerned
    with classification and description. It aimed to bring order to the seem-
    ingly unordered environment in which people lived. Modernist thinkers
    assume that objectivity is possible and that individuals can detach them-
    selves from their biases. Bauman (1991) asserts that many of the inequities
    and social injustices that prevail today are rooted in the modernist world-
    view. With their overarching goal of bringing order to human existence,

modernist paradigms are unsuited to recognizing or accommodating the diversity and complexity present in today's world.

Modernity's reliance on science and human rationality still has a strong hold in the field of early childhood education, particularly in North America. Evidence of this hold can be seen in the enduring influence of the concept of developmentally appropriate practice (DAP), definitions of quality (see chapter 1), and theories of child development that assume universal laws and norms. These ideas, which rest on the concept of normality among all children and families, are part of the intellectual tradition of modernity (Dahlberg, Moss, & Pence, 2007). See also **postmodernism/postmodern theories**.

Neoliberalism / neoliberal forces

Neoliberalism is a loosely defined set of political beliefs and accompanying socio-economic policies that are driven by the view that the government's primary role is to promote individual autonomy by allocating resources through free markets and trade; it is usually accompanied by a belief that government should play a minimal role in social welfare (Thorsen & Lie, 2007). Neoliberalism then is marked by increased privatization and decreased government spending on social services.

The desirable neoliberal subject is shaped and shapes her- or himself according to the values of consumerism. As Thorsen and Lie (2007) explain, individuals are seen as being "solely responsible for the consequences of the choices and decisions they freely make; instances of inequality and glaring social injustice are morally acceptable, at least to the degree in which they could be seen as the result of freely made decisions" (p. 14). In the context of early childhood education, an example of neoliberalism would be the dominant focus on preparing children to be future participants in the labour market (Duhn, 2008, p. 84).

Nomadic

We use Deleuze and Guattari's (1987) term *nomadic* to refer to movement and multiplicity. In this view, nomadic thought, for example, emerges through interconnections and entanglements within **assemblages**. Nomadic practices are those that embrace uncertainty, non-linearity, and the subjectivity and politics of knowledge (Deleuze & Guattari, 1987).

Normative construction

The term *normative construction* is understood as one of the practices of power relations in which rules and truths are produced to organize ideas or behaviours. MacNaughton (2005) explains that *normative construction* is accomplished through "comparing, invoking, requiring, or conforming to a standard that expresses particular truths about, for example, the developing child" (p. 31). We engage in *normative construction* when we observe children and compare their behaviours with developmental guidelines. See also **power/knowledge** and **dominant discourse**.

Othered, the Other

French philosopher Emmanuel Levinas (1985) based his work on the ethics of *the Other*. For him, the Other is not knowable and cannot be made into an object of the self, as is done by traditional metaphysics. We use the word *Other* in our work as a verb to describe processes of **racialization** and marginalization.

Pedagogical documentation

Pedagogical documentation is the term used in some contexts, perhaps most notably the Stockholm Project and Reggio Emilia, for what we in this book call **pedagogical narration**.

Pedagogical narration

Pedagogical narration, simply put, is a way to make children's learning visible. It can take the form of:

- anecdotal observations of children
- children's works
- photographs that illustrate a process in children's learning
- audio and video recordings of children engaged in learning
- children's voiced ideas

In addition to the children's words and images, educators include their reflections and questions and invite their colleagues, the children, and the children's families to add their thoughts. Pedagogical narration thus provides a focus for concrete, meaningful adult and child reflection on children's learning experiences and processes. Through dialoguing, listening, and reflecting with others, understanding can be deepened.

In our work, however, we see pedagogical narration as more than this. We see it as a productive space for complexifying early childhood education practices. We use it as a tool, both to complexify our practice and to make visible the complexity of our practices. In our collaborative work with early childhood educators, we use pedagogical narration for reflection,

deconstruction, planning, experimentation, and action within **a discourse of meaning-making**. Please note that pedagogical narration is a term used in British Columbia. Similar processes are called pedagogical documentation in Sweden and Italy; learning stories in New Zealand; and action research in parts of Australia.

Pedagogy of listening

Reggio Emilia pedagogue Carla Rinaldi (2001) describes a *pedagogy of listening* as follows:

> How can we define the term listening? Listening as sensitivity to the patterns that connect, to that which connects us to others; abandoning ourselves to the conviction that our understanding and our own being are but small parts of a broader, integrated knowledge that holds the universe together.
>
> Listening, then, as a metaphor for having the openness and sensitivity to listen and be listened to—listening not just with our ears, but with all our senses (sight, touch, smell, taste, orientation).
>
> Listening to the hundred, the thousand languages, symbols, and codes we use to express ourselves and communicate, and with which life expresses itself and communicates to those who know how to listen.
>
> (Rinaldi, 2001, p. 78)

Through a pedagogy of listening, Rinaldi says, it is important for educators to become listeners to children's words, interests, and actions.

Positivism

Positivism refers to the philosophical system of the French philosopher Auguste Comte, which recognizes only non-metaphysical facts and observable phenomena (*Oxford Canadian Dictionary*, 2nd ed., 2006).

Postcolonial theories

Postcolonial theories make visible the linkages between historical colonial pasts and current systemic inequities in formerly colonized regions and among marginalized groups in the West (Stoler, 2008; Viruru, 2005). Postcolonial theories critique the dominance of Western knowledge and imperialistic Western economic and political influences in colonized locations.

Postfoundational theories

Foundational ideas allude to ideas from **modernity** that privilege the rational human subject as the basis of knowledge, and which can be expressed through language that conveys pure truth unfettered by values, beliefs, politics, and power (Moss, 2006a). *Postfoundational theories* challenge these ideas. Postfoundational theories include poststructuralist, queer, postcolonial, and sociomaterial theories, among others, all of which interrogate how "their effects have been devastating to many people on the wrong side of humanism's subject/object binaries ... [who] have struggled to reclaim and rewrite untold histories, to subvert what counts as knowledge and truth, and to challenge those who claim the authority to speak for them" (St. Pierre & Pillow, 2000, p. 5).

Ryan and Grieshaber (2005) explain:

> Drawing on a range of theoretical perspectives (e.g., critical theory, postcolonial theory, poststructuralism) and tools of analysis (e.g., deconstruction), postfoundational scholars question the modernist belief in the power of science to objectively determine the universal laws of human development. Instead, science is viewed as a social construction, imbued with the values of its creators and therefore enacting a particular set of power relations in its application (Lubeck, 1998). (p. 35)

As Lather (1991) explains, postfoundational perspectives make visible how "the dualisms which continue to dominate Western thought are inadequate for understanding a world of multiple causes and effects interacting in complex and non-linear ways, all of which are rooted in a limitless array of historical and cultural specificities" (p. 21).

Postmodernism/postmodern theories

Postmodernism is a complicated set of ideas that emerged as a reaction to **modernism**. Postmodernism disrupted arguments and structures that were part of the project of **modernity**. Bauman (1991) asserts that many of the inequities and social injustices that prevail in today's society are the products of modernity (which looks for order, certainty, truth, pure science). With its goal to order human existence, modernity has been unable to recognize and accommodate the diversity and complexity present in today's world. The postmodern condition has given rise to postmodernism as a system of thought. The postmodern condition provides no underlying order to guide individuals, no absolute knowledge, no absolute reality to be uncovered. According to Corson (1998), the postmodern condition has two main features: "an almost universal trend away from things like centralization, mass production, specialization, and mass consumption . . . and an almost universal trend towards the development of flexible technologies that are developed and used in smaller and more diverse units" (p. 2). Postmodernism reveals opportunities for uncertainty, complexity, diversity, subjectivity, non-linearity, multiple perspectives, and spatial and temporal specificities (Lather, 1991).

In early childhood education, postmodern lenses bring awareness to the inequitable potentials of developmentally appropriate practice (DAP), particularly in homogenizing children's and families' knowledges and experiences and in privileging Euro-Western norms (Ryan & Grieshaber, 2005).

Poststructuralism/poststructural perspectives

Just as **postmodernism** rejected objectivity, so too did the emerging school of *poststructuralism* by rejecting the objectivity of social fact (Cannella, 1998). Within a *poststructural perspective*, language is considered a **discursive** system of signs that are interpreted in a social context, a meaning-filled practice, rather than what might be referred to as modernity's instrument for delivering reality. Language does not constitute an absolute representation of reality. Meaning is part of a complex linguistic negotiation among individuals and, as such, it is one of the most important practices through which cultural production and reproduction take place (Cannella, 1998). In light of recognizing the discursive nature of language, the term *young children* can be viewed as a social construct with which we infer or build meanings. A *universal child* **discourse** has been created through strategies and techniques of power in accordance with political, social, judicial, and economic conditions of society.

Poststructuralism also questions binary or dualistic thinking (Dahlberg, Moss, & Pence, 2007). Oppositions have been set up between rational and irrational, ordered and unordered, objective and subjective. Poststructuralists talk about "both/and" rather than "either/or." In education, we discuss the distinction between included and excluded, empowered and disempowered, and voice and voiceless as being natural. However, these distinctions are contingent upon dualistic conceptions of power struggles and, as such, are problematic. The issue is that systems of knowledge have been taken for granted.

See also **discourse, power dynamics, power/knowledge, material and discursive effects.**

Power dynamics

Michel Foucault (1978) teaches us new ideas about how power works in our society:

> Power must be understood in the first instance as the multiplicity of force relations immanent in the sphere in which they operate and which, through ceaseless struggles and confrontations, transforms, strengthens, or reverses them; as the support which these force relations find in

one another, thus forming a chain or a system, or on the contrary, the disjunctions and contradictions which isolate them from one another; and lastly, as the strategies in which they take effect, whose general design or institutional crystallization is embodied in the state apparatus, in the formulation of the law, in the various social hegemonies. (pp. 92-93)

Foucault (1977) defines power as being "exercised" and "circulatory"; as a network of **discursive** relations which move from numerous points through individuals, rather than being held by a particular group or social class. This power "is not exercised simply as an obligation or a prohibition on those who 'do not have it'; it invests them, is transmitted by them and through them; it exerts pressure upon them, just as themselves, in their struggle against it, resist the grip it has on them" (Foucault, 1977, p. 27).

In addition, Foucault (1980) argues that power functions at the level of the body, at the *micro* level of bodies: "Power reaches into the very grain of individuals, touches their bodies and inserts itself into their action and attitudes, their discourses, learning processes and everyday lives" (Foucault, 1980, p. 39).

Power also involves resistance. "Where there is power," Foucault (1978) argued, "there is resistance, and yet, or rather consequently, this resistance is never in a position of exteriority in relation to power" (p. 96). The actual resistance that the exercise of power meets is largely of its own creation due to the discursive nature of power. Its dissemination always means intrusion into the language games that it touches upon (Corson, 1998). The resistance to DAP, and to its multiple **discourses**, is another exercise of power not localized to one specific place or person but part of discourses. This resistance plays an important role in legitimizing the discourses around the care and education of young children.

Power/knowledge

The term *power/knowledge* is borrowed from Michel Foucault. Both histori-cal and power structures in a society determine and legitimize knowledge. Foucault's (1977, 1978) work has been central in understanding the construc-tion of legitimate knowledge. **Poststructuralism** conceives of knowledge as socially constructed, context specific, and value laden. The role of power is key in the organization of knowledge. According to Foucault (1977, 1978), **discursive** power relations involve the formation and regulation of meanings and understandings, disciplining how people act. This view of power and knowledge challenges the idea that power is a thing to be exercised by "powerful" people or groups.

"Power produces knowledge," Foucault (1977, p. 27) said. Wherever power rela-tions exist, a field of knowledge is constituted. Reciprocally, wherever a field of knowledge exists, power relations are constituted. Foucault (1977) states that "it is not the activity of the subject of knowledge that produces a corpus of knowledge, useful or resistant to power, but power-knowledge, the processes and struggles that traverse it and of which it is made up, that determines the forms and possible domains of knowledge" (p. 28). The effects of discursive power relations involve the formation and regulation of meanings and understandings, disciplining how people act. Knowledge also creates possibilities and capacities for action. As Popkewitz (1998) explains in relation to education, the knowledge that organizes schooling is manifested in what educators believe, feel, and discuss about schooling. Social relations of power and knowledge are central to understanding how various **discourses** function to produce and legitimize a body of knowledge around, for example, the idea of young children within early childhood education.

Queer theory

The term *queer theory* emerged in the early 1990s to describe a new body of thought arising from feminist theory. It continued the **poststructural** feminist tradition of challenging gender binaries by locating these binaries within the field of sexuality, thereby focusing attention on the mutually constitutive nature of gender and sexuality. Also see **heteronormativity** above.

"Race"

We use quotation marks for the term *"race"* to emphasize that race is a socially constructed phenomenon with no biological basis. It is also more than socially constructed; processes of racialization are materially and discursively enacted.

Scholars in Australia, examining the social construction of whiteness and considering the critique of multiculturalism, have done extensive work with young children by exposing the racial power games as well as the reconfiguration of these games in early childhood classrooms (see MacNaughton & Davis, 2009). In a study entitled "Preschool Children's Constructions of Racial and Cultural Diversity," MacNaughton, Davis, and Smith (2009) explored how young children use race in the processes of actively constructing their complex, multiple, shifting identities.

They also used observation in order to explore the hierarchies of race and the dynamics of race relations that are commonplace in early childhood classrooms. Specifically, they observed how children grouped themselves during playtimes, the characters they chose to play during free time play, the roles that different children chose to take during play, and the dynamics of inclusion/exclusion evident during play.

Finally, the researchers used storytelling with persona dolls. They developed stories containing instances of inclusion/exclusion based on the data they gathered through other methods and used persona dolls to tell the story back to the children. Then, they interviewed the children and asked the following questions: What they thought about what had happened in the story, whether they had seen something like this happen before, how the doll character could attempt to respond to the situation, and what the children themselves could do about it (MacNaughton et al., 2009).

In our work, anti-racist scholars—and particularly anti-racist feminist scholars—inspire us to think of reflection as a critical literacy of "race," racisms, anti-racisms, and racialization. Lee and Lutz (2005), for example, point to "the need for critical readings of how power operates and how it transforms, and reforms, social relations, through racial categories and consciousness":

> We call attention to the particularities of racializations as they mutate and take hold on new ground. To counter the insidious, commonsensical nature of racial consciousness, new critical literacies must involve processes of "cognitive decolonialization," so that it is possible to really see, hear, and understand where that consciousness comes from. (2005, p. 4)

Racialization

Racialization is understood as a possible effect of encounters with racial difference. Racialization refers to both the **discursive** and **material** processes by which social significance is attached to categories of difference in ways that are potentially divisive and discriminatory (Crutcher & Zook, 2009; Pacini-Ketchabaw, White, & Armstrong de Almeida, 2006). These categories include differences in skin and hair colour, language and accent, clothing, religious markers, citizenship status, performance and intelligence measures, and inferred "personality" traits, among others (de Finney, 2010, p. 485).

Reconceptualist movement

The *reconceptualist movement* in the field of early childhood education is one facet of **postfoundational** thinking. The reconceptualist movement uses postfoundationalist ideas to challenge the view of early childhood educators as neutral and situated in apolitical contexts. This shift has been spurred by scholars who have called for a disruption of decontextualized and prescriptive pedagogies that rely on the science of developmental psychology as the dominant source of knowledge from which to understand all children and construct early childhood pedagogies (Pacini-Ketchabaw & Pence, 2005). Reconceptualist scholars question the existence of a singular truth and, consequently, of universality. They critique the use of terms such as *best* and *appropriate* as misleading in their suggestion that a single best response can be found in our diverse and complex world. Reconceptualists argue that reality does not exist independent of the knower and the process of knowing, and that it is essential to acknowledge the importance of context and values when making decisions. Reconceptualist thinkers also question dualistic thinking; they talk about *both/and* rather than *either/or*.

Reconceptualizing

When we use the term *reconceptualizing*, we're talking about more than merely thinking about something in a new way. Our use of the word implies the meaning we attach to the **reconceptualist movement** in early childhood education, as defined above.

Reflexivity

Reflexivity refers to the process of engaging in **critical reflection**. It implies a political intent in that it allows educators to question how meanings are constructed and what those **constructions** might imply.

Representational thinking

Those working with posthumanist ideas challenge *representational thinking*. We engage in representational thinking when we think in analogies. Law and Benschop (1997) tell this story to explain a humanist understanding of representation:

> A faithful representation of the world understands the point of view of the observer as an eye that looks through an imagined windowpane onto the world. The canvas becomes the imagined windowpane. The world that is transformed to fit onto the canvas/windowpane is a Euclidean volume. The objects making up the world may be viewed through that window in accordance with a set of geometrical rules. Representation is a matter of projection from the observer's eye of the geometrically determined three dimensions of the world onto the two-dimensional surface of the windowpane. (p. 3)

> It may be said of *representation* that it is:

> *illustrative* because the world and its narratives are separate from the depiction. They pre-exist their depiction. The stories are as it were out there, in reality. Depictions illustrate that world—a world apart.

limited, finite. It is a revealed perspective on the world. As we've already noted, other perspectives are possible. This means that the world is *inexhaustible* with respect to representation. Other constructions are always possible. (p. 5)

Rhizomatic thinking/rhizome

We borrow the term *rhizome* from Deleuze and Guattari (1987) to describe approaches in early childhood that create movement, that are always becoming, and that hold potential for multiple trajectories and **lines of flight**. Think of a rhizomatic plant which spreads without a central root, a place of origination or even a logical pattern. A mushroom, for instance, has no obvious centre, is able to move in all directions, and has no parent–child relationship between its different parts. *Rhizomatic thinking* embraces nonlinearity and disrupts the fixities and deficit views that characterize **modernist discourses** (Goodley, 2007). We also think of the image of the rhizome as an illustration of the complexities of early childhood pedagogies—pedagogies that are always in motion, proliferating new ways of knowing and becoming with children in relationship with the things and spaces that come together in the everyday **assemblages** of practice. Deleuze and Guattari (1987) liken the image of the rhizome to "weeds, grass, swarms and packs" (p. 7) in contrast to the tree, which is marked by "hierarchies, linearity and extreme stratification" (p. 7). They write:

A rhizome has no beginning or end; it is always in the middle, between things, interbeing, intermezzo. The tree is filiation, but the rhizome is alliance, uniquely alliance. The tree imposes the verb "to be," but the fabric of the rhizome is the conjunction "and ... and ... and ..." This conjunction carries enough forces to shake and uproot the verb "to be." (pp. 27–28)

Rhizomatic thinking thus both frees the forces that create wholes (or entities) and opens up multiple possibilities for approaching any thought or potential action (Sellers, 2010).

Rhizoanalysis

Rhizoanalysis is "a way to explore the politics of a text in order to create new texts" (MacNaughton, 2005, p. 89). Following Glenda MacNaughton, we use rhizoanalysis in our work with early childhood educators as a strategy for understanding children's meaning-making. MacNaughton writes:

Rhizoanalysis both deconstructs and reconstructs a text. It deconstructs a text (e.g., a research moment or a child observation) by exploring how it means; how it connects with things "outside" of it, such as its author, its reader and its literary and non-literary contexts (Grosz, 1994, p. 199); and by exploring how it organizes meanings and power through offshoots, overlaps, conquests and expansions (Deleuze & Guattari, 1987, p. 21). Rhizoanalysis reconstructs a text by creating new and different understandings of it; and it does so by linking it with texts other than those we would normally use. For example, we can use rhizoanalysis to replot the links between an observation of a child, and a child development text, a feminist text and a popular culture text. (p. 90)

In chapter 5, we give an example of how we use rhizoanalysis to assist us in our collaborative critical reflections on pedagogical narrations.

Subjectivity/subject formation

Lenz Taguchi (2006, 2010), Davies (2000), and MacNaughton (2000, 2005) have contributed a useful lens for understanding children's identities through their work with **deconstructive** feminist **poststructural** theories. They have explored the concept of *subject formation* (also referred to as *subjectivity*), which holds that an individual becomes a subject in the world through processes of social interaction, "not as a relatively fixed end product, but as one who is constituted and reconstituted through the various discursive practices in which he or she participates" (Davies, 2000, p. 89). This view provides an alternative to the rational, conscious, unitary human being described in psychological **discourses** (Davies, 2000; Robinson & Jones-Diaz, 2005). Feminist poststructural perspectives theorize that we become subjects in a simultaneous process of being subjected to **dominant discourses** and subjecting ourselves to them by picking up normalized meanings. Alternatively, we might go against the grain of these meanings and formulate resistant meanings and discourses. In this perspective, human beings are thought of as having multiple, complex, and contradictory ways of being and acting in the world.

Social constructionism

See **construction/constructs**.

Social justice perspectives

Social justice perspectives identify relations of power and knowledge that contribute to and sustain inequities related to "race," class, gender, sexuality, disability, and age, among other sources. Several scholars in early childhood education have provided very useful theoretical and pedagogical resources for thinking about and acting toward social justice practices (Butler & Davies, 2007; Davies, 1989; MacNaughton, 2005; MacNaughton & Davis, 2009; Ryan & Grieshaber, 2005; Taylor, 2007).

Their work has brought attention to the ways in which "race" and gender are **socially constructed** and produced through **discourse**. In this understanding, children's **racialized** and **gendered** identities or **subjectivities** are constructed by the **dominant discourses** in their particular social context. While children exert agency in what they see as desirable as they actively construct, perform, and choose their identities, this agency is mediated and constrained by the available discourses constructing "race" and gender (MacNaughton, 2005). Anti-racist, postcolonial, feminist poststructural, and ecological perspectives are some of resources we can draw on in working toward social justice in early childhood settings.

Sociomaterial (or material–discursive) perspectives

Sociomaterial (or material-discursive) perspectives bring attention to the role of the physical (or material) in creating **subjectivities**. These perspectives suggest that subjectivities, including gendered and racialized subjectivities, are not only created through language or **discourse**, but emerge in the very moments of encounter between bodies, things, and discourse.

Sociomaterial perspectives help us to complexify the concept of **subject formation**, which we described above. From these perspectives, subject formation can be understood not only as the processes by which we position ourselves (in both normalizing and subversive ways) and are positioned within **dominant discourses**, but also in terms of the *material* processes that come into being in conjunction with, or preceding, linguistic and symbolic representation (Grosz, 2005; Lenz Taguchi, 2010; Rossholt, 2009). In other words, bodies are "not merely blank slates for inscription by society and not biologically given entities with particular destinies" (Slocum, 2008, p. 853). As bodies and their actions, perceptions, and affects interact with objects, spaces, and **discursive** elements, our subjectivity emerges as an (embodied) **assemblage**. This assemblage has multiple belongings and is in constant change: it is made, remade, and transformed through relational connections (Braidotti, 1998; Deleuze & Guattari, 1987; Gallacher & Gallagher, 2008).

Theory/practice divide

While **positivist** approaches conceptualize practice in opposition to theory (often theory informing practice), we view practice and theory as inseparable and mutually transformative. There is no practice without theory and no theory without practice (Lenz Taguchi, 2005). We view practice as never final; it is always in flux because young children and the contexts in which they live are also constantly changing.

Universalist

We use the term *universalist* to refer to the prevailing **modernist** idea that knowledge about children and how they develop can be applied to all children everywhere, without regard to their multiplicity and the diversity of contexts in which they live. Like Pence and Hix-Small (2009), we believe that universally applicable theories of child development can result in a "deficit perspective" for children who do not fit with a particular universally defined norm (p. 77). Our resistance to modernist and universalist ways of viewing the world is grounded in **postmodern** theories that value diversity, contexts, and multiplicity (Dahlberg, Moss, & Pence, 2007). For instance, the social, cultural, economic, ethnic (and other) contexts in which children live and negotiate their daily lives are all important considerations.

APPENDIX: PROJECT SUMMARIES

....

Investigating Quality (IQ) Project

The Investigating Quality (IQ) Project is an initiative of the Unit for Early Years Research and Development[1] in the School of Child and Youth Care at the University of Victoria, BC. Its aim has been to broaden and deepen discussions on quality in the early childhood education field at local, regional, national, and international levels (Pence & Pacini-Ketchabaw, 2010, 2012).

We began by identifying where the most innovative work in the field was taking place. We found that Sweden's Stockholm Project, the Reggio Emilia preschools of northern Italy, and groundbreaking programs in New Zealand, among other programs, were working in ways that complexify practice. To explore the possibilities of such programs in our own context, the Unit hosted a series of forums at the University of Victoria, where guests from around the world were invited to discuss pedagogical innovation, democratic engagement, pedagogical documentation, assessment, participatory development, social justice, and other issues (Pence & Pacini-Ketchabaw, 2010, 2012). These dialogues invigorated and enriched our discussions and stimulated many questions. From these starting points, we designed the professional development portion of the IQ Project.

More than 100 early childhood educators have participated in the project to date. These participants work in a wide variety of settings in urban and rural communities in BC, including Aboriginal, multicultural, college- and university-based, preschool, full-time childcare, infant-toddler, family childcare, nonprofit, and small-scale for-profit settings.

---

1 http://www.web.uvic.ca/~eyrd/.

Each educator typically participates for a 10-month period, although many have participated more than once. Together with a facilitator, the educators meet monthly in small groups to dialogue and share their established and emerging practices. These monthly learning circles are critical in creating a community of practice among the project participants. The facilitator's role is to assist the early childhood educators in discussing early childhood practices and investigating postfoundational ideas through reading materials that pertain to the discussions at hand. Following processes of pedagogical narration, the educators collect moments of practice through journal writing, photography, and video and audio recording in their centres and then share their pedagogical narrations with the group. Together, the educators and researchers reflect critically on each narration and on how we might work with postfoundational theories to extend and complexify practices.

Periodic sharing circles bring the educators from the different discussion groups together to interact and discuss the work they have engaged in during the learning circles. A listserv enables the educators and researchers to share ideas and materials of interest between meetings. Members of the research team provide individual support to each educator through visits to early childhood education centres.

Through these processes, our pedagogical understandings are often contested, driving us to change and complexify our practices.

British Columbia Early Learning Framework Implementation Project

The Framework

In 2008, while the IQ Project was underway, the province of British Columbia developed an Early Learning Framework (Government of British Columbia, 2008a) to guide and support early childhood educators, early years professionals, service providers, communities, and governments in providing rich early learning experiences for young children. The framework provided the IQ Project participants with a space to engage in a richer understanding of early childhood education in our monthly learning circles.

BC's Early Learning Framework (ELF) is based on an image of the child as capable and full of potential. This image resonates powerfully with the images of children expressed in respected international early childhood programs such as those of Reggio Emilia, Italy, the Stockholm Project, and others. On the other hand, it contrasts with the image typically expressed in North American early childhood programs, which tend to see children as vulnerable and in need of protection.

The BC ELF envisions early learning as a dynamic process actively supported by families and other adults who care for and teach children in their homes and communities. Children, adults, and environments play distinct but interacting roles in promoting early learning.

Importantly, the framework also recognizes children's strengths and abilities to shape the early learning environment as an important foundation for their growth as future citizens. The framework recognizes the child as an active co-constructor of knowledge and meaning-making. Children and adults both play an active role in the pedagogical process. Co-construction recognizes the child as part of society and culture—a social actor with rights and agency (as supported by the UN Convention on the Rights of the Child). Pedagogical practices that flow from these approaches build on and welcome the knowledge and skills of all players and acknowledge the influence of relationships and interactions as well as the social and cultural contexts in which learning occurs.

The ELF invites critical reflection as a means to transform early childhood education. It offers the tool of pedagogical narration to give educators skills and techniques to deepen their understanding of children's ordinary moments and support the ELF's four areas of early learning:

- well-being and belonging
- exploration and creativity
- languages and literacies
- social responsibility and diversity

The Implementation Project

Her experiences with the IQ Project allowed its co-director, Veronica Pacini-Ketchabaw, to work with colleagues at Selkirk College, Northern Lights College, and Camosun College to create a model for implementing the ELF throughout BC. The implementation project team devised a three-strand, curriculum-focused, train-the-trainer approach in which participant feedback played an integral role.

Strand 1 was a professional development phase focused on developing a team of trainers, called field leaders, who would deliver training about the ELF and its implementation at the local level. Field leaders received the training (through workshops and online activities) in Strand 1 and co-delivered it in Strands 2 and 3.

A key outcome of the field leader training was the production of exemplar materials to demonstrate the process of creating pedagogical narrations.

These exemplars were used in Strands 2 and 3 to build skills in the practitioners trained in Strand 3.

Strand 2 brought the field leaders together with early childhood educator college instructors, first in a workshop format to begin the planning process for co-delivering the training to early childhood educators in Strand 3, and then in their home locations around the province to finalize the plans and deliver the workshops.

In Strand 3, the field leaders and college instructors co-delivered workshops to introduce the ELF to early childhood educators throughout the province. early childhood educator practitioners were broadly defined as people working in the early education field. Practitioners were a diverse group of early childhood educators, assistants in childcare settings, family childcare providers, primary teachers, supported child development consultants, and other community members delivering early childhood services.

The project team chose training materials to reflect the philosophy underlying the BC ELF. A curriculum was developed to introduce critical reflection and pedagogical narration as tools that educators can use as part of an intricate process of deconstructing and then reconstructing the image of the child (see chapter 3).

An implementation guide titled *Understanding the British Columbia Early Learning Framework: From Theory to Practice* (Government of British Columbia, 2008b), developed by the research team, describes the pedagogical narration process and gives detailed practical examples of how the tool was used by field leaders during the training.

REFERENCES

Adichie, C. (2009). *The danger of a single story*. Interactive transcript. Retrieved from: http://www.ted.com/.

Atkinson, K. (2007). Working among the good and the bad. *Island Parent Magazine*. Retrieved from: http://www.islandparent.ca/articles/working.html.

Barad, K. (2003). Posthumanist performativity: Toward an understanding of how matter comes to matter. *Signs, 28*(3), 801–831. http://dx.doi.org/10.1086/345321.

Barad, K. (2007). *Meeting the universe halfway: Quantum physics and the entanglement of matter and meaning*. Durham, NC: Duke University Press. http://dx.doi .org/10.1215/9780822388128.

Bateson, M.C. (1994). *Peripheral visions: Learning along the way*. New York, NY: HarperCollins.

Bauman, Z. (1991). *Modernity and ambivalence*. Cambridge, UK: Polity Press.

Berger, I. (2010). Extending the notion of pedagogical narration through Hannah Arendt's political thought. In V. Pacini-Ketchabaw (Ed.), *Flows, rhythms and intensities of early childhood education curriculum* (pp. 57–76). New York, NY: Peter Lang.

Berger, I. (2013). Narration-as-action: The potential of pedagogical narration for leadership enactment in early childhood education contexts. Unpublished doctoral dissertation. University of British Columbia, Canada.

Bhabha, H.K. (1994). *The location of culture*. London, UK: Routledge.

Blaise, M. (2005). *Playing it straight: Uncovering gender discourses in the early childhood classroom*. London, UK: Routledge.

Bogue, R. (2004). Search, swim and see: Deleuze's apprenticeship in signs and pedagogy of images. *Educational Philosophy and Theory, 36*(3), 327–342. http:// dx.doi.org/10.1111/j.1469-5812.2004.00071.x.

Bowden, P. (1997). *Caring: Gender-sensitive ethics*. Abingdon, UK: Psychology Press.

Braidotti, R. (1994). *Nomadic subjects. Embodiment and sexual difference in contemporary feminist theory*. New York, NY: Columbia University Press.

Braidotti, R. (1998). *Difference, diversity and nomadic subjectivity*. Retrieved from: http:// www.translatum.gr/forum/index.php?topic=14317.0.

Braidotti, R. (2006a). Affirmation versus vulnerability: On contemporary ethical debates. *Symposium: Canadian Journal of Continental Philosophy, 10*, 235–254.

Braidotti, R. (2006b). The ethics of becoming imperceptible. In C. Boundas (Ed.), *Deleuze and philosophy* (pp. 133–159). Edinburgh, UK: Edinburgh University Press. http://dx.doi.org/10.3366/edinburgh/9780748624799.003.0009.

Braidotti, R. (2008). Of poststructuralist ethics and nomadic subjects. In M. Düwell, C. Rehmann-Sutter, & D. Mieth (Eds.), *The contingent nature of life* (pp. 25–36). Dordrecht, The Netherlands: Springer. http://dx.doi.org/10.1007/978-1-4020-6764-8_3.

Brannen, J., & Moss, P. (Eds.). (2003). *Rethinking children's care.* Buckingham, UK: Open University Press.

Bredekamp, S., & Copple, C. (Eds.). (1997). *Developmentally appropriate practice in early childhood programs* (rev. ed.). Washington, DC: National Association for the Education of Young Children.

Britzman, D. (2003). *Practice makes practice. A critical study of learning to teach.* Albany, NY: SUNY Press.

Britzman, D. (2007). Teacher education as uneven development: Toward a psychology of uncertainty. *International Journal of Leadership in Education, 10*(1), 1–12. http://dx.doi.org/10.1080/13603120600934079.

Britzman, D. (2009). *The very thought of education: Psychoanalysis and the impossible professions.* Albany, NY: SUNY Press.

Bronson, P., & Merryman, A. (2009). *NurtureShock: New thinking about children.* New York, NY: Twelve.

Brydon-Miller, M., Greenwood, D., & Maguire, P. (2003). Why action research? *Action Research, 1*(1), 9–28. http://dx.doi.org/10.1177/14767503030011002.

Burman, E. (1994). *Deconstructing developmental psychology.* New York, NY: Routledge.

Burman, E. (2009). Beyond "emotional literacy" in feminist and educational research. *British Educational Research Journal, 35*(1), 137–155. http://dx.doi.org/10.1080/01411920802041848.

Butler, J. (1990). *Gender trouble: Feminism and the subversion of identity.* New York, NY: Routledge.

Butler, J. (1993). *Bodies that matter: On the discursive limits of sex.* London, UK: Routledge.

Butler, J., & Davies, B. (2007). *Judith Butler in conversation: Analyzing the texts and talk of everyday life.* New York, NY: Routledge.

Cadwell, L. (2003). *Bringing learning to life.* New York, NY: Teachers College Press.

Cagliari, P., Barozzi, A., & Giudici, C. (2004). Thoughts, theories and experiences: For an educational project with participation. *Children in Europe 6*, 28–30.

Cannella, G.S. (1997). *Deconstructing early childhood education: Social justice and revolution.* New York, NY: Peter Lang.

Cannella, G.S. (1998). Critical research: Postmodern methodologies for the examination of race, ethnicity, class, and gender in education. *Advancing Women in Leadership, 1*(2). www.advancingwomen.com.

Cannella, G., & Viruru, R. (2004). *Childhood and postcolonization: Power, education and contemporary practice.* New York, NY: RoutledgeFalmer.

Carr, M. (2001). *Assessment in early childhood settings: Learning stories.* London, UK: Chapman.

Carr, M., & May, H. (1992). *Te Whāriki: National early childhood curriculum guidelines in New Zealand*. Hamilton, NZ: Waikato University.

Carr, W., & Kemmis, S. (1986). *Becoming critical: Education, knowledge and action research*. Basingstoke, UK: Falmer.

Chan, K.H. (2010). Rethinking children's participation in curriculum making: A rhizomatic movement. In V. Pacini-Ketchabaw (Ed.), *Flows, rhythms and intensities of early childhood education curriculum* (pp. 39–53). New York, NY: Peter Lang.

Chia, R. (1995). From modern to postmodern organizational analysis. *Organization Studies, 16*(4), 579–604. http://dx.doi.org/10.1177/017084069501600406.

Chia, R. (1999). A "rhizomic" model of organizational change and transformation: Perspective from a metaphysics of change. *British Journal of Management, 10*(3), 209–227. http://dx.doi.org/10.1111/1467-8551.00128.

Clark, A., & Moss, P. (2001). *Listening to children: The mosaic approach*. London, UK: National Children's Bureau.

Clark, V. (2012). Art making as a political and ethical practice. *Canadian Children, 37*(1), 21–26.

Colebrook, C. (2002). *Gilles Deleuze*. London, UK: Routledge.

Common World Childhoods Collective 2014. *Common World Childhoods website*. http://www.commonworlds.net/.

Copple, C., & Bredekamp, S. (Eds.). (2009). *Developmentally appropriate practice in early childhood programs*. Washington, DC: National Association for the Education of Young Children.

Corson, D. (1998). *Changing education for diversity*. Philadelphia, PA: Open University Press.

Crutcher, M., & Zook, M. (2009). Placemarks and waterlines: Racialized cyberscapes in post-Katrina Google Earth. *Geoforum, 40*(4), 523–534. http://dx.doi.org/10.1016/j.geoforum.2009.01.003.

Dahlberg, G. (2000). Everything is a beginning and everything is dangerous: Some reflections of the Reggio Emilia experience. In H. Penn (Ed.), *Early childhood services: Theory, policy and practice* (pp. 175–183). Buckingham, UK: Open University Press.

Dahlberg, G. (2003). Pedagogy as a loci of an ethics of an encounter. In M. Bloch, K. Holmlund, I. Moqvist, & T. Popkewitz (Eds.), *Governing children, families and education: Restructuring the welfare state* (pp. 261–287). New York, NY: Palgrave.

Dahlberg, G., & Moss, P. (2005). *Ethics and politics in early childhood education*. London, UK: RoutledgeFalmer. http://dx.doi.org/10.4324/9780203463529.

Dahlberg, G., Moss, P., & Pence, A.R. (2007). *Beyond quality in early childhood education and care: Languages of evaluation* (2nd ed.). London, UK: Routledge.

Davies, B. (1989). *Frogs and snails and feminist tales: Preschool children and gender*. Sydney, Australia: Allen & Unwin.

Davies, B. (2000). *A body of writing 1990–1999*. New York, NY: Altamira.

Davies, B. & Gannon, S. (Eds.). (2006). *Doing collective biographies*. New York, NY: Open University Press.

Davis, D., & Atkinson, K. (n.d.). *Images of Learning Project*. Retrieved from: http://imagesoflearningproject.com.

de Finney, S. (2010). "We just don't know each other": Racialised girls negotiate mediated multiculturalism in a less diverse Canadian city. *Journal of Intercultural Studies*, *31*(5), 471–487. http://dx.doi.org/10.1080/07256868.2010.513082.

De Lissovoy, N. (2010). Decolonial pedagogy and the ethics of the global. *Discourse*, *31*(3), 279–293. http://dx.doi.org/10.1080/01596301003786886.

Deleuze, G., & Guattari, F. (1987). *A thousand plateaus: Capitalism and schizophrenia* (B. Massumi, Trans.). Minneapolis, MN: University of Minnesota Press. (Original work published 1980).

Derman-Sparks, L., & A.B.C. Task Force (1989). Anti-bias curriculum: Tools for empowering young children. Washington, DC: National Association for the Education of Young Children.

Derman-Sparks, L., Ramsey, P.G., & Edwards, J.O. (2006). *What if all the kids are white? Anti-bias multicultural education with young children and families*. New York, NY: Teachers College Press.

Dirlik, A. (2008). Race talk, race, and contemporary racism. *PMLA*, *123*(5), 1363–1379. http://dx.doi.org/10.1632/pmla.2008.123.5.1363.

Doherty, G., Friendly, M., & Beach, J. (2003). *OECD thematic review of early childhood education and care: Canadian background report*. Ottawa, ON: Organisation for Economic Co-operation and Development (OECD).

Doherty, G., Lero, D.S., Goelman, H., LaGrange, A., & Tougas J. (2000). You bet I care! A Canada-wide study on wages, working conditions, and practices in child care centres. Guelph, ON: University of Guelph, Centre for Families, Work, and Well-Being.

Duhn, I. (2008). Globalising childhood: Assembling the bicultural child in the New Zealand early childhood curriculum Te Whariki. *International Critical Childhood Policy Studies Journal*, *1*(1), 82–105.

Edmiston, B. (2008). *Forming ethical identities in early childhood play*. New York, NY: Routledge.

Edwards, C., Forman, G., & Gandini, L. (Eds.). (1998). *The hundred languages of children: The Reggio Emilia approach to early childhood education—advanced reflections*. Norwood, NJ: Ablex.

Elliot, E. (2010). Thinking beyond a framework: Entering into dialogues. In V. Pacini-Ketchabaw (Ed.), *Flows, rhythms and intensities of early childhood education curriculum* (pp. 3–20). New York, NY: Peter Lang.

Ellsworth, E. (1999). *Teaching positions: Difference, pedagogy, and the power of address*. New York, NY: Teachers College Press.

Escayg, K. (2010). Diverse classrooms, diverse teachers: Representing cultural diversity in the teaching profession and implications for pre-service admissions. *Canadian Journal for New Scholars in Education*, *3*(2), 1–8. Retrieved from: http://cjnse-rcjce .ca/ojs2/index.php/cjnse/article/view/156.

Fendler, L. (2003). Teacher reflection in a hall of mirrors: Historical influences and political reverberations. *Educational Researcher*, *32*(3), 16–25. http://dx.doi.org/10 .3102/0013189X032003016.

Fiske, J. (1996). *Media matters: Race and gender in US politics*. Minneapolis, MN: University of Minnesota Press.

Foucault, M. (1977). *Discipline and punish: The birth of the prison*. New York, NY: Vintage.

Foucault, M. (1978). *The history of sexuality: An introduction*. New York, NY: Vintage.

Foucault, M. (1980). Truth and power. In C. Gordon (Ed.), *Power/knowledge: Selected interviews and other writings 1972–1977* (pp. 109–133). Brighton, UK: Harvester.

Foucault, M. (1991). Governmentality. In G. Burchell, C. Gordon, & P. Miller (Eds.), *The Foucault effect: Studies in governmentality* (pp. 87–104). London, UK: Harvester Wheatsheaf.

Fullan, M. (2001). *The new meaning of educational change*. New York, NY: Teachers College Press.

Gallacher, L.A., & Gallagher, M. (2008). Methodological immaturity in childhood research?: Thinking through "participatory methods." *Childhood, 15*(4), 499–516. http://dx.doi.org/10.1177/0907568208091672.

Garrick, J., & Rhodes, C. (1998). Deconstructive organizational learning: The possibilities for a postmodern epistemology of practice. *Studies in the Education of Adults, 30*(2), 172–183.

Giudici, C., Krechevsky, M., & Rinaldi, C. (2001). *Making learning visible: Children as individual and group learners*. Reggio Emilia, Italy: Reggio Children.

Goodley, D. (2007). Towards socially just pedagogies: Deleuzoguattarian critical disability studies. *International Journal of Inclusive Education, 11*(3), 317–334. http://dx.doi.org/10.1080/13603110701238769.

Goodley, D. (2013). Dis/entangling critical disability studies. *Disability & Society, 28*(5), 631–644. http://dx.doi.org/10.1080/09687599.2012.717884.

Goodley, D., & Runswick-Cole, K. (2012). Reading Rosie. The postmodern dis/abled child. *Educational & Child Psychology, 29*(2), 53–66.

Government of British Columbia. (2008a). *British Columbia early learning framework*. Victoria, BC: Ministry of Education, Ministry of Health, Ministry of Children and Family Development, & Early Learning Advisory Group.

Government of British Columbia. (2008b). *Understanding the British Columbia early learning framework: From theory to practice*. Victoria, BC: Ministry of Education, Ministry of Health, Ministry of Children and Family Development, & Early Learning Advisory Group.

Government of New Zealand (1996). *Te Whāriki: Early childhood curriculum*. Auckland, NZ: Ministry of Education. Retrieved from: http://www.educate.ece.govt.nz/.

Government of New Zealand. (2002). *Pathways to the future: Nga Huarahi Arataki*. Auckland, NZ: Ministry of Education.

Green, B. (2010). The (im)possibility of the project. *Australian Educational Researcher, 37*(3), 1–17. http://dx.doi.org/10.1007/BF03216927.

Grieshaber, S.J., & Hatch, J.A. (2003). Child observation and pedagogical documentation as effects of globalisation. *Journal of Curriculum Theorizing, 19*(1), 89–102.

Grosz, E. (1994). *Volatile bodies: Toward a corporeal feminism*. Bloomington, IN: Indiana University Press.

Grosz, E. (2005). *Time travels. Feminism, nature, power*. Durham, NC: Duke University Press. http://dx.doi.org/10.1215/9780822386551.

Guhn, M., Janus, M., & Hertzman, C. (2007). The early development instrument: Translating school readiness assessment into community actions and policy planning. *Early Education and Development, 18*(3), 369–374. http://dx.doi.org/10.1080/10409280701610622.

Guskey, T.R. (2002). Professional development and teacher change. *Teachers and Teaching, 8*(3/4), 381–391. http://dx.doi.org/10.1080/135406002100000512.

Habermas, J. (1983). Modernity: An incomplete project. In H. Foster (Ed.), *The anti-aesthetic: Essays on postmodern culture* (pp. 3–15). Port Townsend, WA: Bay Press.

Haraway, D. (1991). A Cyborg manifesto: Science, technology, and socialist-feminism in the late twentieth century. In *Simians, Cyborgs and women: The reinvention of nature* (pp. 149–181). New York, NY: Routledge.

Haraway, D. (1992). The promises of monsters: A regenerative politics for inappropriate/d others. In L. Grossberg, C. Nelson, & P. Treichler (Eds.), *Cultural studies* (pp. 295–337). New York, NY: Routledge.

Haraway, D. (2003). *The companion species manifesto: Dogs, people, and significant otherness.* Chicago, IL: Prickly Paradigm.

Heydon, R. (2005). The theory and practice of pedagogical ethics: Features for an ethical praxis in/out of special education. *Journal of Curriculum Studies, 37*(4), 381–394. http://dx.doi.org/10.1080/0022027042000325155.

Højgaard, L., & Søndergaard, D.M. (2011). Theorizing the complexities of discursive and material subjectivity: Agential realism and poststructural analyses. *Theory & Psychology, 21*(3), 338–354. http://dx.doi.org/10.1177/0959354309359965.

Hoyuelos, A. (2004). A pedagogy of transgression. *Children in Europe, 6,* 6–7.

Hughes, P., & MacNaughton, G. (2001). Fractured or manufactured: Gendered identities and culture in the early years. In S. Grieshaber & G.S. Cannella (Eds.), *Embracing identities in early childhood education: Diversity and possibilities* (pp. 114–131). New York, NY: Teachers College Press.

Hultman, K., & Lenz Taguchi, H.L. (2010). Challenging anthropocentric analysis of visual data: A relational materialist methodological approach to educational research. *International Journal of Qualitative Studies in Education, 23*(5), 525–542. http://dx.doi.org/10.1080/09518398.2010.500628.

Hultqvist, K., & Dahlberg, G. (2001). *Governing the child in the new millennium.* New York, NY: RoutledgeFalmer.

James, A., & Prout, A. (1997). *Constructing and reconstructing childhood: Contemporary issues in the sociological study of childhood.* London, UK: Falmer.

Jiwani, J. (2006). *Discourses of denial: Mediations of race, gender and violence.* Vancouver, BC: UBC Press.

Johnson, R. (2000). Colonialism and cargo cults in early childhood education: Does Reggio Emilia really exist? *Contemporary Issues in Early Childhood, 1*(1), 61–78. http://dx.doi.org/10.2304/ciec.2000.1.1.8.

Keddie, A. (2006). Pedagogies and critical reflection: Key understandings for transformative gender justice. *Gender and Education, 18*(1), 99–114. http://dx.doi.org/10.1080/09540250500195184.

Kemmis, S. (2009). Action research as a practice-based practice. *Educational Action Research, 17*(3), 463–474. http://dx.doi.org/10.1080/09650790903093284.

Kessler, S., & Swadener, B.B. (Eds.). (1992). *Reconceptualizing the early childhood curriculum: Beginning the dialogue.* New York, NY: Teachers College Press.

Kim, B. (2001). Social constructivism. In M. Orey (Ed.), *Emerging perspectives on learning, teaching, and technology*. Retrieved from: http://projects.coe.uga.edu/epltt/.

Kind, S. (2006). Of stones and silences: Storying the trace of the other in the autobiographical and textile text of art/teaching. Unpublished doctoral dissertation, University of British Columbia, Vancouver.

Kind, S. (2008, June). *Encountering children's artistic languages*. Paper presented at the Reconceptualizing Early Childhood Education Conference, Victoria, British Columbia.

Kind, S. (2010). Art encounters: Movements in the visual arts and early childhood education. In V. Pacini-Ketchabaw (Ed.), *Flows, rhythms and intensities of early childhood education curriculum* (pp. 113–132). New York, NY: Peter Lang.

Kocher, L. (2008). *The disposition to document: The lived experience of teachers who practice pedagogical documentation*. Unpublished doctoral dissertation. University of Southern Queensland, Australia.

Kocher, L. (2010). Families and pedagogical narration: Disrupting traditional understandings of family involvement. In V. Pacini-Ketchabaw (Ed.), *Flows, rhythms and intensities of early childhood education curriculum* (pp. 177–201). New York, NY: Peter Lang.

Kukla, A. (2000). *Social constructivism and the philosophy of science*. New York, NY: Routledge.

Kummen, K. (2011, October 28). *Making space for disruption: Resisting the discourse of the universal child*. Unpublished paper presented at the 19th Reconceptualising Early Childhood Education conference, London, UK.

Kurtz, J. (2007). *Rapunzel. Fairy tale classics*. New York, NY: Jump at the Sun.

Lather, P. (1991). *Getting smart: Feminist research and pedagogy with/in the postmodern*. New York, NY: Routledge.

Law, J., & Benschop, R. (1997). Resisting pictures: Representation, distribution and ontological politics. In K. Hetherington & R. Munro (Eds.), *Ideas of difference: Social spaces and the labour of division* (pp. 158–182). Sociological Review Monograph. Oxford, UK: Blackwell.

Lee, J.A., & Lutz, J.S. (2005). Introduction: Toward a critical literacy of racisms, anti-racisms, and racialization. In J.A. Lee & J.S. Lutz (Eds.), *Situating "race" and racisms in space, time, and theory. Critical essays for activists and scholars* (Vol. 3) (pp. 3–29). Montreal, QC: McGill-Queen's University Press.

Lenz Taguchi, H. (2005). Getting personal: How early childhood teacher education troubles students' and teacher educators' identities regarding subjectivity and feminism. *Contemporary Issues in Early Childhood, 6*(3), 244–255. http://dx.doi.org/10.2304/ciec.2005.6.3.5.

Lenz Taguchi, H. (2006). Reconceptualizing early childhood education: Challenging taken-for-granted ideas. In E.J. Wagner & J.T. Wagner (Eds.), *Nordic childhoods and early education philosophy, research, policy, and practice in Denmark, Finland, Iceland, Norway, and Sweden* (pp. 257–287). Greenwich, CT: Information Age.

Lenz Taguchi, H. (2007). Deconstructing and transgressing the theory–practice dichotomy in early childhood education. *Educational Philosophy and Theory, 39*(3), 275–290. http://dx.doi.org/10.1111/j.1469-5812.2007.00324.x.

Lenz Taguchi, H. (2008a). An "ethics of resistance" challenges taken-for-granted ideas in Swedish early childhood education. *International Journal of Educational Research*, 47(5), 270–282. http://dx.doi.org/10.1016/j.ijer.2008.12.006.

Lenz Taguchi, H. (2008b). *Doing justice in early childhood education? Justice to whom and to what?* Paper presented at the European Early Childhood Education Research Association, Stavanger, Norway.

Lenz Taguchi, H. (2009). *Going beyond the theory/practice divide in early childhood education: Introducing an intra-active pedagogy*. New York, NY: Routledge.

Lenz Taguchi, H. (2010). Doing collaborative deconstruction as an "exorbitant" strategy in qualitative research. *Reconceptualizing Educational Research Methodology*, 1(1), 41–53.

Lenz Taguchi, H. (2011). Investigating learning, participation and becoming in early childhood practices with a relational materialist approach. *Global Studies of Childhood*, 1(1), 36–50. http://dx.doi.org/10.2304/gsch.2011.1.1.36.

Levinas, E. (1985). *Ethics and infinity: Conversations with Philippe Nemo* (R.A. Cohen, Trans.). Pittsburgh, PA: Duquesne University Press. (Original work published 1982).

Lubeck, S. (1998). Is developmentally appropriate practice for everyone? *Childhood Education*, 74(5), 283–92.

Lyon, S., Osborne, S., Carducci, C., Schendorf-Klinger, M., & Matul, M. (2006). Presidio Child Development Centre: Reflections on transformation and diversity within a Reggio-inspired school in an urban school district. *Innovations in Early Education: The International Reggio Exchange*, 13(2), 12–20.

M'charek, A. (2010). Fragile differences, relational effects: Stories about the materiality of race and sex. *European Journal of Women's Studies*, 17(4), 307–322. http://dx.doi.org/10.1177/1350506810377698.

MacNaughton, G. (2000). *Rethinking gender in early childhood education*. London, UK: Chapman.

MacNaughton, G. (2001). Action research. In G. MacNaughton, S.A. Rolfe, & I. Siraj-Blatchford (Eds.), *Doing early childhood research: International perspectives on theory and practice* (pp. 208–223). Maidenhead, UK: Open University Press.

MacNaughton, G. (2003). *Shaping early childhood: Learners, curriculum and contexts*. Maidenhead, UK: Open University Press.

MacNaughton, G. (2004). The politics of logic in early childhood research: A case of the brain, hard facts, trees, and rhizomes. *Australian Educational Researcher*, 31(3), 87–104. http://dx.doi.org/10.1007/BF03249530.

MacNaughton, G. (2005). *Doing Foucault in early childhood studies: Applying poststructural ideas*. New York, NY: RoutledgeFalmer. http://dx.doi.org/10.4324/9780203465332.

MacNaughton, G., & Davis, K. (Eds.). (2009). *"Race" and early childhood education: An international approach to identity, politics, and pedagogy*. New York, NY: Palgrave Macmillan. http://dx.doi.org/10.1057/9780230623750.

MacNaughton, G. Davis, K., & Smith, K. (2009). "Exploring 'race-identities' with young children: Making politics visible." In G. MacNaughton & K. Davis (Eds.), *"Race" and early childhood education: An international approach to identity, politics and pedagogy* (pp. 31–48). New York, NY: Palgrave Macmillan.

MacNaughton, G., Hughes, P., & Smith, K. (2007). Young children's rights and public policy: Practices and possibilities for citizenship in the early years. *Children & Society, 21*(6), 458–469. http://dx.doi.org/10.1111/j.1099-0860.2007.00096.x.

MacNaughton, G., Hughes, P., & Smith, K. (Eds.). (2008). *Young children as active citizens: Principles, policies and pedagogies.* London, UK: Cambridge Scholars.

MacNaughton, G., & Smith, K. (2008). Engaging ethically with young children: Principles and practices for consulting justly with care. In G. MacNaughton, P. Hughes, & K. Smith (Eds.), *Young children as active citizens: Principles, policies and pedagogies* (pp. 31–43). London, UK: Cambridge Scholars.

Malaguzzi, L. (1993). History, ideas, and basic philosophy. In C. Edwards, L. Gandini, & G. Forman (Eds.), *The hundred languages of children: The Reggio Emilia approach to early childhood education* (pp. 41–89). Norwood, NJ: Ablex.

Mar, P., & Anderson, K. (2010). The creative assemblage. *Journal of Cultural Economics, 3*(1), 35–51. http://dx.doi.org/10.1080/17530351003617560.

Mayhew, S. (2004). Governmentality. In S. Mayhew (Ed.), *A dictionary of geography.* Oxford, UK: Oxford University Press.

Miller, P., & Rose, N. (2008). *Governing the present: Administering social and personal life.* Cambridge, UK: Polity Press.

Mol, A. (2002). *The body multiple: Ontology in medical practice.* Durham, NC: Duke University Press.

Morss, J.R. (1996). *Growing critical: Alternatives to developmental psychology.* London, UK: Routledge. http://dx.doi.org/10.4324/9780203130797.

Moss, P. (2001). *Beyond early childhood education and care.* Paper presented at the Starting Strong OECD-Conference, Stockholm, Sweden.

Moss, P. (2005). Dedicated to Loris Malaguzzi, the town of Reggio Emilia and its schools: A presentation by Peter Moss, February 26 2004 in Reggio Emilia. *Refocus, 1,* 23–25.

Moss, P. (2006a). Structures, understandings and discourses: Possibilities for re-envisioning the early childhood worker. *Contemporary Issues in Early Childhood, 7*(1), 30–41. http://dx.doi.org/10.2304/ciec.2006.7.1.30.

Moss, P. (2006b). Listening to young children: Beyond rights to ethics. In *Let's talk about listening to children: Towards a shared understanding for early years education in Scotland* (Vol. 2), (pp. 17–23). Edinburgh, UK: Learning and Teaching Scotland.

Moss, P. (2007). *Bringing politics into the nursery: Early childhood education as a democratic practice. Working Paper 43.* The Hague, The Netherlands: Bernard van Leer Foundation. Retrieved from: http://www.bernardvanleer.org.

Moss, P., & Dahlberg, G. (2008). Beyond quality in early childhood education and care: Languages of evaluation. *New Zealand Journal of Teachers' Work, 5*(1), 3–12.

Moss, P., & Pence, A. (Eds.). (1994). *Valuing quality in early childhood services: New approaches to defining quality.* New York, NY: Teachers College Press.

Moss, P., & Petrie, P. (2002). *From children's services to children's spaces: Public policy, children and childhood.* New York, NY: RoutledgeFalmer.

Munsch, R. (1980). *The paper bag princess.* Toronto, ON: Annick.

New, R. (1993). *Reggio Emilia: Some lessons for U.S. educators.* Champaign, IL: ERIC Clearinghouse on Elementary and Early Childhood Education. ED354988.

New, R. (2007). Reggio Emilia as cultural activity theory in practice. *Theory into Practice, 46*(1), 5–13. http://dx.doi.org/10.1080/00405840709336543.

Noddings, N. (1984). *Caring: A feminine approach to ethics and moral education.* Berkeley, CA: University of California Press.

Oliver, M. (1990). *Politics of disablement.* London, UK: Macmillan.

Oliver, M. (1996). *Understanding disability: From theory to practice.* Basingstoke, UK: Macmillan.

Olsson, L. (2009). *Movement and experimentation in young children's learning: Deleuze and Guattari in early childhood education.* New York, NY: Taylor & Francis.

Pacini-Ketchabaw, V. (2007). Child care and multiculturalism: A site of governance marked by flexibility and openness. *Contemporary Issues in Early Childhood, 8*(3), 222–232. http://dx.doi.org/10.2304/ciec.2007.8.3.222.

Pacini-Ketchabaw, V., & Berikoff, A. (2008). The politics of difference and diversity: From young children's violence to creative power expressions. *Contemporary Issues in Early Childhood, 9*(3), 256–264. http://dx.doi.org/10.2304/ciec.2008.9.3.256.

Pacini-Ketchabaw, V., & Bernhard, J. (2012). Revisioning multiculturalism in early childhood education. In N. Howe & L. Prochner (Eds.), *New directions in early childhood education and care in Canada* (pp. 159–181). Toronto, ON: University of Toronto Press.

Pacini-Ketchabaw, V., Kocher, L., Sanchez, A., & Chan, C. (2009). Rhizomatic stories of immanent becoming and intra-activity: Professional development reconceptualized. In L. Iannacci & P. Whitty (Eds.), *Early childhood curricula: Reconceptualist perspectives* (pp. 87–119). Calgary, AB: Destilig.

Pacini-Ketchabaw, V., Kummen, K., & Thompson, D. (2010). Becoming intimate with developmental knowledge: Pedagogical explorations with collective biography. *Alberta Journal of Educational Research, 56*(3), 335–354.

Pacini-Ketchabaw, V., & Nxumalo, F. (2010). A curriculum for social change: Experimenting with politics of action or imperceptibility. In V. Pacini-Ketchabaw (Ed.), *Flows, rhythms and intensities of early childhood education curriculum* (pp. 133–154). New York, NY: Peter Lang.

Pacini-Ketchabaw, V., & Nxumalo, F. (2012). Unpacking racialization through pedagogical documentation. In A. Fleet, A.C. Patterson & J. Robertson (Eds.), *Conversations: Conversations about early childhood pedagogical documentation* (pp. 259–272). Castle Hill, Australia: Pademelon Press.

Pacini-Ketchabaw, V., & Pence, A. (2005). Contextualizing the reconceptualist movement in Canadian early childhood education. In V. Pacini-Ketchabaw & A. Pence (Eds.), *Canadian early childhood education: Broadening and deepening discussions of quality* (pp. 5–20). Ottawa, ON: Canadian Child Care Federation.

Pacini-Ketchabaw, V., White, J., & Armstrong de Almeida, A.E. (2006). Racialization in early childhood: A critical analysis of discourses in policies. *International Journal of Educational Policy, Research, and Practice. Reconceptualizing Childhood Studies, 7*(1), 95–113.

Paley, V.G. (2005). *A child's work: The importance of fantasy play.* Chicago, IL: University of Chicago Press.

Parr, A. (2005). The deterritorializing language of child detainees: Self-harm or embodied graffiti? *Childhood, 12*(3), 281–299. http://dx.doi.org/10.1177/0907568205054923.

Pence, A. (1989). In the shadow of mother-care: Contexts for an understanding of child day care in North America. *Canadian Psychology*, *30*(2), 140–147. http://dx.doi .org/10.1037/h0079806.

Pence, A., & Hix-Small, H. (2009). Global children in the shadow of the global child. *International Critical Childhood Policy Studies Journal*, *2*(1), 75–91.

Pence, A., & Pacini-Ketchabaw, V. (2010). The Investigating "Quality" Project: Opening possibilities in early childhood education policies and practices. In N. Yelland (Ed.), *Contemporary perspectives on early childhood education* (pp. 121–138). Maidenhead, UK: Open University Press.

Pence, A., & Pacini-Ketchabaw, V. (2012). The Investigating "Quality" Project: Innovative approaches in early childhood. In N. Howe & L. Prochner (Eds.), *Recent perspectives on early childhood education in Canada* (pp. 229–244). Toronto, ON: University of Toronto Press.

Pinar, W. (2012). *What is curriculum theory?* (2nd edition). New York, NY: Routledge.

Popkewitz, T. (1998). *Struggling for the soul: The politics of education and the construction of the teacher*. New York, NY: Teachers College Press.

Project Zero. (2004). *Making learning visible: Children as individual and group learners*. Reggio Emilia, Italy: Reggio Children.

Project Zero (2006). *Making learning visible: Understanding, documenting, and supporting individual and group learning*. Retrieved from: http://www.pz.harvard.edu/mlv/.

Puttayuk, A. (2008). *Caribou*. Montréal, QC: Avataq Cultural Institute.

Rinaldi, C. (1993). The emergent curriculum and social constructivism: An interview with Leila Gandini. In C. Edwards, L. Gandini, & G. Forman (Eds.), *The hundred languages of children* (pp. 101–112). Norwood, NJ: Ablex.

Rinaldi, C. (2001). *Making learning visible: Children as individual and group learners*. Reggio Emilia, Italy: Reggio Children & Project Zero.

Rinaldi, C. (2003). The teacher as researcher. *Innovations in Early Education*, *10*, 1–4.

Rinaldi, C. (2006). *In dialogue with Reggio Emilia: Listening, researching and learning*. London, UK: Routledge. http://dx.doi.org/10.4324/9780203317730.

Ritzer, G. (1993). *The McDonaldization of society*. Thousand Oaks, CA: Pine Forge Press.

Robinson, K.H., & Jones-Diaz, C. (2005). *Diversity and difference in early childhood education: Issues for theory and practice*. Maidenhead, UK: Open University Press.

Rose, N. (1985). *The psychological complex*. London, UK: Routledge.

Rose, N. (1990). *Governing the soul: The shaping of the private self*. New York, NY: Routledge.

Rose, N. (1996). *Inventing ourselves: Psychology, power and personhood*. Cambridge, UK: Cambridge University Press. http://dx.doi.org/10.1017/CBO9780511752179.

Rossholt, N. (2009). The complexity of bodily events through an ethnographer's gaze: Focusing on the youngest children in preschool. *Contemporary Issues in Early Childhood*, *10*(1), 55–65. http://dx.doi.org/10.2304/ciec.2009.10.1.55.

Rowan, M.C. (2010). Disrupting colonial power through literacy: A story about creating Inuttitut-language children's books. In V. Pacini-Ketchabaw (Ed.), *Flows, rhythms, and intensities of early childhood education curriculum* (pp. 155–176). New York, NY: Peter Lang.

Ryan, J. (1999). *Race and ethnicity in multi-ethnic schools: A critical case study.* Toronto, ON: Multilingual Matters.

Ryan, S., & Grieshaber, S. (2004). It's more than child development: Critical theories, research, and teaching young children. *Young Children, 59*(6), 44–52.

Ryan, S., & Grieshaber, S. (2005). Shifting from developmental to postmodern practices in early childhood teacher education. *Journal of Teacher Education, 56*(1), 34–45. http://dx.doi.org/10.1177/0022487104272057.

Saldanha, A. (2006). Reontologising race: The machinic geography of phenotype. *Environment and Planning D, Society & Space, 24*(1), 9–24. http://dx.doi.org/10.1068/d61j.

Salée, D. (2006). Quality of life of aboriginal people in Canada. *IRRP: Choices, 12*(6), 1–38.

Seidel, S. (1991). *Collaborative assessment conferences for the consideration of project work.* Cambridge, MA: Harvard Project Zero.

Sellar, S. (2009). The responsible uncertainty of pedagogy. *Discourse, 30*(3), 347–360. http://dx.doi.org/10.1080/01596300903037077.

Sellers, M. (2010). Re(con)ceiving young children's curricular performativity. *International Journal of Qualitative Studies in Education, 23*(5), 557–577. http://dx.doi.org/10.1080/09518398.2010.500629.

Semetsky, I. (2009). Deleuze as a philosopher of education: Affective knowledge / effective learning. *European Legacy, 14*(4), 443–456. http://dx.doi.org/10.1080/10848770902999534.

Singer, E. (1992). *Childcare and the psychology of development.* London, UK: Routledge.

Skattebol, J. (2003). Dark, dark, darker: Negotiations of identity in an early childhood setting. *Contemporary Issues in Early Childhood, 4*(2), 149–166. http://dx.doi.org/10.2304/ciec.2003.4.2.5.

Slocum, R. (2008). Thinking race through corporeal feminist theory: Divisions and intimacies at the Minneapolis farmers' market. *Social & Cultural Geography, 9*(8), 849–869. http://dx.doi.org/10.1080/14649360802441465.

Smith, A., & May, H. (2006). Early childhood care and education in Aotearoa-New Zealand. In E. Melhuish & K. Petrogiannis (Eds.), *Early childhood care and education: International perspectives* (pp. 95–114). London, UK: Routledge.

Smith, C., & Gillespie, M. (2007). Research on professional development and teacher change: Implications for adult basic education. In J. Comings, B. Garner, & C. Smith (Eds.), *Review of adult learning and literacy: Connecting research, policy, and practice* (pp. 205–244). New York, NY: Routledge.

Springgay, S. (2008). An ethics of embodiment, civic engagement and a/r/tography: Ways of becoming nomadic in art, research, and teaching. *Educational Insights, 12*(2). Retrieved from: http://www.ccfi.educ.ubc.ca/.

Stoler, A.L. (2008). Imperial debris: Reflections on ruins and ruination. *Cultural Anthropology, 23*(2), 191–219. http://dx.doi.org/10.1111/j.1548-1360.2008.00007.x.

St. Pierre, E.A. (1997). Circling the text: Nomadic writing practices. *Qualitative Inquiry, 3*(4), 403–417. http://dx.doi.org/10.1177/107780049700300403.

St. Pierre, E.A., & Pillow, W.S. (2000). Inquiry among the ruins. In E.A. St. Pierre & W.S. Pillow (Eds.), *Working the ruins: Feminist poststructural theory and methods in education* (pp. 1–23). New York, NY: Routledge.

Sullivan, G. (2005). *Art practice as research: Inquiry in the visual arts.* Thousand Oaks, CA: Sage.

Swadener, B., & Mutua, K. (2008). Decolonizing performances: Deconstructing the global postcolonial. In N.K. Denzin, Y.S. Lincoln, & L.T. Smith (Eds.), *Handbook of critical indigenous methodologies* (pp. 31–44). Singapore: Sage.

Taylor, A. (2007). Playing with difference: The cultural politics of childhood belonging. *International Journal of Diversity in Organisations, Communities and Nations, 7*(3), 143–149.

Taylor, A., & Blaise, M. (2007). Editorial. [Special queer issue.] *International Journal of Equity and Innovation in Early Childhood, 5*(2), 1–4.

Thompson, D. (2010). A story to unsettle assumptions about critical reflection in practice. In V. Pacini-Ketchabaw (Ed.), *Flows, rhythms and intensities of early childhood education curriculum* (pp. 77–94). New York, NY: Peter Lang.

Thorsen, D.E., & Lie, A. (2007). *What is neoliberalism?* Retrieved from: http://folk.uio.no.

Tsoukas, H., & Chia, R. (2002). On organizational becoming: Rethinking organizational change. *Organization Science, 13*(5), 567–582. http://dx.doi.org/10.1287/orsc.13.5.567.7810.

UNICEF (2008). *The childcare transition: A league table of early childhood education and care in economically advanced countries.* Florence, Italy: UNICEF Innocenti Research Centre. Retrieved from: http://www.unicef-irc.org/publications/pdf/rc8_eng.pdf.

Vandenbroeck, M. (2004). Diverse aspects of diversity: A European perspective. *International Journal of Equity and Innovation in Early Childhood, 2*(2), 27–44.

Vintimilla, M.C.D. (2012). *Aporetic openings of living well with others: The teacher as a thinking subject.* Unpublished doctoral dissertation, University of British Columbia, Canada.

Viruru, R. (2005). The impact of postcolonial theory on early childhood education. *Journal of Education, 35*(1), 7–29.

Walkerdine, V. (1984). Developmental psychology and the child-centered pedagogy. In J. Henriques, W. Hollway, C. Urwin, C. Venn, & V. Walkerdine (Eds.), *Changing the subject: Psychology, social regulation and subjectivity* (pp. 153–202). London, UK: Methuen.

Walkerdine, V. (1990). *Schoolgirl fictions.* London, UK: Verso.

Weedon, C. (1987). *Feminist practice and poststructuralist theory.* Cambridge, MA: Blackwell.

Wohlwend, K.E. (2009). Damsels in discourse: Girls consuming and producing identity texts through Disney princess play. *Reading Research Quarterly, 44*(1), 57–83. http://dx.doi.org/10.1598/RRQ.44.1.3.

Zembylas, M. (2009). Global economies of fear: Affect, politics and pedagogical implications. *Critical Studies in Education, 50*(2), 187–199. http://dx.doi.org/10.1080/17508480902859458.

Zembylas, M., & Vrasidas, C. (2005). Levinas and the "inter-face": The ethical challenge of online education. *Educational Theory, 55*(1), 61–78. http://dx.doi.org/10.1111/j.1741-5446.2005.0005a.x.

INDEX

curriculum-making, 36
  children's participation in, xx, 55–57
  emphasis on the process (rather than product), 56, 114
  keeping curriculum alive, 128–129
  standards-based programming, 57
  what the child wants to learn, 129
curtailing play. *See* regulating children's play

Davis, Danielle, 136
decolonial perspective, 156
deconstructive analysis, xxi, 29, 145
Deleuze, Gilles, "Treatise on Nomadology—The War Machine," 187
democracy, 13, 55, 134–135
development theories, 4, 15, 23, 130
  alternative pedagogies, 14, 25
  contextualizing and politicizing, 25
  critical perspective, xx, 23–26
  early childhood education's reliance on, 24, 181
  limitations, 178–179
  looking beyond, 13
  "natural" development path, 29
  reconceptualizing, 24–25
developmental approaches, 17, 49, 52, 64, 145
  curriculum-making and, 55
developmental psychology, 145
developmentally appropriate practice (DAP), 120, 145
  assumptions embedded in, 25
  heteronormativity and, 160
  quality and, 121
  silencing other ways of thinking, 24
difference, 95–96, 170–171, 180, 192
  ethical encounters with, 183
diffraction, 41–44, 164, 167, 170
diffractive engagement, 123
discourse of meaning-making, xx, 14, 16–17, 113, 121–129
discourse regarding ideal beauty, 88, 90, 94–95

discourses of care, critical thinking about, 25
diversity, xx, 3, 15, 24, 60, 64, 73
  cultural and linguistic, 32
  moving beyond diversity perspective, 57–61
documentation. *See* pedagogical documentation
Doing Foucault in Early Childhood Studies (MacNaughton), 120
dominant discourses, 36, 46
  challenging, 17, 40, 54, 133, 146–147
  making visible, 145
  powerful influences of, 16
  role in children's understandings, 26
  solidifying inequitable power relations, 182
dominant gender discourses, 26, 34, 51–53
dominant images of the child, 45–46
  "independent child," 4
  rethinking, 46–48, 54, 96
dominant images of the educator, 62–64
dominant pedagogical practices. *See also* developmentally appropriate practice (DAP)
  limiting children's meaning-making, 18

Early Childhood Environment Rating Scale (ECERS), 12
Early Development Instrument (EDI), 12
Edmiston, Brian, 185
  Forming Ethical Identities in Early Childhood Play, 127
educator, 15, 133, 175
  "as an incomplete project," 67
  as authoritative, interventionist, 17
  complexifying our image of, 64–66
  as custodian, 63
  as expert, 28, 40, 56, 63, 70–71
  as facilitator, 55
  part of the image of the child, 53–54
  as researcher, 64–66, 74, 117, 171
  as substitute maternal care, 62
  as technician, 63–64